I0166511

The Elder or Poetic Edda,

COMMONLY KNOWN AS

SÆMUND'S EDDA.

by Saemund Sigfusson

EDITED AND TRANSLATED WITH INTRODUCTION AND NOTES

BY

OLIVE BRAY.

ILLUSTRATED BY

W. G. COLLINGWOOD.

PRINTED FOR THE VIKING CLUB,
KING'S WEIGHHOUSE ROOMS, LONDON.
1908.

CONTENTS.

LIST OF ILLUSTRATIONS.

INTRODUCTION.

A translation is only a compromise at best, and effected with a sense of resting in defeat. It has therefore always some need of apology, especially to those who are already acquainted with the original, and for a work which is entitled to a high place in international literature. Such place we claim for the Edda, not only as the fountain head of Germanic mythology and tradition, but for its own beauty of expression—the art of the Scandinavian poets. They sent it forth long since armed with winged words and girded with power, and only for want of speech in different tongues has it remained so little recognised. Two previous renderings into English by Thorpe and York Powell might well have proved its worth, but the first was allowed to fall out of print while interest was only beginning to awaken, and the second is included in the Corpus Poeticum Boreale with other less worthy material in a form that cannot appeal to the general reader. Both have been used in preparing the present book, which is offered less to scholars and students than to all who have sufficient taste for mythology, and understanding of old lore, to recognise the truth and beauty which are not expressed in precisely the forms and language of to-day; but who are also insistent, like ourselves, that old books are not true because of their age, nor old lamps beautiful unless they can be polished anew. To satisfy truth and for fear of doing injustice to the original, we have endeavoured to keep the translation as literal as possible, though ambiguity in the original occasionally necessitates interpretation by a somewhat freer rendering. Where we have failed to catch the spirit of the Icelandic or to find for it worthy English expression, we hope that the illustrations will suggest that a wealth of beauty is waiting to be represented in modern art by the painter as it was pictured of old by the Icelandic poets. For their style is so essentially graphic without being descriptive that the more familiar we are with their works the more difficult does it seem to translate them into words instead of colour and form.

A A

Sæmund's Edda bears a title under which its first editor would have failed to recognise it.   Sæmund, a well-known Icelandic scholar of the twelfth century, had no part in its composition, although, according to popular tradition, he was the author of a work on mythology.   Nor was the name of Edda given to it before the seventeenth century : we find this word attached to a collection of mythical stories made by the great Icelandic historian, Snorri Sturluson (1181-1241).   Its earliest meaning was "great-grandmother," and it is thus used in Rigsþula ; what were the intermediate steps in sense development we little know, but "great-grandmother's stories" like "old wives' tales" was deemed by some sceptic a fitting title for Snorri's account of the Old Norse gods and goddesses of Asgarth ; and it was deemed equally suitable by Bishop Brynjolf Sveinsson (1643) for the more venerable work which from that time was called Sæmund's or the Poetic Edda.*

It exists in several MSS., none of which were brought to light before the Icelandic Renaissance of the seventeenth century.   The finding of the first and most complete MS. was somewhat dramatic, and resembled the long awaited discovery of the planet Neptune. Magnus Olafsson had suggested the former existence of a more "ancient Edda," and we soon find this hypothetical work regarded in the light of a hidden treasure of wisdom and ancient lore, of which all existing fragments were but "the bare shadow and the footprint." We know nothing of how it was tracked and at last discovered, but by 1643 the Codex Regius was in the hands of Bishop Brynjolf.   This most important MS., known as R, is in the Copenhagen library : it is an octavo volume consisting of five parchment sheets belonging to the thirteenth century, and containing nearly all the poems given below. The others are found in MSS. of the fourteenth century, which were brought to light by the same scholars.   The Codex Arnamagnæanus (A) supplied Baldrs Draumar ; the Codex Wormianus includes Rigsþula with Snorri's Edda ; Hyndluljoþ is found in one of the great Saga books, the Flateyjarbók ; Grógaldr ok Fjölsvinnismál are only known in paper MSS. of the seventeenth century.

---

* *Many scholars, however, incline to the theory put forth by Mr. Eiríkr Magnússon in his paper on* Edda *(Saga book of the Viking Club, vol. i., p. 219), that the name, whatever later meanings may have been given, meant originally "the book of Oddi," or* Codex Oddensis ; *and that Edda is merely a feminine form, agreeing with* bók, *of Oddi, the home of Snorri, where his love for history and literature first was kindled.*

Thus, with a few modern additions, Sæmund's Edda is an early collection of much older lays, some mythical and some heroic: the mythical lays only are given here, although, as regards style and authorship, no line of distinction can be drawn between them. Brief passages in prose have been added at some later period; the poems themselves belong to somewhat different dates, and show the work of different hands; some are fragmentary, and have suffered from re-arrangement and interpolation; all are more or less obscure. They point back to lost traditions, forgotten creeds, and, it is suggested, a wealth of early poetic literature and mythology which are common to the Germanic race: they lead us forward also to the more intelligible account of Snorri's prose book, which is the earliest commentary on the subject. This cannot rank with the primitive sources of tradition except in so far as it quotes old fragments from lost poems and strophes of those found in the Edda. Christian and foreign influence, the orderly mind of the scholar, the shaping hand of the artist have left their traces behind. In one or two cases we can even correct his misinterpretations where an earlier and perhaps grander myth, less understood in the narrow light of mediæval learning than by the broader and more comparative knowledge of to-day, has become over-grown by some later fairy tale. We are obliged, however, to rely on Snorri's version where all other explanation is wanting for gaps and obscurities in the poems; indeed there is little else to throw light upon the subject.

Iceland has a magnificent prose literature in the Sagas of the thirteenth century, which are records of the old Norse kings, stories of family life in Iceland or the mother country, and Viking expeditions both romantic and historic. They treat of times past when the mytho-logy of the Edda was still living, but they show only the cult and worship of the principal deities—Odin, Thor, and Frey—who differ widely from the heroic beings of the myths. The skalds or court poets, save Ulf Uggason and Thiodwolf, rarely chose such subjects for their songs, but in praising their lords they made use of a poetic diction based on mythical lore, and full of allusions which sometimes bear out what is written in the Edda, though often too obscure to be of much service. The only other contemporary source of information is a not very reliable history of Denmark by Saxo Grammaticus (1185 A.D.), who, to honour his native land the more, has stolen the traditions of neighbouring peoples, and brought the Old Norse gods upon the scene as heroes only, or as vanquished foes. It is the unwritten literature, the folk-lore and fairy tales of Germanic nations and of other races, which often supply us with the motive, and help us to an understanding of the Eddic myths.

But the poems are not so obscure as they appear at first sight; when taken together and compared and fitted one into the other they become intelligible and reveal much concerning themselves, their nature and their history. From internal evidence alone we must seek an answer to the question: "When and where were they composed?" The MSS., as we have seen, belong to the thirteenth and fourteenth centuries, but the poems themselves are clearly older. An atmosphere of heathendom pervades them, and suggests a time before 1000 A.D., when Christianity was established in Iceland: the evidence of language, the Icelandic dialect, and of metre shows on the other hand that they were not written earlier than the ninth century, when the Old Norse tongue underwent definite changes. Between these dates therefore, 850-1000 A.D., it is now generally agreed that the Edda was composed. During this period the Icelanders, in their intercourse with Norway and in Viking expeditions or more peaceful settlements in the British Isles, had every opportunity of drawing from all the mediæval springs of language and literature, and the question has now become "How far do the poems belong to Iceland and the North?" Altogether, Olsen thinks; Finnur Jónsson gives them to Norway; but in contrast to the early critics, who held these myths and legends as the heirloom of the whole Germanic race, the tendency is now to regard them as mainly borrowed from Christian, classical, and other foreign sources. Thus Bugge and Vigfússon will not allow that they belong to the North at all, but rather to the West, where they were composed under the influence of international literature by settlers in the British Isles. This theory cannot be wholly accepted, but their researches have at least shown that the vocabulary and descriptions of life are not exclusively Icelandic or even Northern, and they enable us to view the poems in better perspective. Few traces will be found of the immediate history of the Icelanders, their settlement in the ninth century, their life as depicted in the sagas with its strange mixture of law at home and lawlessness abroad. The stage of the Edda is filled with kings and earls such as those who once ruled in Norway or figured in heroic legends of the past. Strange fables, old-world charms and saws, where wisdom works by spells and knowledge is immersed in magic lore, barbarous customs, savage heathen rites all harmonise in the picture of an earlier life, and suggest that the writers were repeating the traditions of their mother country, or even, as Jessen holds, those of the primitive Germanic race. It is only when we come to the individual style and treatment that the setting becomes truly Northern: the *kennings* used, the descriptive details, the atmosphere and scene alike are characteristic of Iceland; and here we meet with foreign words such as plóg, plough; tresc, tress; which show the influence of European civilisation and mediæval romance. The myths likewise in their broad outlines do not belong to Iceland alone, but to other Scandinavian countries, and to Germany and England. Odin or Woden, Thor, Hel, Frigg, Tyr were known to all the tribes, as were dwarfs and elves; even the Jötun, a being so familiar in the Edda, is met in old English as a monster, "eoten." Their presentation, however—Hel, no longer as the underworld, but a northern land of mist and cold, the Jötuns, who have become Frost giants, and Odin as the War-father, a Viking in spirit—can only be creations of the Icelandic poets; while the conception of a new world and higher Powers and the figure of Baldr betoken the near approach of Christianity. It seems most reasonable, therefore, to adopt Mogk's theory that the poems were composed mainly on old themes which had been brought from the mother country into Iceland, where they took their present form with traces of Old English and Celtic influence.

But the wealth of interest in the Edda has been disclosed by the manifold researches and conjectures of different scholars pursuing each his own theory, perhaps, to extinction: Uhland, Hoffory, Müllenhoff, tracing the delicate outlines of some nature myth; Grimm and Max Müller finding links in mythology and Heinzel in poetic form between the Indo-Germanic nations; Rydberg attempting, without even attaining complete success, to prove that one grand historic saga and a few heroic forms of Germanic origin are the source of all the late and varying traditions; Schwartz, Mannhard, Meyers, distinguishing the fancies born of superstition from the religious creeds of more developed man; Kauffmann and Fraser revealing how once savage rites are still remembered and transfigured in poetic myths. But no one has done more towards proving the value of the Edda than Bugge, who has shown that all its interests in literature, history, mythology, religion are not drawn from one barren source alone, but from the wisdom of the world.

Partly for this reason, because its interests are too wide and deep
to yield themselves at once, and partly because the Edda has suffered
too much from the chances and changes of time, we offer suggested
explanations of the different poems for readers who are not previously
acquainted with Eddic literature.   We should like to have avoided all
the vexed questions which leave their scars behind and spoil appreciation of the art and spirit of the work ; but too often these questions
ask themselves, and the many possible answers give depth and large-
ness to the subject.   To those, however, who would read it without
commentary we offer the translation only, with notes of reference
between corresponding passages which may possibly serve as guides in
following the right thread, and occasionally find an end for a story
begun ; though they will not, nor will any commentary, unravel all the
tangles in the Edda.

For mythology itself is a tangled garden of thought unless it has
undergone complete transformation in the hands of the artist.   It is
nothing less than the mind of the nation laid bare, which, like the
mind of the individual, discloses a mass of inconsistent, incongruous
ideas, childish notions, mature thoughts, fleeting fancies, high imagin-
ings, borrowed opinions, lying side by side, all stamped by past
experience, but never blended into unity.

It is for some artist or historian to reveal the mind of his nation ;
if a true artist, his own sense of beauty will discover something which
is immortal and which, like the sculpture of the Greeks, he can leave
in fixed abiding forms ; if a true historian, he will disclose some one
phase or stage of development ; or if a prophet, he will declare the
ideals of his nation, and show mythology in the light of religion.   But
no such influence has given unity to the mythology of the North.   The
Edda discloses only a mixture of rational and irrational ideas, folk-
lore, and fairy tale.   Savage heathen ritual, symbolic acts, and mystic
legends are found as different expressions of the same human instinct,
and even associated with the same deity.   For the gods themselves are
continually changing their characters and forms ; well defined one
moment, the next they are shifting, shapeless beings, sometimes
appearing as types of thought, statuesque and classic in repose, or as
natural forces in their workings, full of almost human life and passion.
We seek in vain for the Indo-Germanic Heaven or Sky god, by which
is meant no unalterable personality who lives on in tradition from
age to age, but merely the conception of an over-ruling power, now

inhabiting, now symbolising, and now identified with the heaven itself. Odin, the Wind god, the High One, is set on his throne as the All-father whom all other gods obey and serve, but soon we find him parting with his weapons or attributes of Heaven god—his sword of light to Heimdal or to Frey, his thunderbolt to Thor.

We could scarcely hope for unity in a mythology which is handed down in old wives' tales and scattered fragments of art; but in a work as poetic as the Edda, and a collection which was almost co-existent with the myths themselves, we might have looked for some funda-mental idea, some one aspect whether of art or history or religion, in which they would present themselves. But we have already pointed out that the Edda is too diffuse in its interest to confine itself to one side of life: it is like some old building in which many hands and many ages have taken part: its charm lies in all its varied features and claims, and to follow the poems in an appreciative way we are obliged to dip into a world of fancy and emerge into one of fact, only to plunge and be lost in mysteries of thought: a specialist will find no satis-faction in studying it, nor can he appreciate its merits. To con-sider its myths as in any way representative of Old Norse religion would lead us very far astray. They hint now and then at acts of worship, sacrifice and rites, but the narrative or dialogue is never interwoven with prayers or hymns of praise, and seldom broken by moral teaching. The connection between the mythology and the religion of the people is obscure, and probably very slight; for the poet's hand has been at work, adding grace and humour, reinterpreting in the light of fancy rather than of truth. History also, after tracing with delight some ancient custom, distinguishing Scandinavian features from Germanic origins, and filling in a background of contemporary life in the Viking period, rejects the rest as fiction. And art will not forbear to criticise a cycle of poems which show a total lack of unity, which are manifestly by different authors and of different dates, full of obscure allusions, half forgotten tales, discrepancies, inequalities of style. But here censure will be lost in praise of the almost unique qualities of the individual poems—the dramatic power, suggestiveness, humour which seldom appears conscious of itself, vigour and swift-ness of expression, where word follows hard after word with a kind of impetuous eagerness, and where all the force of the ballad-writer is often combined with the grace of a finished artist. Nor will admira-tion pause: for there is colossal grandeur about the whole subject which inspires reverence and awe, a material grandeur, such as men loved and feared until civilisation taught them the minuteness, and also the pettiness of life, an entire contrast to the intellectual delicacy of the Greeks, and yet a mythology even more fitted than theirs for an epic poem.   The Germanic ideal naturally expressed itself in large heroic action; its huge forms and simple outlines allow infinite space for the play of power, and a skilful hand might have wrought these poems into an epic cycle as fine and much stronger than the Arthurian legend.   But they approach most nearly—in fact, only for want of the one shaping hand, they just miss being—the mightiest drama that has ever been written.   The characters Odin, Baldr, Loki, Njörd, Frey, Freyja are capable of infinite development ; they possess even now all the steadfastness of the type, all the life of the individual ; they are godlike in their power and majesty ; they are girt about with the freshness and vigour, the tenderness and youth, the breadth and atmosphere which belongs to them as forces of nature, and yet they are intensely human in their passions, in their actions, and their speech.

It is indeed as we pass from the drama and get closer and closer to a representation of life itself that a principle of unity appears in the Edda.   It is seen at last in a thread which is woven through all the poems—that of Fate, or rather Weird ; for the power of Germanic mythology is not the Fate which takes revenge on the individual and which can be seen to interpose in the fortunes of men ; it is a sweeping world-force set free by the first born beings, the Jötuns, and left to work itself out in the life of the universe.   It knows no law except that of consequence, and obeys no impulse except that of nature.   It is Weird which renders the meeting of Menglod and Dayspring as inevitable as the sunrise at dawn ; Gerd must surrender to Frey as earth must ever respond to the wooing of summer ; Thor will recover his hammer as surely as spring will return.   But Weird is seen at work on a yet mightier scale in the whole cycle of the Edda.   It is as inevitable for the Æsir, the war gods, to perish as it is for all imperfect ideals to be shattered ; and they are destroyed, before even the coming of mightier powers, as a result of their own weakness and folly, and by forces which they have long held at bay.   At intervals in the poems Doom is foretold, the Weird motive is heard.   But only in Völuspá does there seem any conscious attempt to trace its power through all the history of the gods.   This poem stands first in the Codex Regius, a place which it merits, for it is the grandest of all the works in the Edda, and is necessary for a full comprehension of the spirit which moves and lives throughout, and the unity which binds all the fragments together. But it is full of allusions whose significance is not understood except by those already familiar with the various myths and their interpretations. For this reason, and because the attitude of the writer is essentially one of summing up and estimating the value of old-world thoughts in the light of new, we have placed it last. The other poems have been arranged where possible in their right sequence in the history of the gods, but more often, for they are seldom closely related, to introduce scenes and characters most conveniently to the reader. This scheme is perhaps made clearer by the explanatory notes. Grimnismál stands first, for in it we meet with much that is most characteristic of Old Norse mythology, the chief gods and goddesses, their homes, the rude war-faring life in Valhöll, the Valkyries, and the great World-tree, Yggdrasil. Odin, the All-father, is shown in the manifold forms in which he must henceforth be recognised. Alvíssmál and Vafþruþnismál complete the description of cosmology, and make us familiar with the inhabitants of different worlds and the history of the earliest times. These poems place us at the outset in a right attitude towards the type of mythology found in the Edda: its myths have their place in evolutionary history among those drawn by the poets from a religion in the transition stage between a worship of nature and of more anthropomorphic gods. In Hávamál, the High One reveals himself by relating the mysteries of his own experience and the wisdom he has gained. Hymiskviþa, Thrymskviþa, and Skirnismál are less didactic narratives of Thor and Frey, told with a simple love for old themes, and still in touch with nature myths; but in the next poems Fjölsvinnismál, Rigsþula, Hyndluljoþ and Harbardsljoþ, the myth is associated with some new theme, and used merely as a setting; veiled meanings suggest themselves, and the gods have become more conventional forms. Their power is waning, and in Baldrs Draumar and Lokasenna the Weird motive is heard waxing stronger and louder, proclaiming the near approach of Doom or Ragnarök, for once more the Icelandic word is required to express a Doom which is but the last of life's issues. The first of these poems, with its tone of solemn warning, is like a return to faith in the old gods; the second, with the mocking laughter of a sceptic, reviews and criticises their history and their characters. Völuspá also

B B

is a retrospect, but seen with a tender discerning eye, and, as we have noticed, an attempt to find unity and truth.

The text has been included more for the sake of comparison with the English than for the use of scholars and students. The version is based on that of Gering (Padeborn, 1904), whose spelling and metrical corrections have generally been adopted. The spelling is to some extent simplified : '*ö*' is used both for the 'i' umlaut of 'o' and the 'u' umlaut of '*a*' ; '*œ*' represents the 'i' umlaut of '*ó*' ; the '*u*' umlaut of '*á*' is neglected as in all later MSS. Different readings of the more important passages are noted below with the same abbreviation of names which are found in the best German commentaries. Emendations and all changes in order of strophes are also noted with a reference to the MSS. as given by Detter and Heinzel (Leipzig, 1903), whose edition, it should be observed, is arranged in half lines.

No precise attempt has been made in the translation to render the original metre, which follows strict laws of its own ; the long line is divided by cæsura into half lines, which are connected by alliterative staves falling on the most emphatic words, and occasionally by rhyme. Two forms of strophe are found : the Fornyrþislag resembles most nearly the oldest epic metre of the Germanic race; it is used in Völuspá, Thrymskviþa, and other epic lays, and consists of four such lines as described ; the Ljoþaháttr, which is peculiar to Old Norse, has greater rhythm and flexibility ; variety is given by the alternation of long lines with and without cæsura. It is more suitable for the dramatic poems like Skirnismál, or for dialogue as in Lokasenna. Alliteration has been retained or introduced where possible, and the rhythm, which is hard for modern ears to catch, has been slightly emphasised—all, we freely admit, resulting in a compromise which satisfies neither the new nor the old, but which seems the only means of introducing the one to the other.

It is with great hesitation that a translation (based mainly on suggestions by Detter, Gering, Finnur Jónsson, Vigfússon, and other authorities) has been given of the names, many of which are of doubtful meaning. By-names often seem to be used only for the sake of alliteration ; in such cases (Grm., st. 8) it has sometimes been considered advisable to substitute the better known title. On the other hand, we ourselves have occasionally introduced a familiar by-name for metrical convenience. In every case, however, the text will supply the original form even to those unacquainted with Icelandic. Where the meaning of the names is wholly obscure they are given in their original form in the translation; 'd' is adopted for Icelandic 'þ,' or '*th*,' since this has been done in previous versions, and a few names, such as Odin, which have already become familiar to English readers, are retained. The nominative case ending '*r*' ('*l*,' '*n*') is dropped except in the case of '*ir*'—as Fenrir; or where '*r*' forms part of the stem—as *Baldr*.

We would here express our gratitude to Prof. Ker, Mr. W. G. Collingwood, and Mr. A. F. Major, whose corrections and suggestions have been of inestimable value in the translation, commentary, and general plan of the work.

THE SAYINGS OF GRIMNIR.

It has been suggested that Grimnismál is one of the oldest poems in the collection, and it may well have been such in its original form, for there is a grand simplicity in expression and an absence of any seemingly borrowed ideas. It touches only on the main features of Old Norse mythology, and has no knowledge of later stories which grew up around the separate gods and goddesses, and which form such frequent subjects of allusion by the poets, supplying them with a wealth of obscure poetical imagery. But the confused arrangement, which we have altered only for the sake of giving more sequence to the ideas, and such details as those which surround the original conception of the World Tree, suggest revision and interpolation, and give ground for the supposition that the poem as it stands is of late origin, and an attempt to revive a belief in the old religion by the teaching of old myths. The setting of the poem, too, bears the mark of a different and more skilful hand. It is wonderfully dramatic in contrast to the quiet rehearsal of old-world knowledge and traditional lore. Odin and Frigg appear first as humble peasants, who give shelter to the sons of a certain King Hraudung. Next the Sky god is pictured in Heaven, sitting on his throne of Window-shelf, from whence he can view all the worlds. "Odin," says Snorri, "is highest and first born among gods. He rules over all things, and the other gods, however mighty, serve him as children serve their father." Beside him is Frigg, his wife, who is also a power of the sky, and perhaps the ruler of the clouds. The scene changes, and Odin is found once more upon earth

as a stranger at Geirröd's doors.   He appears in the form best known
to men—grey-bearded, and clad in blue mantle and broad-brimmed
hat, but he is unrecognised by Geirröd.   Here the poem opens with
the tortured god sitting between the fierce heat of two fires, craving for
one draught of water from Agnar's hands to cool his parched lips
before he can answer the questions of his tormentors concerning the
secret and holy places of the world.   From time to time the narrative
is broken by a cry from the god—to his faithful Valkyries, who even
now bear refreshing ale to the Chosen warriors in Valhöll—to his
kinsmen who are assembling, as was their wont, to drink in the sea
halls of Ægir.   How he is at last delivered from his painful situation
is left uncertain, owing to the obscurity of sts. 42 and 45.

To a like skilful hand belong the magnificent strophes in which
Grimnir reveals himself to Geirröd as Odin, the highest god; where
the poet shows him as the One, who in different ages and for different
beings has many aspects and many names.   In his character as
Heaven god, he is Odin, Wafter, Tree-rocker, Wind-roar; as ruler in
Asgarth, they call him the High One, Equal-ranked, Third Highest.
He is the life and source of all things—the Maker, the All-father.   He
rules the World as the Watcher from Window-shelf.   He comes forth
from Valhöll as the Death-father, and goes to battle as War-father,
Host-leader, Helm-bearer.   To evil giants he appears as the Dread
One, Bale-worker, Flashing-eyed, Flaming-eyed.   Both gods and men
know the Wanderer, Grey-beard, Long-beard, Broad-hat.   As Well-
comer he has many a love adventure; as Hoodwinker, Form-changer,
Wizard, he is the great master of magic.   He is moreover the god of
culture, the Sage and Wise One, the Counsellor or Poet who has won
the Song-mead, and even bestowed the gift of poesy upon men.   This
glorious monotheistic hymn reminds us of some Indian poet singing of
Krishna, "countless mystic forms unfolding in one Form."   In such
Protean fashion the supreme god of every mythology has the right to
change his shape, and assume the powers and attributes of lesser beings.
It is unusual, however, for an old Northern mythologist to show such
appreciation of this truth.   He is usually content with presenting a
god now in this light, now in that, and each of the different poems
which relate to Odin will reveal him more fully in some one of the
above characters.   Here the "Masked One" has veiled his god-head
and suffered torment in order to instruct and enlighten mankind.

Grimnir begins his recital of old lore by enumerating the homes of

the gods, which usually correspond with the characters of their owners. All the principal deities are mentioned except Frigg, who, as we are told elsewhere, has her dwelling in the "Halls of Moisture," where perhaps she rules the clouds. Loki also is omitted, for the airy fire demon had no resting place until he was bound in the underworld. Odin is here the War-father, who shows the true Viking spirit of an old Norse hero. His home is Valhöll, the Hall of the Slain, described in sts. 8-10, 20-24. It is seen from afar, standing high in Asgarth, overshadowed by Yggdrasil, and surrounded by the air river Thund, which roars and thunders when the dead are brought through by the Valkyries. This dwelling is reserved for the chosen sons of Odin who have been slain in strife; other dead folk pass to the underworld of Hel. Snorri says, drawing his information mainly from this passage and other extant poems, "all the warriors who have fallen in battle since the beginning of the world come to Odin in Valhöll. A great host is there assembled, and more shall gather; yet they will seem too few when Fenrir, the Wolf, is let loose at Ragnarök, the Doom of the gods. They have for food the flesh of a sooty-black boar called Sæhrimnir, which will never be consumed, however great the throng in Valhöll. Each day he is boiled in Eldhrimnir (the fire-smoked cauldron) by Andhrimnir (the sooty-faced cook), and every evening he becomes whole again. But Odin partakes not of the same food as his Chosen Warriors. He gives the portion from his table to two wolves, Greed and Ravener, for he himself needs no food, but wine is his meat and drink. Two ravens sit perched on his shoulder, and whisper to him tidings of what they have seen and heard. Thought and Memory are their names. He sends them flying each day over all the world, and at breakfast-time they return. Thus he is made ware of the things which come to pass, and is called by mortals the Raven god. The Chosen Warriors have a drink which, like their food, is never failing; but they drink not water, for how should All-father bid kings and earls and other mighty men to his halls and give them nought but water? A great price would it seem to those who had suffered wounds and death to get such a draught for their pains. But there stands a she-goat called Heidrun over the roof of Valhöll, biting leaves from the Shelterer's boughs. Mead flows from her teats into a vessel so huge that all the Chosen Warriors can drink their fill. When they are not drinking they hold sport. Each morning they put on their war-gear and take their weapons, and go forth into the court-yard and there fight and lay one another low, and play thus till breakfast-time, when they go back and sit them down to drink." These daily conflicts, it would seem, are but a preparation for the last great conflict at Ragnarök. Valhöll as a paradise is the ideal of the West in contrast to that of the East. It is no home of rest, but one of conflict and strenuous endeavour, where the warriors fight on higher planes the same battles that they fought upon earth, still with the same hope of achievement and honour, still with a delight in the struggle itself, which is never finished. Even the alternating periods of bliss have no resemblance to the passive Nirvana state, but are like the ale which the Old Norsemen drank at their revels, deep and intoxicating draughts of active material enjoyment.

In st. 7 Odin, as husband of Saga the seeress, is a god of wisdom, and perhaps the by-name which we omitted, Hrópt, the One who Utters, was used with intent. But the story attached to it is unknown. It is perhaps only another version of the Mimir myth, where the god draws his wisdom from sacred waters (p. 287). Full of pictorial beauty is the scene of Odin and Saga drinking peacefully from the fount of knowledge.

Three sons of Odin are mentioned: Thor (st. 4), who, as wielder of the great thunder-hammer, owns the Home of Strength; Vidar (st. 17), called by Snorri "the silent god," who lives in wild Wood-home; and Baldr (st. 12), whose dwelling-place is fair and shining as his face, and pure as the heart of him who is the best, and the most loved of all the gods.

Two gods, Ull and Forseti (sts. 5 and 15), play little part in Old Norse mythology, but were well known among other Germanic tribes. Ull, as the great archer, owns the land of yew-trees which were used for making bows. He is called Ollerus by Saxo, and is said to have been given both the name and kingdom of Odin when the latter was banished for practising magic. Forseti is the son of Baldr and Nanna. His cult may be traced among the Frisians. In Heligoland, which is called by Latin writers "Forsiti's land," the god had his temple and holy places, and the people told legends of a culture hero, sprung from the gods, who came once and taught them justice and "Frisian right."

The owner of Vala-shelf (st. 6) is not clearly indicated.

Many obscure myths have attached themselves to the name of Heimdal, who was primarily a god of light. As such "he is warder of the gods, and sits at the end of heaven to guard the bridge Bifröst against the giants." Loki taunts him with this arduous life (p. 263), but he had also his pleasant home of Heaven-hill. Frey and Freyja, with their father Njörd, belong to the gentler tribe of gods called Wanes (Vanir), distinguished from the war-gods, or Æsir. Frey (st. 5), as god of summer fruitfulness, dwells in a home of sunshine among the elves. Freyja (st. 14), who has here assumed the powers of Frigg, rules in Folk-field; while Njörd, the peaceful sea-god, has made his home in Noatun beside the ocean.

One dwelling-place, Sound-home (st. 11), is not found in Asgarth, the gods' realm, but in Jötunheim, or Giant-land, which is always associated with the stirring, sounding elements of nature. The famous story of Thiazi and his daughter Skadi is given later on.

After describing his own home and the joyous life there, Grimnir, tortured by fiery heat, calls to mind the cool, rushing waters which flow from Roaring Kettle, the central fountain of the world, which brings him to the holiest of all places, the Doomstead of the gods, where they assemble daily to hold council and judgment. Here also are two other fountains—the well of Mimir, whence Odin draws his wisdom, and the well of Weird, with the Norns who dwell beside it shaping the lives of men. Overhead rises the World-tree Yggdrasil, which Grimnir has just called by the name which in his torment most appealed to him—the Shelterer. He remembers now its sufferings: the fair, green boughs which stretch over the heavens, and whence fall the dews of life, are being gnawed by spiteful harts; the roots, springing no man knows how deep, are torn by the fierce dragon of the under-world; and the mighty stem which rises like the central column of the universe, rots and suffers from decay. In all ages and among many peoples has been traced this reverence for a tree—first, as the embodiment of the tree-spirit, the home of vegetative life; and, lastly, as typifying the source of spiritual life. Yggdrasil is sometimes the World Tree, which embraces the Universe of space and time. Here, behind the poetic fancies, which are peculiar to Old Norse mythology, it stands in grand outlines as the symbol of all creation—groaning and travailing together in death, but quickened and renewed with never-failing life.

A well-ordered scheme of Old Norse cosmology meets with a difficulty in st. 31. The realms of Hel, of Jötunheim, and of mankind, which lie beneath the three roots of Yggdrasil, are there clearly conceived as on one level and bordering on each other, but elsewhere (pp. 240, 291) Hel is stated to be underground. Other passages suggest that there was a confusion between an old Germanic idea of Hel situated beneath the earth and the Scandinavian notion of Hel and Jötunheim in the bleak and terrible regions of the north and east, divided from Midgarth, the home of men, and Asgarth, the home of gods, by great rivers which flowed from Roaring Kettle.

It is now that Odin (st. 36) cries aloud to his war-maidens, the Valkyries. They are Choosers of the Slain, winged beings who attend the conflict, who slay the "fey" or doomed ones, and bring them to Odin's hall. A song worthy of these battle-maidens is given to them in Njáls Saga :—

> Let us wind, let us wind the web of darts !
> fare we forth to wade through the host
> where our friends are crossing weapons.
> Let us wind, let us wind the web of darts
> where the banners of the warriors are streaming !

And thus weaving the web of war, they foretell who shall stand and who shall fall on the bloody field. Their more peaceful office is to serve the Chosen Warriors at their feast in Valhöll.

Grimnir then resumes his narrative. Still craving for coolness and shelter from the burning heat, he tells of the weary Sun horses, refreshed in their labours by a delicious chill which is given by the gods to lighten their toil ; of earth, protected by a mysterious shadow-maker whose nature is unknown ; of Sun herself, "who fares swiftly as one in fear," but has a home of refuge where she may hide herself from her tormentor, the grim wolf Sköll.

The next strophes which recount the creation of the world are best considered with the Words of the Mighty Weaver, where they are also found (p. 47). 43 and 44 have little bearing on the context. The story of the Wielder's sons is famous in Old Norse mythology, and a frequent topic of allusion. Snorri relates how Loki, the mischief-maker, had once cut off the golden hair of Sif, the Thunderer's wife, and to appease the latter had gone down to the dwarf race called Dark elves, the Wielder's sons, and persuaded them to forge her a wig of gold. They made this with other treasures so wonderful that Loki, never weary of stirring up strife, wagered his head with two dwarfs called Brokk the Badger and Sindri the Sparkler that they could not make aught as fine. Thereupon the twain set to work and forged three treasures, although Loki sought to hinder them, and changed himself into a fly, which settled upon Brokk and stung him as he was blowing the furnace. When all were complete Loki and the dwarfs brought the treasures to Asgarth to settle the wager, and "the gods went to their thrones of doom to hear the judgment of Odin, Thor, and Frey, which none could gainsay."

The work of the Dark elves was first set forth, and to Odin Loki gave Gungnir, the spear which never failed to hit the mark; and to Thor the golden hair for Sif, "which would grow into the flesh as soon as it was placed upon her head;" and to Frey the ship Skidbladnir, "which was followed by a fair wind when the sails were set wheresoever it went. It was so huge that all the gods could find room in it with their weapons and war gear, and yet one could fold it up like a cloth and put it in one's pocket." Then Brokk brought out his treasures, and gave to Odin the ring called Draupnir, saying that eight rings would drop from it every ninth night; to Frey he gave the Boar which could run through air and sea, by night and day, swifter than any steed, for never was night so dark nor the underworld so murk but there was light enough to go on from the gleaming of its golden bristles. But the hammer which was called Mjöllnir, Brokk gave to Thor, and told him that he might strike with it as hard as he willed, no matter what lay before him, and the hammer would not fail; that if he hurled it away it would never miss the mark, nor fly so far but he would find it there when he felt with his hand; moreover that it would become so small that he could hide it if he liked in his bosom. There was but one flaw in the hammer; it was somewhat short in the handle. Then the gods gave judgment that Mjöllnir was the best of all treasures, and the mightiest weapon of defence against the Frost giants.

Perhaps Meyers is right in tracing an Indo-Germanic myth in this tradition of the dwarf forgers; they were, like the Cyclopes of Greek mythology and the air beings of the Vedas, personifications of natural forces, who wrought weapons to aid the gods in subduing the ruder and more hostile powers. Most precious in each case was the thunder-hammer or thunder-bolt.

Bifröst (st. 44) is a bridge between heaven and earth, which, Snorri says, is woven out of the colour of the rainbow. Its name signifies the "trembling way," from its nature as light. It will scarce bear Thor, and must be broken at Ragnarök. Sleipnir, Odin's eight-footed steed, is seen in Baldr's Draumar; Bragi, the mythical poet, at the great banquet scene of Lokasenna; Garm, the Hel hound, with his loud baying, announces Doom to the gods. This strophe sounds like a conventional Song of Saws with which Grimnir ends his recital.

THE WISDOM OF ALL-WISE.

In Alvíssmál we pass from the fearful scene of a god in anguish to the elf-land of poetic fancy. Here the author is little bound by traditional ideas, but may exercise all his imagination and skill in describing nature, who has ever fresh beauties to offer and fresh poetic themes. In two particulars only has he borrowed from mythology—he shows himself familiar with all mythical beings in the worlds of the Edda, and he has taken for the setting of his poem some possibly well-known story which told how Thrym, the daughter of Thor, was pledged to a dwarf by the other gods in the absence of her father. This dwarf, All-wise, is discovered hastening to the home of his betrothed, rejoicing too soon at the good fortune which has won him a bride born of gods. Thus, lost in love-musing, he is met by a rude and way-worn traveller—Thor returning on foot from some weary journey into the land of giants. All-wise does not recognise the father of his bride, and is much injured at the harshness of Thor's address. He has doubtless, if such vanities are permitted to dwarfs, clothed himself in his best as a bridegroom, and now he is taunted with the disfigurements of his race, the pallor of beings who may never see the sun, and the shortness of stature which gives rise to fear and hatred of their giant foes. Swelling with pride he stands upon his rights, and even answers the irony of the ill-clad wanderer by admiring his rich attire. But the god of Thunder declares himself, and the dwarf seeks to propitiate him by a display of wisdom. Thor detains him in conversation—strange behaviour in one whose wonted speech is brief and stern—until the sun has risen and All-wise is turned into stone, which is the fate of all foolish dwarfs who are caught by the first morning beam above ground.

Thor questions All-wise on the different names which are given to objects of nature by the beings of different worlds, all of whom are well known to Old Norse mythology, and reappear so constantly that it will be worth our while to make their closer acquaintance.

Mankind occupy Midgarth, the middle dwelling of Germanic cosmology, between Heaven and Hel. The gods born of Odin's race, or adopted as his children, have their home in Asgarth. In this poem and elsewhere they are called Æsir, to distinguish them from the other god tribe, the Wanes. The Jötuns are best known as giants, but this name little describes their true character. They appear sometimes, it is true, as three-headed monsters who walk the earth in anthropomorphic form, much like the giants of Grimm's fairy tales. They are seen, too, as beautiful human creatures, such as Skadi, who know the loves and sorrows of human kind. But in Old Norse tradition they still retain something of what they have lost in the folklore of other Germanic tribes—their original character as wild forces of nature, born before the controlling, ordering power of the gods had been established. As such they are akin to the Titans, or the Fomors of Celtic mythology. Their home was once in the storm, in the waters, amid the tumultuous elements; but by the poets of the Edda they have already been given a fixed habitation, Jötunheim, a waste and desolate realm situated in the north or the east. Skadi alone still dwells in Sound-home. As beings of nature they are clearly shown in the Frost giants, and the Mountain giants, in Hymir, lord of the dusky sea, in Sköll and Hati, the wolves of darkness, and the giant eagle who makes the wind. They are the great opponents of the gods, but not all, for some have lent their powers to be used with skill and purpose for the good of all living things. Ægir, ruler of the sea in its milder moods, provides the gods with drink, and is even numbered among them. Mimir gives a draught to Odin from his fount of wisdom. The Norns who dwell by the Tree of Fate are weaving strands of life. Asgarth itself is built by a giant smith. Odin learns the fate of Baldr from a giantess, and seeks giant maidens as his wives; for the gods cannot dispense with the power of the Jötuns. They are dependent, moreover, on another race of beings, the dwarfs, who forge their treasures and cunning weapons. For this myth also we must seek an explanation in the instinctive beliefs or intuitions which man keeps with him from his earliest days till superstitious fancy ends in knowledge—his sense of unity with Nature, the feeling that earth and air are filled with a life in some way akin to his own, but made visible only in its workings. The dwarfs and elves are, in contrast to the Jötuns, the secret, silent forces, unseen agents who toil beneath the ground and possess the hidden treasures of the earth; or creatures of air, who make their homes in mountains, woods, and fields, and who appear in such fairy form that "beautiful as an elf" became a customary phrase in different tongues. Snorri speaks of the Dark elves or dwarfs and the Light elves who inhabit Elf-home and those future realms of Paradise which he calls Far-blue and Long-life. In early folk-lore they were usually beneficent beings, and their presence was held as a safeguard to men; but later on, through Christian antagonism to all heathen superstition, they were regarded as malevolent sprites, and became confused with evil-working trolls.

Of the other races mentioned, the Powers and High Powers are mysterious; the word "regin" is often used for the gods, from whom they are here distinguished. Hel-folk are the dead who have not perished in war, and who have therefore no place in Valhöll, but must pass to those regions of the underworld called Hel, which in later tradition was given to a goddess of that name.

Thor questions All-wise concerning thirteen different objects which fall into pairs—Earth and Heaven, Moon and Sun, Clouds and Wind, Calm and Sea, Fire and Wood, Corn and the Ale which is brewed from barley. Night alone is without her fellow Day, either because dwarfs may not see him, or because, too soon, he will appear. Each object is described in six different terms, such as might be used by the inhabitants of the different worlds, though to us their fitness is not always apparent. Sometimes, however, they show careful discrimination on the part of the poet. Men use the more ordinary names, and Thor also employs these. Elves call Heaven the Fair-roof, because it stretches over their home in the air. Jötuns call Moon the Hastener, for he is pursued always by one of their own kindred, the great wolf Hati, while dwarfs who are permitted to look on his soft light call him the "Shimmerer;" but Sun, who plays hide and seek with them, is the Dallier's playmate. The synonyms do not belong to the ordinary poetic diction of skalds; but with a dainty touch and a delicate play of language the poet of Alvíssmál employs an art which is clearly his own, showing individual love and observation of nature.

THE WORDS OF THE MIGHTY WEAVER.

Vafþruþnismál, like Alvíssmál, is a song of nature, but more in accordance with traditional ideas. It is a poetical interpretation of

Old Norse mythology, which has suffered change from that existent among the people with its unquestioning belief in elves and giants, dwarfs and trolls as veritable beings who helped and hindered their doings; for Day and Night, Winter and Summer are here the wonderful giants of a fairy tale; Rimy-mane and Shining-mane are never found in folk-lore, nor the great eagle who makes the wind.

The most life-like figure in the poem is that of Mighty Weaver, a giant sage, unutterably old and unutterably wise; the personification of all Experience, who sits on his throne throughout the ages, waiting to be questioned by those who dare enter his presence.   In Old Norse tradition there are no legends of inspired prophets who in visions have been allowed to look into the future of the world, or of singers who have been given utterance in divine madness.   The mysteries of nature are hidden deep in her own bosom, and shared only by those beings who are nearest akin to her and draw their wisdom from its source, or those who by long familiarity have learned her ways.   Knowledge must be sought from bird or beast, from souls of the dead who have gone back to their home in nature, but above all from the giants, that ancient race who were born even before the earth, and were made of like substance.   There was one other way, indeed, though scarce permitted, in which it was deemed possible to attain wisdom, through magic spells such as those used by witches when they "sat out," enchanting like the Vala (p. 287), and compelled the night powers to give up their secrets.

Odin has now resolved to contend with the giant whose knowledge is a race heritage; but Frigg is fearful as to the issue, for the contest is no mock one.   Odin, though a god, is not all-wise by nature, but has to learn, borrow, buy, and even steal his wisdom.   Disguised as Riddle-reader he enters the giant's hall, and stands on the floor with an assumption of humility until he has proved his right to sit beside the Mighty Weaver.   If the latter had known the nature of his guest he would scarce have asked the Wind god concerning powers of the sky and the steeds of light and darkness, which Odin well knows. Day and Night in this form, as we have already noticed, are only a late invention of poets, though they were undoubtedly objects of superstition among Germanic races, and sometimes conceived as animals. In German poetry Day is a beast or bird who tears the clouds of darkness with his claws; in Anglo-Saxon he is a raven who "blithe-hearted announces the joy of heaven."   The language used in all time

to describe the ever-recurring phenomena of day and night show that
they were felt as living personalities, whose presence was not merely
visible, but could be heard in its mysterious movements.   In Old
English, Day glides and climbs, clangs and hastens and pushes on ; in
modern English, it still breaks and peeps.   In German, it gathers
strength (erstarket) or turns aside (ervendet).   Night sinks and falls,
and in Anglo-Saxon wears a shadow helm.   The Old Norse lay of
Sigrdrifa has a greeting to dawn, which sounds like an ancient hymn
and prayer for divine aid :—

> Hail Day,   hail sons of Day,
>   hail Night and the daughter of Night !
> With eyes of blessing   behold us now
>   and grant us victory who sit here.

    Sun and Moon belong to Part II. of this poem, but may be
mentioned here, for they have undergone a change corresponding to
that of Day and Night.   Cæsar notes their worship among the old
Germans, whose religion, in a period better known, was far removed
from any pure nature-worship, and one in which Sun and Moon no
longer play any prominent part.   Their humiliation is recounted by
Snorri in a myth.   The gods were wroth because the Sun and Moon took
to themselves such mighty names, and set them in their places in heaven
where they could only move on their appointed course.   Sol or Sunne
is still a goddess, the sister or companion of the Moon god.   She is
drawn in her chariot by the horses Early-woke and All-fleet, and is
pursued by the wolf Sköll, while Mani, who rules the changes of the
moon called Ny and Ni (st. 25, Grim.), is followed by Hati.   But the
glory of Sun, the myths which tell of her ever-renewed conflicts and
triumphs over darkness, her wealth and her bounty have been transferred to the more anthropomorphic gods Baldr, Odin, Frey, and
Freyja, who each in turn represent the sun deity.

    Though openly deprived of their dominion, traces of Sun and
Moon worship linger in old customs and folk-lore.   The power of
Moon, though somewhat impersonal, is apparent in superstitious
practises, which have hardly died out.   His waxing and waning was
regarded as influential for good and ill on the doings of mankind.
That which required growth and increase was undertaken while he
was waxing ; money was counted, weddings took place, and seed was
planted which bore fruit above ground.   But with the waning Moon

timber was felled, grass was mown, charms were used against pestilence, and the seed planted whose fruit ripened beneath the ground.

St. 27 is the only passage in the poems which speaks of Winter and Summer as personal beings, though at one time they were doubtless regarded as such. The custom of crowning a May king or queen, and the expulsion of Winter, represented by a victim or an effigy, are recollections of the days when both were powers who had to be propitiated and coerced by ceremonies and magic. The conflict between Winter and Summer has become in the Edda a struggle between the gods and the Jötuns, and especially one between Thor and the Frost giants.

The last question of the giant (st. 17) concerns the future. When this is answered he admits the wisdom of his guest, and invites him to a seat on the throne. But Riddle-reader has so far only proved himself equal to his opponent; he must now show himself superior. The first questions are comparatively easy. Who should know better than the old giant how earth was framed from his forefather, Ymir. In the beginning, relates Snorri, there was nought but Muspell-home, the world of fire in the south, and Mist-home, the region of ice and snow, in the north, and between them the yawning Deep called Ginnunga Gap. Then Ymir, the first Jötun, was born. He arose from the melting poison-drops of the chill river Stormy-billow, which flowed southward towards Muspell-home. In due time he begot children (st. 33), but before long arose another race of nobler kind. Once when the cow called Audumbla was licking salt from a rock there appeared a man's hair, then his head, and at length his whole form. This was Bur, father of Bor, whose son by the giantess Bestla was Odin. Thus the gods were born or evolved, like those of many other mythologies, after a first imperfect creation. They slew Ymir, and made the world out of his mighty frame; while all the other giants were drowned in his blood except Bergelm, who was laid in some mysterious object (here rendered as cradle, st. 35), and thus saved from the flood. Snorri has many details which are not given in Vafþruþnismál, and modern critics have still further completed a picture of the deluge, with Bergelm floating on its bloody billows in a Noah's ark, perhaps of Scandinavian type; or, translating Icelandic luþr as *flour-bin*, of a great world-mill in which the giants were ground up for the making of the world.*

---

* *See* Rydberg, *pp. 387-395*; Hamlet in Iceland, *by I. Gollancz, pp. xi.-xvi.*

But the poem is aware of no such studied myth; it alludes vaguely to some great epoch when the everlasting war began between the gods and the Jötuns, when natural powers were first made subject to god-like ends.

The Mighty Weaver has now proved his knowledge of giant-lore, and is asked concerning the history and life of the gods. He remembers the first great war between their kindred races, the gentle Wanes or gods of culture and the war-like Æsir (see also p. 283), which ended with exchange of hostages and the admittance of Njörd among the Æsir.

He knows too, as well as humble earth-folk, that when the wind is heard roaring overhead on stormy nights, Odin, the lord of Valhöll, the Victory Father, is holding sport with his Chosen warriors. This most famous of Old Norse myths is not peculiar to Scandinavia. It is found in Britain in connection with King Arthur, and among the superstitions of Somerset, where, however, a somewhat close resemblance suggests direct borrowing from Old Norse sources.* More original is the wide-spread superstition among German peasants of the Furious Host or Wild Hunt which was heard passing through the air, led by an old man, sometimes visible in his broad-brimmed hat, who rode a white or black horse, and was called by the name of Wode or Wote. Both versions have arisen from the blending of different ideas. The souls of those who died appeared to be withdrawn into the world of nature from whence they had come; in woods, by streams, among mountains their presence was detected, and they dwelt in companion-ship with elves and watersprites, but most of all they haunted the air. Odin as Wind god became lord of these spirits, but especially of the dead warriors, since he was also the god of battle, and those slain on the field were dedicated to him and called "guests of Odin." His valkyries, as we have already mentioned, used to ride through the air at his bidding, and choose from the battlefield those who were worthy of a summons from the War-god.

The questions now become more abstruse. They touch on the future history of the world, and the reign of new powers after the Great Doom, which is foretold in the Soothsaying of the Vala. Even in the present untroubled lay, which seems only to rejoice in the life and

---

* As shown by the Rev. C. W. Whistler, Saga Book, vol. ii., part i., pp. 46, 48, 49; vol. v., part i., p. 146.

powers of nature, Weird is already visible to the giant, he knows its end. But there is one secret which he does not know, and which all have failed to divine, a secret hidden between god and god, which Odin whispered in Baldr's ear, as he laid him on the bale-fire, in words which only the dead could hear. The very question reveals the personality of the god; the Weaver admits his defeat; and it is shown that Odin has thus far attained all the knowledge which can be won by experience and learned by tradition. In the next poem it will be seen how, in mysterious fashion, he attains the wisdom which more properly belongs to him as a god.

THE WORDS OF ODIN, THE HIGH ONE.

Another poem introducing some of the more remarkable and interesting myths is Hávamál, or The Words of the High One. It has been subjected to almost more discussion than any other poem of the Edda, but all the ingenuity of critics and scholars has not cleared it from mystery and confusion. It has served rather to show how superficial and fragmentary is our knowledge of the history, the myths, and the soul-life of the early Germanic races. For although this poem, with its wisdom of yesterday and to-morrow, myths which are purely Scandinavian, ideas which can only be Christian, may belong to different periods, it seems to be archaic in the main. The same half obsolete words occur in the various parts, and the teaching is traditional, proverbial, such as might have been handed down by word of mouth. Moreover, Odin or Woden appears, not as the War-father of the Skalds, but in his more universal character as the god of culture. As such he was best known to all the Germanic tribes and to the Romans, who identified him with their god Mercury—Wednesday or Woden's day corresponding with " dies Mercurii."

The varying metre and style of the poem, its discrepancies, and abrupt changes of subject prove it to be a collection of once separate fragments. Attempts have been made to distinguish between these, but there are only three well-marked divisions: 1 (st. 1-108), the Guest-rules, in which are included ethical laws and Odin's love adventures; 2 (st. 108-136), the Counselling of Stray Singer; 3, Odin's quest after the runes. Parts II. and III. are linked together by the entrance of Stray

D D

Singer into both, and all the three by a poetical fiction in which it is assumed that Odin, the High One, is speaker throughout, and that the precepts are given with divine authority.   It is, indeed, in the person of Odin himself that a real unity can be claimed for the poem.   It would seem that its final author, who was more teacher than poet, possibly a Christian monk with a taste for antiquarian knowledge, had a mind not merely to collect the wise sayings of heathen lore, but to show forth Odin, the heathen god, in a higher and more spiritual aspect than that of the War-father.   He had none of the poetic imagination of the author of Grimnismál, to picture in rainbow strophes the manifold nature of the god.   In a loose and inartistic way he has associated traditional sayings and mythical stories, freely admitting the later and more Christian-seeming ideas to a place beside the old.   He has not, however, altogether failed in his aim.   For notwithstanding the signs of Christian influence, which have caused the poem to be rent in pieces by criticism and held as a haphazard collection of fragments new and old, Odin reveals himself still a heathen, and emerges from a web of heathen thought steeped in the magic of old charms and runes.   In the whole teaching of the poem, which is filled with sober beauty and wisdom, there is no creed save that of humanity.

In Part I. Odin comes as guest to a hall, and, it is assumed, gives friendly counsel to those assembled within.   In his character of Wind-wanderer he often passes thus unrecognised through all the worlds. With Loki and Hönir he is often found adventuring in Giant-land, and comes to the dwellings of men calling himself "Gest."   The Sagas tell how he visited many kings and rulers of Norway under this title. To the Christian king Olaf the Holy he was an object of terror and hate, as the dread heathen god of enchantments who still lived and could be exorcised only by the more potent spell of the mass-book.

"Far have I fared, much have I ventured," said Odin, and it was thus as wanderer, beggar, guest, that he learned the ways of the world and the hearts of men.   Laws of love, friendship, and war are expressed, often with epigrammatic humour, sometimes with a tender, half-pitying knowledge of life.   The first Part, and the advice given to Stray Singer in the second, are full of sayings and maxims which agree almost word for word with the wisdom of Solomon or other ethical teachers, for they are of the nature of those simple truths which take up their abode with mankind so soon as he has learned humanity and fellowship.

But, unlike the teaching of the Eastern prophet, there is nothing of religious duty, no aspiring after an ideal of perfection. The sober precepts of common sense are never interrupted by sudden upward soarings and yearnings of passion. The wisdom of Odin, in this Part, is the wisdom drawn from experience.

Historically, the poem is of immense value. We are taken far back into real life, and meet people no longer in a world of myth and speculation, but on the firm ground of daily existence. Customs, manners, social duties, and relations are brought before us, corresponding closely sometimes with what Tacitus wrote in the *Germania* about the race in the first century, and it is seen from his descriptions that sts. 11, 17, 41, allude to what was especially characteristic of the old Germans. St. 155 also refers to a curious practice mentioned by him. The German warriors advanced to meet their foes, like the giant Hrym (p. 293), with shields lifted to the level of their lips as a sounding board for their song. They sung gently at first, letting the sound swell out until it became like the roar of the sea, inspiring terror and rousing their own courage. Other customs are typically Northern. The word for court mentioned in st. 61 is þing, a name for the great assembly or parliament of the Norsemen, which was most democratic in character. Here were settled the laws of the land, and private cases were tried with no lack of ceremony and red tape, though matters frequently ended in a duel or a free fight between the two parties.

In st. 84 we come to the love quests of Odin, in which the High One has descended from his height, and laid all dignity aside. His love is not even the idealised love of the mediæval knight errant, but like that of Zeus, the pastime of the god. There may once have been some underlying motive in these tales of Odin and his giant wives, explaining his conduct as that of some fickle power of nature, but here he figures only as the favourite of the skalds, the love adventurer, who knew as well as any the chances and mischances of love. We may imagine that our author selected one of these skaldic poems which contained the famous story of how Odin won the art of poesy for men by making love to the giantess Gunnlod, but unfortunately for the dignity of the god, he included also the other episode with Billing's daughter. But here, too, he may be intending to record one of the most important incidents in Eddic mythology, which led to the birth of Vali, Baldr's avenger. We have allusion in the Edda (pp. 159, 243)

to Odin's courtship of Rind.   Saxo Grammaticus tells more fully of
his ardent wooing in a story which so closely resembles the above as to
suggest that Billing's nameless daughter is Rind, although the one is
seemingly of dwarf Rind, the other, according to Saxo, a giantess.*
The tale of this crafty maiden, who thrice outwitted Odin, is here told
in delicately suggestive scenes, enlivened by amused disappointment or
passionate regret, according as we choose to regard it.

For the explanation of the other story Snorri's help is required,
although, as usual, we find a myth so disguised by later additions that
any interpretation is doubtful.   In the peace treaty between Æsir and
Wanes the gods created a wise being called Kvasir, who was slain by
certain dwarfs, and from whose blood was brewed the mead of poetic
inspiration called Soul-stirrer.   This passed into the hands of Suttung,
a giant of the underworld, who gave it into the care of his daughter
Gunnlod to guard deep down in the earth.   Odin, in the character of
Bale-worker, hired himself to Suttung's brother, and was promised the
mead as his wage.   He must fetch it, however, for himself, and after
boring his way through the rock with Rati, the awl, he gained admittance to Gunnlod.   Three nights he lay with her, and three draughts
she gave him of the mead, in which he drank the whole.   Then,
disguised as an eagle, he bore it safely to Asgarth, despite the giant
who followed so hard after him that a few drops of the precious liquid
were spilt, and thenceforth deemed worthy only for the makers of
bad poetry.   Snorri does not finish the story, nor tell how the Frost-
giants came storming to Asgarth knowing that Bale-worker was there
who had stolen the mead.   It was thus that poesy was won for gods
and men, and was given the name so often used by skalds, "Odin's
craft" or "Odin's drink;" and thus, as ever, a great power is first
found in possession of the Jötuns, and must be won by the gods before
it becomes serviceable to man.   In Soul-stirrer we meet with the most
primitive ideas: a drink producing a divine madness is found among
many peoples, and familiar is the notion that intellectual or spiritual
powers can be gained by drinking the blood of their owners.

Odin's discourse is now broken off by the writer of Part II., who
states that while listening in the most sacred spot, the Well of Weird,
he was able to see and hear what went on in the world of men and in
the High One's hall, where Odin was giving instruction to a mythical

---

* Mr. A. F. Major has pointed out that this theory of Rydberg's has some foundation.

poet called Loddfafnir or Stray Singer. But the Well of Weird is the fount of Wisdom, known to all poets and seers, a secret place of communion with the divine, where all the strands of life—present, past, and future—are revealed, and the writer is merely claiming divine authority for his words by the use of mythological language. He describes inspired moments when things hidden to others were made known to him. The counsel to Stray Singer is of much the same character as the last set of maxims, though in expression they seem less archaic. Especially when compared with strophes such as 80-82, 84, 86, they sound more like skaldic verses than the saws of old time, which are again heard in the charms of st. 136.

Very different in tone is the solemn opening of Part III. In the midst of half-humorous, half-serious words of warning and advice, a recital of love tales and charms, we come suddenly upon this awful and mysterious scene of a god offering himself in sacrifice upon the World Tree in order to attain the maturity of his wisdom and power.

The whole passage is full of mystery, which we have not attempted to elucidate by rearrangement or ingenious translations. Nor is this the place to discuss the vexed question as to whether (with all the earlier authorities) in some old and mystic legend we are entering the very sanctuary of heathendom, or whether (with Bugge, Meyer, Golther) it is merely a scene borrowed from the Christian sacrifice, where Tree and spear must be identified with cross and lance. There is no other record of the deed in Northern mythology except an old song from the Shetland Isles, quoted by Bugge in confirmation of his own theory; whether it is genuinely archaic we cannot say :—

> Nine days he hang pa da rutless tree,
> For ill wis da folk, in gud wis he.
> A bludy maet wis in his side,
> Made wi a lance 'at wid na hide.
> Nine lang nichts in da nippin rime
> Hang he dare wi' his neked limb.
> Some dey leuch,
> Bitt idders gret.

This, without doubt, is a description of the crucifixion, but leads

---

* On the discovery of this song, see article by Dr. Karl Blind, Saga Book, vol. i., p. 166.

to no conclusion as to which of the two has borrowed its details from the other. The sacrifice depicted resembles in many points the human sacrifices that were offered to Odin. In this, if we may take that of King Vikar described in Gautreks S., c. 7, as typical, the victim was hung on the branch of a tree and stabbed with a spear, which is as intimately associated with Odin as the hammer with Thor.*

There will be better hope of an explanation of this passage, or at least of more fruitful .result. when the discussion no longer centres around the exact meaning of Yggdrasil, and of the " windy tree."

The labours of research will then perhaps be given to finding the origin of a strange and world-wide legend, without which no mythology seems complete. This legend, in outline, is of a god—call him Odin, Baldr, Osiris, Ishtar, Adonis—who must be sacrificed or voluntarily die in order that he may rise again in fulness of power, or even give place to some new god. Sometimes it is clear that he typifies the beneficent powers of nature, whether as the sun or the spring or summer fruitful-ness; but occasionally, as here, his significance is more doubtful. When our knowledge of comparative mythology is extended, and when all these legends have been arranged in due order, beginning with the early superstitious rite of savages, ending with the reinterpreted idea of philosophy, some rightful place will then be claimed for the myths of Baldr and of Odin.

The sacrifice of the god was made for the sake of attaining the Runes. By this word is usually understood the letters of the old Ger-manic alphabet, but its earliest meaning must have been something softly spoken, whispered, or " rounded " in the ear; it was especially used for those metrical charms which preserved from all danger whoso-ever whispered or chanted them. As civilisation advanced and the art of writing was learned, these charms were inscribed in characters cut in stone or wood, and thus seemed to lend to the characters themselves a magic power. The transmission of thought by writing must have seemed strange and supernatural to the uninitiated, and the name of runes was soon applied to letters of the alphabet.

Among many nations of the past there has been a lawful and unlawful use of the supernatural, a distinction between "white magic" and "black magic." To the latter class belonged the evil spells which

---

* See " Cult of Othin," by H. M. Chadwick.

one man wrought for the destruction of another (st. 150). Such practice of magic was the unpardonable sin in the old ethical code of the Germans, and was punished by burning. According to Saxo, Odin himself was banished for a while from Asgarth because he won Rind, his giant wife, by magic craft. But the use of supernatural power was permitted in prayer, or in the divine rites performed by priests; and in this passage runes also seem to have been a lawful agent through which a power above nature could be compelled and used by the individual. Kauffmann suggests that runes of this kind were mystic names for objects which expressed their essence and being, and which gave control over nature to the initiated.

In strophes 138, 139, are recorded Odin's attainment of three kinds of wisdom upon which he grew and throve: 1, the runes; 2, Mimir's wisdom, for which he pledged his eye; 3, Soul-stirrer, the mead of song. With regard to the last it is clear that we have here some variant and perhaps older myth than that of 103-108. A passage in the heroic poem of Sigrdrifumál, although it cannot be fully explained, throws suggestive lights on the subject, and shows the intimate connection of the threefold wisdom and the purpose of Odin's sacrifice. With the help of moisture from Hoddrofnir—that is, a draught from Mimir's well—Odin is said to have read, graved, and thought out the runes. Then they were cut off and mingled with Soul-stirrer, or the gift of song, and "sent on far ways, where they are found with the gods, and found with the elves, some with Wanes, and some with men." In the different accounts there seems to be one fundamental idea. By self-sacrifice and toil Odin drew a shapeless and unordered knowledge from nature upon which he grew and throve, and then gave it back through the medium of his divinity interpreted and rendered serviceable to all beings. It is unlikely that the earliest thinkers ever arrived at a defined notion of this kind, but they uttered in the language of fairy tale their belief that the gods were saving, ordering powers who stood between them and nature.

With the spells which begin in st. 145 there is change of tone and style, suggesting that they belong to a once separate poem. St. 158, where Odin can hardly be the speaker, seems to confirm this view. The second poem was added to supply the "nine mighty rune-songs" alluded to in st. 139, although eighteen are thus given. The songs mentioned below, whose words are unknown, must have been such as those sung by Gróa to Day-spring (p. 159), or like the old Merseburger

Spruche, which is found in a German MS. of the tenth century. In this Odin or Wodan heals the foot of Baldr's foal, singing :—

> Bone to bone,   blood to blood,
> limb to limb as if they were limed.

St. 158 seems the utterance of the poet himself, if Müllenhoff's explanation is correct, that Folk-stirrer is the dwarf who day by day is surprised and vanquished by the dawn, and who in some wondrous song of praise announces the conquering powers of light and life. The poet himself claims knowledge of this mystic song to give dignity to his own.

The reappearance of Stray Singer in st. 162 is a clumsy device of the author to unite the different parts, and st. 164 an epilogue such as those with which skalds were wont to end their recitals.

THE LAY OF HYMIR.

Hymískviþa has been chosen to introduce and illustrate the character of Thor, because it shows him in truer though less familiar aspect than the famous Lay of Thrym.

Two, or perhaps three, motives are combined in this lay. The first recounts how Thor fetches the great cauldron for the gods to drink. They are all assembled, after their hunting expedition, to consult the oracle, and learn where they shall make their banquet. According to old Germanic custom the twigs, which have been sprinkled with sacrificial blood and graven with runes, are cast on a cloth, and by the manner of their falling it is shown to the gods that they will find plenty in the halls of Ægir. It is a momentous occasion, for not only have they chosen their banqueting-room for all time, but they must win the alliance of the wild sea-giant Ægir, who from henceforth will be numbered among them as the god of ocean in its gentler moods. His fierce wife Ran, who remains hostile and catches drowned men in her net, is well known to skald-letters, also his nine children, the waves.

Thor, a strange ambassador of the peace, is sent to greet the giant, who is found sitting on the rock, a dire in proud contemplation of his daughters, the merry, sparkling water class tumbling one over the other in their sport, when his peace is _____ by the harsh voice of the Thunderer demanding the wealth of for the gods. Small wonder that he takes offence, and bids them wick. cauldron for their drink.

As usual, the wants of the gods must be supplied by the Jötuns; the only kettle large enough is in possession of the Frost-giant Hymir. Who shall be sent on this new errand but much-enduring Thor? He sets forth with Tyr, who is here called "kinsman of giants," but elsewhere the son of Odin, though perhaps only one of the chosen sons of the War-father. Speedily they harness Thor's famous goats Tooth-gnasher and Tooth-grinder, and swiftly they drive to the borders of Giant-land where the rumbling car and goats must be left behind, while they cross the river which flows between Asgarth and Jötunheim, and fare on foot to Hymir's halls. The Frost-giant refuses to give up the great kettle until Thor has proved his might by breaking a cup of wondrous strength, and this the god, not without help from the friendly wife, at last performs. Thus, having won the cauldron, Thor and Tyr return to the banquet.

But while they are still in Jötunheim another episode is introduced—that of Thor's fishing expedition. He has consumed all Hymir's store of provisions with an appetite like that which he displays in the courts of Thrym, and therefore volunteers to go fishing the next day. In a manner characteristic of the god, whose deeds are all on colossal scale, he fares to the wood and slays the biggest ox he can find, called Heaven-hitter, to provide the fishing bait. Thor has designs upon a nobler prey than mere fish or even whales, and he compels the reluctant giant to row further and further out to sea; but Snorri, who has already supplied some of the particulars, must be allowed to describe this incident in his graphic manner :—"They made such way that soon Hymir said that they had reached the place where he was wont to stop and fish. But Thor was fain to row much further, and they fared swiftly onward with vigorous strokes. Presently Hymir said that they were so far out now that it would be perilous to stay on account of the great World Serpent, called Midgarth's Worm. But still Thor declared that he must row on a while and did so, while the giant waxed sullen and was filled with gloom. At length Thor laid up his oars, and made ready a fishing line exceedingly strong, with a hook no slighter and not a whit less strong. He baited it with the ox-head and cast it overboard, where it sank to the bottom. Now in truth, it may be said, that the World Serpent was beguiled, for he opened wide his jaws and gaped at the ox-head, and the hook stuck fast in his gums. As soon as he became aware of this, he lashed out and tugged so furiously that Thor's hands slid over the gunwale. Then was the Thunderer wroth. He girt him

E E

with all his god's might, and stamped so hard that with both his feet he leapt through the bottom of the boat, and found himself standing on the ground. He pulled the monster up to the gunwale, and it may well be said that none has ever seen a more fearful sight than this—when Thor set eyes on the serpent, and the serpent glared back at him from below and breathed out poison. 'Tis said that Hymir changed hue and grew pale, for he was appalled when he beheld the serpent and saw the waves flowing into the boat. At the very moment when Thor raised his hammer aloft, the giant groped for his knife and cut the line in twain over the side, and the serpent sank back into the sea. Thor threw his hammer after it and, some say, struck his head off, but others say, with truth, that the World Serpent still lives and lies beneath the sea." Snorri goes on to tell how Thor slew the giant, which would not have suited our present author's design, who, as already noticed, completes the first story and introduces an episode to which Snorri refers, another of Thor's adventures, which occurred when he was on his way to Utgarth-lóki. He had stopped for the night at a peasant's (probably Egil, mentioned in st. 5) where, as usual, he killed his goats for the evening meal, but ordered the bones to be carefully preserved. The peasant's son, however, broke one to get at the marrow, and in the morning when Thor brought his goats to life again by hallowing the bones with his hammer, one of the animals was found to be lame. The peasant trembled when he saw the Thunderer grow wroth, and draw his bushy brows down over his eyes. In atonement he was obliged to give his children, Thialfi the Digger and Röskva the Swift One, to be thenceforth the servants of Thor. In the poem, st. 39, this takes place on the return journey with the cauldron.

At first sight the Lay of Hymir seems to have lost its connection with mythology and to be a mere fairy tale about giants who are real giants, and heroes with human appetites and human passions. Common fairy tale motives are introduced, such as the good wife who conceals guests from her husband and betrays his secrets. The writer scarcely regards his story from a humorous or artistic point of view, but, like some child, he tells it with a simple air of conviction, and a delight in the incidents which obscure the original nature myth. But the outlines of this nature myth may still be traced, the more clearly because of the faithful repetition of strange and impossible facts. It is the story of how the god of Thunder goes to release the storm clouds from their winter bondage and brings them into summer realms, filled with summer showers of rain. Explanation might also be found for some of the details—the cup which had to be broken is perhaps the ice-bound sea—but there is so much which is mere fancy that further interpretation becomes dangerous. It is mainly through combining the separate adventures of Thor that the poet has secured for his fairy tale a high place among the mythological poems. For, whether consciously or unconsciously, he has given us the most complete picture of Thor, the god.

The latter, as son of Odin and Jörd, is the offspring of Heaven and Earth, and his character is twofold—human and divine. Thor, whose name is derived from þunor (thunder), shows himself to men in the aspect of a heaven god when they hear the rushing of his chariot wheels in the storm, and in the lightning see the swift blow of his hammer; for, like Indra, Zeus, and Jupiter, he is armed with the destructive thunderbolt. But though terrible in his might, he is feared only by evil beings. To those who ally themselves with the gracious gods his appearance is ever welcome, for it means that the winter powers are dispersed, and in his fierce accents they hear the promise of summer rain. Among the gods he is protector of Asgarth and Midgarth. The giant forces of nature quail before him, and even Loki, the elusive fire-demon, is obedient to his word. In such form he is shown in the myth of the cloud cauldron.

But Thor is rightly called by the poets a "Son of Earth." He is the most human of all the gods, a Hercules in Old Norse mythology, who is continually exerting himself in the service of man. We can see his mighty form striding over the wastes of Jötunheim, where endless labours and conflicts with the giants demand his presence. Rude featured, with gleaming eyes beneath his bushy brows, with quivering red beard, clad in toil-worn garb, for ever attempting the impossible—to unbind earth, to empty ocean, to conquer old age, he is alike glorious in victory and defeat. It is this figure which is presented to us in Thor's fishing adventure, and in the various incidents of the poem. One after another, he proves himself equal to the tests of the giant—he slays the oxen; unaided, he lands the boat, and bears home the tackle and the whales; he breaks the cup, and finally carries off the cauldron. But all these are only stupendous human tasks, proofs of mere physical strength and daring; yet more human is Thor in his failure to catch the World Serpent and in his baffled rage, which is childish rather than godlike. Perhaps it was this weakness, this striving to perform the impossible, and inability to admit defeat—for once again Thor met with the Serpent—that appealed to the Old Norse seafarers and peasants, and made him their favourite among the gods.

Not only is this myth characteristic of the North, but also the manner in which it is told or rather pictured in scenes, while the curtain is allowed to drop over all the uninteresting details. With the Saga writers a national method of story-telling grew into a self-conscious, artistic style, but they never surpassed the poet of Hymir's Lay in impressionistic realism. The entrance of the Frost-giant, with the icicles clinging to his beard, is like the sudden blast of the wintry storm; sudden, too, and alarming is the fall of the row of mighty cauldrons, and the shivering of the ice cup into a thousand pieces. But most striking of all is the majestic picture of the Thunderer as he strides forth with the great cloud kettle upon his head. It is one which Carlyle loved to recall:—"Thor, after many adventures, clapping the pot on his head like a huge hat, and walking off with it—quite lost in it, the ears of the pot reaching down to his heels—a kind of vacant hugeness, large awkward gianthood, characterises that Norse system; enormous force, yet altogether untutored, stalking helpless with uncertain strides."

The language of the poem is rude; words and sentences are ill-strung, and the use of clumsy epithets make it difficult to translate without losing its almost savage vigour and life. But in the original the strength and simplicity have a wild attractive power, and render it a favourite in Northern literature.

THE LAY OF THRYM.

In Thrymskviþa we come to one of the best known and best sung of all the Scandinavian myths. Strong and vigorous like Thor striding into Jötunheim, crisp and clear as a northern snow-scene in the sunlight, this narrative poem is very perfect of its kind, and needs but little explanation. Like the more modern Saga writers, the author shows an appreciation of the spirit and peculiar qualities of Scandinavian literature which appear in the Lay of Hymir. But his arrangement and choice of details is made with more conscious design. He handles his subject as an artist, and plays with it as a humourist; throughout retaining a simplicity and rudeness which is strong, but never crude.

Thor is discovered in helpless plight, his red beard quivering in impotent rage, a Thunder-god searching vainly for his thunder-hammer, "which the Frost-giants and Mountain-giants well know when they see it uplifted, and small wonder, for many a head has it broken of their forefathers and their kindred." But now it is stolen, and none must be told the dire secret except Loki, the mischievous fire-god and the swiftest of all messengers, who on this occasion uses his cunning in the service of the gods, and soon discovers the lost treasure. The hammer, like the thunderbolt of superstition, which is silent during the winter months, is deep hidden below the earth in the keeping of the Frost-giant Thrym; nor will he surrender it until he has seen the fair Spring-goddess Freyja coming as bride to his dark realms like the sunshine which she impersonates. He has never yet beheld the bright maiden, though he may have heard her light footfall overhead. Thor hastens to her court and bids her at once put on her bridal veil, not dreaming that, with Asgarth in danger and the precious hammer stolen, she will refuse to go meekly into Jötunheim. But she is not so poor spirited, and flies into a rage as god-like as that of Thor himself when the great sea-serpent refused to be caught upon his fish-hook. Thor must himself fetch the hammer. Then Heimdal who, though one of the warlike Æsir, is as wise and far-seeing as the Wanes, counsels that Thor should deceive the Frost-giant disguised as Freyja. In this scene one can almost hear the laugh that goes through Asgarth at the rueful picture of the Thunderer thus decked with jewels and feminine trifles, his sturdy figure draped in woman's weeds. Thrym seems to accept his strange bride without expressing surprise, perhaps because Frost-giants and Spring-goddesses have seldom a chance of meeting. But Thor can control his appetite as little as his temper, and the giant wonders much at its capacity. He wonders yet more when he stoops to kiss her, and sees beneath the veil those flaming eyes, half hidden by the bushy brows. The wedding, however, must be completed. The hammer which hallowed the wedding feast of man is brought forth, and Thor seizing it becomes once more the god—and summer is first announced by the crashing thunder peal.

This poem is worthy of all praise for its realism and humour; but it is responsible, with others of its kind, for the comic, even ridiculous figure which has always passed for Thor.   In the ruder Lay of Hymir the heroic outlines of the god are more clearly discerned.   The nature myth too, suggested above, would be unrecognisable, if Thor and his hammer had not elsewhere played such parts.   Mjöllnir is one of the mythical treasures forged by the dwarfs.   A belief in it was not confined to Old Norse mythology, for it appears in many traditions and fairy tales of Germany.

Two other famous objects are mentioned—Freyja's feather coat in st. 3, and her necklace called Brisinga-men in st. 12.   If the story of the last could be reconstructed, it might prove to be one of the most poetical in mythology.   It is undoubtedly old, though it may not, as Müllenhoff suggests, date back to Indo-Germanic times.   It was known in England, the earliest reference to it being in *Beowulf*, and in Denmark, where Saxo mentions it as the property of Frigg.   In the Sörlaþattr we have the following story:—Once Freyja, mistress of Odin, spied a necklace lying in a cave.   It was the work of certain dwarfs, perhaps the Brisings, and when she looked at it she longed to possess it.   They promised to give it her if she would stay with them four nights, and this she did.   Odin was angry when he discovered it, and caused Loki to steal the necklace from her chamber, and would only give it back to her on condition that she stirred up war between two kings, whence the legend of the " Everlasting Battle."   The poet Ulf Uggason tells in the following lines of the battle between Loki and Heimdal :—" The famous and skilled one of the bridge of the Powers (Bifröst) wrestled with the evil and cunning son of Farbauti (Loki) at Singastone, ere the mighty son of nine mothers gained the shining necklace of sea-stones."

What is the meaning of this fragmentary tale?   The shining necklace must have been a symbol of light, especially the light cast upon the ocean waves.   We can scarcely venture, like some critics, to define it as the moon, the morning and evening star, or the rainbow.*   It belonged to the Sun goddess, whether called Freyja, Frigg (wife of the heaven god), or Gefjon, for that the three were originally one is suggested by the frequent confusion between them, in Saxo, in Sörlaþattr, and in Ls., st. 20, 21.   But Brisinga-men in Old Norse tradition is the property of Freyja, who is also called Mardöll,

---

* See *Z.f.d. A. 30, p. 220 ; (Bugge) Arkiv f.n. fil. IV., p. 121 ; E. Mogk, p. 140.*

or Sea-shining, and Menglöd, the Necklace-glad. Freyja loses her necklace, and Heimdal, the god of light, wins it back for her in some conflict with darkness, which was possibly confused with the last fight between Loki and Heimdal at the Doom of the gods, or it may have given rise to this latter incident, which is only told by Snorri. Müllenhoff pursues the myth of Brisinga-men through the story of Hildr and Hogni, and other heroic lays which belong to more recent times.

THE STORY OF SKIRNIR.

The Song of Skirnir, like those of Thrym and Hymir, is a simple narrative poem, but less severe in its outlines. It is full of sentiment, and even romantic in its love motive, while a soft-tinted nature myth still clings to it, and lends a mysticism which is absent in the others.

It is the spring-time, and Frey, the lord of light and heat, longs to embrace Gerd, the fair earth, and to draw her away from her father's wintry halls, that together they may bring forth the rich summer fruits. Whom shall he send as his herald but Skirnir, the Light-bringer, to bear the first greeting of the Sun to Earth after the long winter darkness in the North? But Earth is wilful and reluctant; hardly will she forsake her frost-bound halls. She dallies with the first tender caresses and bribes, until the Sun grows fierce and impatient, and her heart melts in love to him who had once seemed as alien to her as the summer warmth to the winter cold.

The story is told in true Northern fashion in a series of dramatic scenes—Frey, discovered alone in the hall, wandering aimless and love-sick, and refusing speech with his kind; Skirnir, holding speech with his horse, sustaining his courage in the fear and mystery of the night journey; his parley with Gerd in words aflame with such passion that one sees his slight form quivering, and hears his voice rise higher and higher as he passes from gentle pleading to fierce denunciation.

The curse itself pictures the hell of Northern belief, which is widely different from the fiery kingdom of other mythologies. It is a far stretching waste, hemmed in by snow-clad mountains, bleak and cold, dark and desolate of all inhabitants save three-headed monsters or eagles rending corpses, and the dim form of Frost-giants stalking to and fro, and binding all things in their chains of ice. Small wonder that Gerd is threatened with raving madness in this lonely land, without speech with human kind, without love, without the good cheer which gladdens winter in the North.

There are, however, indications that this poem is not exclusively Icelandic or Norwegian. The romance and sentiment are more fully expressed than is usual. One or two familiar forms and objects suggest that the author had a knowledge of international literature, and the best known motives of legend and mythology. There is the watcher who greets Skirnir, the newcomer, and demands the reason of his coming; magic, flickering flames are one of the perils of the way; the sword which he borrowed from Frey must have been one like that in *Beowulf*, or that of Sigurd or other ancient weapons, forged with magic craft, and graven with stories of old battles and runes of protection and victory. The golden apples of youth, which were the property of Idun, and either borrowed or stolen by Skirnir, are scarcely known to the Edda, though mentioned by Snorri. They were a fruit little known in Norway and Iceland, and the poet, it seems, also has been borrowing, perhaps from the golden apples of the Hesperides. More peculiar to the North is another object, the ring Draupnir, which was forged by the dwarfs. It belongs to Odin, and the allusion shows that Baldr is already slain. All the different treasures are symbols of light, growth, fertility, and other beneficent powers, and the passing of them from hand to hand is commonly found in the myths of polytheism, where no god is ever truly individualised, but is apt to melt away in shadowy outlines, assuming the form and attributes of some other god, unless indeed, like Thor, he has become so anthropomorphic as to have lost already something of his god-head.

Frey, the hero of the story, was better known in Sweden than in other northern lands. There he was worshipped as the highest god; temples were built, and yearly sacrifices were offered to him. Frey's cult, though perhaps less evident in folk-lore, is more noticeable in history than that of Odin. He was especially regarded as the patron of harvests, and in this aspect he is known to the Eddas. Snorri says:—" Frey rules over the rain, and the shining of the sun and the growth of fruits in the ground." Hence the symbols of fertility and light which Skirnir is allowed to carry with him, and hence too the gods' gift of Elf-home to Frey, where the elf-folk work his kindly will in nature (see Grm., st. 5). In this poem his more original character is apparent. He is the Sun-god who awakens earth out of her winter

sleep, too weak at first to melt her frozen heart (st. 4) ; and Skirnir is
not merely his messenger, but himself in disguise.   The sword or sunbeam which he sent as gift to the earth maiden is now lost for ever to
the gods, and in the possession of their giant foes.   At Ragnarök he
will seek for it in vain (see Lok., st. 42).   But here, as everywhere,
there is a discrepancy between the myth and its nature interpretation ;
the symbol in the one must pass away, but year by year the power of
which it is the emblem will be renewed.

DAY-SPRING AND MENGLÖD.

Grógaldr and Fjolsvinnismál are found in several MSS., none
older than the seventeenth century, as two separate poems, but they
have been associated for many reasons.   The one without the other is
fragmentary ; together they give a story which is told in a Danish
ballad of the sixteenth century called " Young Svendal."   In the first
part the hero is starting forth upon a dangerous mission ; in the
second he has accomplished his journey, and arrived upon the scene of
action, where he attains his object.   No details are given of the perils
of the way, but it is not even necessary to assume that the strophes
recounting them have been lost, for a sudden dramatic opening, a swift
passing over of incidents, are sufficiently common in the Edda, and
require only some brief line of explanation, such as " Then Day-spring
fared into Jötunheim."   Here and there are found connecting links
between the poems.   The object of search in Part I. is *menglöþum*,
those joyous with necklaces (st. 4) ; and Day-spring, in Part II., wins
Menglöþ, the Necklace-glad.   If, as most authorities take it, both are
proper names, the identification is complete.   In st. 14 is prophesied
Day-spring's dispute with the giant warder Much-wise.   The same
motive runs through the whole action, which from beginning to end is
ruled by destiny.   In st. 4 of Part I. and st. 47 of Part II. this is
openly expressed—" The issue must follow fate," " The doom of Weird
may no wight withstand."   In no poem is the Weird motive heard
more clearly, in none is it more distinctly seen to work in obedience to
natural law.

Menglöd is often met in fairy tales as the princess who sits on a
glass mountain, and is won by a princely lover ; but with the help of

F F

"Young Svendal," the story can be reconstructed in its more original form.   Day-spring has been sent by his step-mother to seek Menglöd, a fair giant-maiden who owns a shining necklace, and is of such renown that she has long been sought by lovers in vain.   Day-spring comes for help to his own mother's grave, and stands calling her at the doorway, for she has promised to aid him with the wisdom of the dead.   She comes forth reluctantly, like all who are compelled by love or enchantments to re-enter their old haunts, and standing at the gates of the tomb, she sings him magic songs to render him victorious in all the difficulties which lie before him ; bonds shall not hold him, foes shall not slay him, bitter frosts on the mountains, storms on the sea, mists on the night journey, even the spirits of dead women shall not dismay him—one thing alone can hinder his desire, the doom of Weird, which nor gods nor men can withstand.   The charms which she sings are rune songs, such as Odin knew, and one which he had even used to win his giant-wife Rind.   This scene between Gróa and her son is characteristic of the attitude of the Old Norsemen towards their dead, who were still regarded as a power for good or evil in their lives, and whose constant presence among the living was loved or feared, but never a matter of wonder, or an occurrence different in kind from the ordinary events of life.   This supernatural influence had to be met with one of a corresponding nature ; hence the charms and spells cut in runes which men used against one another and to combat difficulties.

Here ends the first fragment ; before the opening of the second a long interval has elapsed, during which Day-spring has endured untold perils, and prevailed through the spell songs of his mother.   He has, moreover, though this incident is veiled in mystery, met with Menglöd (st. 5 and 49), and has lost her.   She sits waiting for him on the mountain top, knowing that he will come back ; and he is seeking her, with the assurance that he can break down every barrier between them.   The next scene opens abruptly ; Day-spring has arrived in the gloom of night at his journey's end.   In the dim flickering light of magic flames he sees the giants' hall rising up before him, and in front, passing to and fro, is outlined the dark figure of the warder.   The ring of fire has here a deeper signification than the wonted circle through which the princes of romance had to pass to their princess ; it is inherent in the myth.   Day-spring hails Much-wise the watcher, and is refused admittance ; but he will not now turn

back, his love is almost within sight, and he stands conversing with
Much-wise under the assumed name of Wind-cold. Gradually he
leads up to a revelation of his true name, before which all barriers will
fall and leave the way open to Menglöd, his beloved, who is destined
for him alone. He questions Much-wise concerning all that lies in
front of him, and one by one, interwoven, the obstacles are seen.
Outside is the fiery ring of flames, and round the castle a huge rock-
wall with but one entrance, the barred gate called Sounding-clanger.
Yggdrasil, the tree of life and fate, stands overshadowing all things ;
and in its boughs sits Golden-comb or Wood-snake, the cock whom the
giants watch in dread, for when he crows their Doom will be at hand.
Fierce dogs are guarding the courts, and can be eluded only when
feasting on Wood-snake's wings ; but Wood-snake himself can be
slain by a magic wand alone, which is in the keeping of the giantess
Sinmara, and she will not lend it except for a tail feather from that
same cock. Thus the chain of difficulties is complete. But still Day-
spring asks concerning Ember, the flaming hall, built by wondrous
beings (of whom we know only Loki the fire-god and Delling the dwarf
of dawn), until he comes to Menglöd herself. A contrast to the ruthless
spirit of Old Norse literature and to all other descriptions in the Edda
is this patient figure—a tender, gracious woman, waiting and yearning
in heart for her lover, but shedding meantime contentment and peace
on those around. Day-spring at last reveals his name, and they meet
like the lovers of all time, first with trembling doubt, " Will she have
me ? " and " Is it he ? " then with the certainty that they have known
and have been destined for one another through all eternity.

The whole scene is so complete in its human passion that it seems
almost superfluous to ask for any further interpretation ; but those
which suggest themselves are so natural and fitting that, just seen,
they fade away in delicate ethereal colours, and form a background of
opalescent light.

The underlying allegory which Cassel suggests is not wholly false,
although far-fetched in some of its details. The idealist sets forth in
search of perfect love and beauty, which he sees far off on some high
mountain top, and longs to gain. The difficulties appear insurmount-
able to those who strive with them in the spirit of worldly wisdom, but
to him who follows the true instincts of his heavenly nature they give
way, and he attains.

Much also may be said for the view which sees in this myth only another presentation of that concerning Gerd and Skirnir, the oft-repeated wooing of the imprisoned earth by a summer god. If, however, the interpretation lies in natural phenomena, it must be the one suggested by the names. It is a radiant light picture—Day-spring or Day-hastener, child of Sun-bright, comes as Wind-cold (the cool, fresh breeze which springs up at dawn), to wed Menglöd on the mountain tops; while she, the bright sun goddess and her shining necklace are well known to us as Freyja and Brisinga-men. The sudden revealing of Day-spring is that earliest moment in the dawn which can be called day rather than night. Still a few moments pass before Sun herself comes, and the inevitable meeting takes place between her and the Day. No myth so poetical and so fitting could be told of this union, as that of two predestined souls.

We cannot well compare the poem or associate it with any other in the Edda. It is different in spirit, more romantic, more tender, with a passion which cannot be limited to any one age or locality. Everything tends to show that it is of late origin. The writer makes frequent use of the peculiar type of synonym known as the "kenning," in which some other person or object is employed to represent and describe the particular one in view. The name of a god or goddess serves often as a general term for man or woman; thus Eir (st. 28), who in the Prose Edda is a goddess of healing, means only a fair woman, in the present case a giantess. The old mythology had become a conventional system, technical rather than imaginative; and names which once belonged to personal beings had lapsed into mere words expressing abstract qualities. The question of poetic diction is of importance here, for it is possible that many difficult passages could be explained in this light. St. 18, as we have given it, alludes to Golden-comb, who will first announce Doom to all giants and giant-wives; but if the names of Surt and Sinmara must be retained, the passage is meaningless to any modern reader. Not only in language and sentiment does the writer stand apart from the other poets of mythology, but his knowledge of its most famous objects is defective and obscured. The mistletoe which Loki plucked (st. 26) seems confused with Golden-comb and the Doom of the World; the cock itself, who has his station in the scene of dawn, resembles the Christian symbol of watchfulness, whose cry dispels the power of darkness. The description of Yggdrasil, with its fruits which are instrumental in the birth of men, is so different from the old Tree of life and fate that some critics have denied their identity. The nature myth itself seems to wear a modern garb, quite unlike the old-fashioned and improbable stories of a less critical age.

GREYBEARD AND THOR.

Hárbarþsljóþ is one of the old flyting scenes which are so familiar in the sagas of history and romance, where hero mocked hero, hurling frank abuse across the hall in language which might be softened, but was little disguised by a rude strophic form. Two such flytings are recounted among the gods—the present scene, and the more famous one in Ægir's halls (p. 245). There is a wide difference between the clumsy dialogue of the first with its mixture of prose and metre, and the polished strophes of the second. The wit is of a different texture. Here it is rude and forcible, but sometimes merely abusive; there it is keen, artistic, swift and sparkling as Loki himself. No one has yet been able to discover any definite principle in the metre of Hárbarþsljóþ. We have therefore made Thor speak in Fornyrþislag, abrupt and trochaic like the harsh-spoken god, while Greybeard uses the more musical Ljóþaháttr. As in the Song of Rig, mythology is used to outline a sketch of social life, but once again the contrast is striking. Old world stories and nature myths serve but to illustrate topical allusions. The gods themselves are mere exponents of different social ideals. In treatment of their characters and in the real humour of the situation the author redeems himself for any lack of brilliance in the dialogue, but the skit, for it can be called nothing less, presents little attraction to us, although it may have seemed witty enough to contemporaries, who knew all the obscure traditions of the poem, and shared the intense feeling and bitterness which underlie its humour. For us the colours are faded, and the stories half forgotten.

We can, however, still recognise certain features of history and mythology. The historical background, indeed, scarcely needs to be recalled, for it is ever present with us—that of struggle between the aristocracy and the people. This began at a much earlier date in Norway and Sweden than among other mediæval nations, and had a more immediate and decisive result. The Viking who had tasted the sweets of freedom in his wild seafaring life refused to submit to dependence when a "bóndi" at home. Tyranny had once been enforced by the right of conquest, and feudalism strove to maintain it by the authority of law, successfully for a while in the South, but vainly in the North. Strife on the battlefield, strife at the Thing, and strife in skaldic verse between class and class was the order of the day.

The two figures on either side of the stream, though caricatures of the gods as we are wont to meet them, are easy to recognise. A weary traveller arrives on the banks of the fjord which flows between him and his home. Unwilling to wet himself by wading through the flood, he hails a ferry-man whom he spies over by the further shore. But the latter, an old man with a grey beard and a tongue which might have learned to wag more kindly, in a spirit of pure contradiction refuses to aid the traveller. Both reveal their names. Greybeard shows an intimate knowledge of the other's antecedents in the uncomplimentary dialogue which follows, and the story ends where it began, with Thor raging on the further shore, vainly longing to get within reach of his tormentor, who has just described the length and weariness of the journey.

Thor shows the same character that we know well in other poems. Had he called himself by some other title he would not have escaped recognition, and could scarce have gone in disguise as Greybeard suggests—a veiled reminder of how Thor once wore woman's weeds. Rude in his appearance and harsh in his speech as when he met All-wise the dwarf, straightforward and simple in his thoughts and actions, he takes literally the sneer of Greybeard when told that his mother must be dead or she could scarce have thus neglected his appearance. He has just been engaged in the never-ending, somewhat thankless task, of fighting the giants. Many of the labours which he proudly boasts and the failures with which he is taunted are well known. The battle with Hrungnir, mentioned in st. 15, is one of the world-famed contests of Old Norse mythology, and is told by Snorri in Skaldskaparmál. It happened that the giant Hrungnir, whose name, like that of other Jötuns, means the Sound-maker, and whose head and heart were of stone, had been invited to feast with the gods in Asgarth. There they plied him with drink till he grew boastful and threatened to destroy them all save Freyja and Sif, whom the giants had oft tried to win. At last the gods grew weary of such mighty words and uttered the name of Thor, who was then warring in Jötunheim. Forthwith entered the Thunderer, all wrathful, swinging his hammer and asking, "Who had let a crafty Jötun drink ale with the gods? who had made peace with Hrungnir that he was now within Valhöll? and why was Freyja thus filling the ale-cup as she was wont at the gods' banquet?" Then answered Hrungnir, and looked at Thor with no friendly eyes, "Odin bade me drink with him in Valhöll, and he is surety for me." Thor refrained for the moment from slaying Hrungnir, and accepted his challenge. Armed and thirsting for battle they came to the appointed spot—Hrungnir with Mokkr-kalfi, a giant made out of clay, to support him; Thor, with his trusty servant Thjalfii. His arrival on the scene is thus described by Thjodulf:—

> The son of Earth, with swelling heart,
> drove forth unto the play of swords,
> and Moon's path rumbled beneath him.
> Before him blazed all the realms of space:
> the ground was dashed with hail, and earth rent asunder,
> as the mighty-hoofed goats of his chariot
> drew him forth to the meeting with Hrungnir.
> Then Baldr's brother spared not the rocky foe,
> while the mountains trembled and were cloven,
> and ocean blazed.

Thor slew Hrungnir, while Thjalfi despatched the clay giant. The god was wounded by a stone splinter, which stuck fast in his head. He besought the giantess Groa to extract it by singing a charm over him, but she forgot the charm in her joy when she heard that Thor had brought back her lost husband, Aurvandil, in a basket from the icy realms of the North—safe except for one toe, which had been frozen and thrown up into the sky to make the morning star.

Many incidents in this story have been interpreted by Uhland. Hrungnir is the stony ground which vainly resists the thunder showers. Mokkr-kalfi is the less stubborn clay, which submits to Thjalfi the Delver; Groa is nature's power to heal the rents and sears that have been made in the storm conflict; and Aurvandil, whose name belongs to the morning star in Old English, is a summer being imprisoned in Jötunheim during the winter, perhaps some constellation which is seen with joy when it appears on the horizon as the herald of summer. Our poet seems to have confused him with Thiazi (st. 19), whose death was a yet more famous event in the chronicles of Asgarth. Thor, however, played little part in it, and the full account is best reserved for the appearance of Idun, in Lokasenna. In both incidents Thor is redeeming the faults of other gods—of Odin, who had invited Hrungnir; of Loki, who had stolen Idun. The deeds of st. 29, 37, 39 are unknown; but they were all of like nature—the destruction of Jötuns, and their yet more terrible wives. St. 39 has perhaps some connection with Geirröd's daughters (see p. 275). St. 26 is an allusion to one of the most humorous of Thor's adventures which Snorri recounts, although "it is not well for mortals to speak of those powers which the Thunderer could not subdue." He was journeying once with Loki and Thjalfi, whom he had just taken for his servant (see p. xxxiv.). Presently they came unawares into the land of Utgarth-loki, in the uttermost parts of the earth, and there many wonderful things befell them. One night they sought rest in a large and empty hall, but about midnight they were disturbed by a great rumbling and earthquake. "Then Thor arose, and called his companions. They groped around them, and found on the right of the hall about half-way down an outhouse, where they entered. Thor sat him down in the door, while the others, who were sore afraid, went further within. But he kept a grip on the handle of Mjöllnir, for he had a mind to defend himself." So the night passed, and in the morning the adventurers found that their hiding place had been the thumb of a giant's glove. This giant, Utgarth-loki himself, is called by various names—Fjalar (the Dissembler) and Skrymir. He plays many tricks on the three companions, and unwittingly they race with thought and wild fire, strive with ocean and with old age, and inevitably suffer defeat; but, as we have noticed, defeat without dishonour was the privilege of Thor. Throughout the poem the author shows a complete understanding of the god's nature, as seen in its human aspect, from the side which made him loved by the Norwegian and Icelandic peasants. He was the companion of their labours when they prepared and softened the hard earth. He hallowed their soil, he blessed their marriage feasts with his hammer, and showed himself ever the friend of churls, as Odin was the patron of lords and earls.

This brings us to the figure on the other side of the stream, who gives only the name of Greybeard. Some critics have suggested that he is Loki, the mocking demon, who knows better than any the misdemeanours of the other gods, and who now reviles Thor as he reviles them all at Ægir's banquet. But the name alone reveals him as

Odin in his usual disguise of a grey-bearded old man, unrecognised by Thor. The deeds mentioned can very rarely be identified with those told in other poems, but they are such as belonged to Odin in his various characters. As god of war, he is seen with battle-flag and reddened spear, wasting the fair meadows of All-green (16), rousing hatred between nation and nation, and inciting men to slay one another (24). As love-adventurer he keeps secret trysting with the gold-bright maiden (30), who perhaps is Billing's crafty daughter (p. 87), and well he knows how to gain the love of women with fair speeches and a false heart. As master of magic he does not scorn to win giant maidens by spells like those he had practised on Rind (p. 159), or by sporting aloft with dark witch riders at night (20). He has attained knowledge in his usual way, by fair means or foul (st. 20), and from all beings, even the dead (44) whom, like the Vala, he has called up from the grave.

Thus a contrast is drawn between Thor, the patron of the hard-working tillers of the soil, and Odin, the god, and here the representative, of the aristocratic and cultured classes, whose lives were given to love-making and expeditions of plunder and war. "Odin has earls who fall on the battlefield, Thor has the race of thralls." The oppression of the rich could never be "atoned for by a ring," nor the strife of classes settled by arbitration (42). Thor's bitter reply to this mocking suggestion, "Where didst thou learn such scornful speeches!" seems to give voice to the discontent of the people, which is evidently shared by the poet, who leaves us in little doubt as to his own views in the portraits which he has drawn of the gods. That of Odin is bloodthirsty, lustful, unscrupulous, not unlike the fiend and sorcerer that he became to early Christians, while they still half believed in him as a god. Thor, on the other hand, is not painted in such dark colours. He is caricatured, and stands no longer equipped with all his god's might, the grand outlines showing beneath the rough exterior; he is only pathetic in his discomfiture, and even ridiculous, the uncouth giant who lives on in popular notions of to-day. But the sympathy of the poet is always with Thor. He is still shown as the Warder of Midgarth, whose lot is to redeem the faults of others; and he still retains a mortal glory which was ever his in defeat.

One reproach of Odin's is mysterious and unexplained (34). Thor is accused of having once broken faith, which he does not deny. Does this refer to an incident in mythology, such as Thor's slaying of the

G G

giant smith in Asgarth, to whom the gods were bound by oath (see Introd. to Vsp.); or is it some topical allusion to an occasion when the people had turned against their leaders, and betrayed them to a foe?

If the realism of this scene is at times too great for the dignity of the gods, they are at least viewed in an aspect little known to modern readers of mythology. The presentation of Thor and Odin as familiar types, if we may trust our poem, shows in what light they were regarded by the masses, what place they occupied in the hearts of men. Thor was their protector; he was the author of all that was good and kindly in nature, and was worshipped less from awe than from love. Odin, on the other hand, was feared, and perhaps hated, by the peasants for his destructive violence as war-god, and for his magic wonder-working power, which was as little comprehensible to them as the culture which lay beyond their range. Just for a moment, by the hand of a sceptic, the curtain seems withdrawn, and we look into the obscurity of past thought, and see something of the relationship between the mythology and the religion of the people.

THE SONG OF RIG.

Rigsþula is not included in any of the best MSS. of Sæmund's Edda, but only in the Codex Wormianus with the Prose Edda. Partly for this reason, and because its connection with Heimdal, the god of light, seems obscure and improbable, the poem is sometimes put aside as a late invention of the skalds. It is without doubt a skaldic song, one of those lays which were sung in the hall by a court poet in praise of his royal master, whose descent he traces from the gods. Unfortunately the final strophes are missing, or we should perhaps learn the name of this king of famous race. Harald the Fair-haired has been suggested, and the date of composition is certainly that of the Viking period. But the poet is evidently not drawing on his own imagination, except for details. The art of the skald lay in taking some old theme and singing it, like an old melody, with variations to suit the occasion.

The myth in question tells how once of old the god Heimdal, who was not wont to leave the seat where he kept watch in heaven, came to earth as a kingly being called Rig. He is described as passing through all the world, and visiting first the dwelling of the serf and thrall, then that of the peasant landowner, and lastly the hall of the rich and nobly born. To each home he brings the birth of children, who are reared, who pursue occupations, and who wed according to their station. From the highest rank of the earls is born a king, who is given the name of Rig. Thus Heimdal is the originator of different classes of men, but kings especially have their right to claim descent from the god.

Snorri knows nothing of this story, but the Vala (p. 277) speaks of Heimdal as the father of all "holy kindreds," and in the "Shorter Soothsaying," although no name is mentioned, he is called "the kinsman allied to all races."

The attempt to explain the myth any further, and to identify Rig, as Rydberg has done, with Skef or Scyld, the culture hero of the Germanic race, is unsatisfactory. The motive, indeed, is common, for it is primitive and world wide; and some such myth arose everywhere (see Introd. to Hdl.) when man began to wonder whence he had come, and why he was man with a knowledge of good and evil. Not having yet learned his kinship with the ape, he invented a race founder, sometimes a god in human form. He made up stories which, oft repeated, were soon told as true, and were believed because they took place so "long ago"—of a culture hero who came to be king over men, to awaken them out of their first sleep of ignorance, and teach them to rule nature by wisdom and knowledge, until, as in the poem, wisdom itself became regarded as the divine inheritance of kings. Sometimes the scene is more poetical than the green roads and the hasty striding figure of Rig. Scyld, the Danish hero, came as a child drifting in a boat to shore, and when he had accomplished his work he passed back to unknown regions beyond the sea. "From the great deep to the great deep" King Arthur came and went in mystic fashion.

But the present poet has another end in view than dreaming. He is answering man's next question, which was in truth the demand of his socialistic countrymen—"Who thus made men of high and low degree?" "They were born so," is his answer, and he shows by mythic lore that such an order was established by divine authority. His contempt for the low-born seems to indicate that he would not change it if he could.

The political setting of the poem has already drawn it out of the realms of fancy upon historical ground; and in its details, the description of the customs and manner of life among the different classes, it is most valuable. Some features of life which the poet depicts are out of date, as though he were going back to an older period, or were very conservative in his views.

The first-born son (st. 6) is Thrall. The Old Norse thralls were serfs, little better than slaves, who could be sold at the will of their master. In the Viking period they were often prisoners of war. It was sometimes possible for them to obtain freedom, but never any share in the government, or influence in the popular assembly. As their names indicate, their social condition and occupations were very low. Great-grandfather's table is set with coarse brown bread and broth, which are the best that he can lay before his guest.

In the home of Grandfather and Grandmother there is more comfort; their appearance and clothing are neat, and even ornamental; their work and that of their children requires skill; the son who is born to them has a fair and ruddy skin, his bride does not travel on foot, and she is graced by a wedding veil. Churl in st. 18, which is a cognate form of Icelandic " Karl," does not give a true idea of the position of the latter, who here represents the class of free-born peasant proprietor called " bóndi " or " bui," a name which was given to his offspring, and which was used in Viking days to designate the emigrants to Iceland. These formed a kind of hereditary aristocracy, self-governed, and absolutely independent. The Karl of this passage scarcely takes so high a position, but belongs to an earlier age.

Mother and father are found (st. 21) in a lordlier dwelling; she has no task but to admire and adorn her fair white neck and arms; his work is the honourable pursuit of warfare, and the fashioning of weapons. They have a son, Earl, with bright eyes and shining hair, who lives the glorious life of a conqueror, distributing spoils and wealth among his dependents. Yet more than Churl he belongs to ancient days, and resembles one of the great lords who are mentioned in Hyndla's Lay, or those who give rise to the epithets used by poets, "the ring-breaker " and "gold-giver." The Old Norse ideal was fixed before the rise of any kind of feudal rule; the power of earls passed into the hands of the collective *bœndr*, and they too become subject to the laws and customs of the *Thing*.

Earl weds the fair daughter of Ruler, and their children—Son, Offspring, Descendant, &c.—are required only to inherit the rights and follow the customs which belong to their noble birth. But to Kon the youngest, who becomes a king, is given a higher heritage, not of his father Jarl, but from Rig, who bestows his own name upon him, and endows him with the wisdom of gods. He shares their powers, he learns to understand and use the sacred runes, he interprets nature, and is alone the true son of Heimdal and the father of all kings.

This poem has little beauty and grace, but a quaint charm in the original. The swift movement of the metre keeps time with the striding march of Rig, and throughout there is an air of superiority which disdains all the polish and delicacies of art for so fine a theme.

THE LAY OF HYNDLA.

The Shorter Soothsaying is included in the MS. with the Lay of Hyndla, but is now, by general consent, regarded as a distinct poem. The main theme of Hyndla is the recitation of a family history, but suddenly, with an abrupt change of style, the subject passes to a genealogy of mythical beings; then again it reverts to the original theme. Snorri quotes from this interpolation (st. 6) as though from some old and famous song, and mentions as his authority a poem called "The Shorter Soothsaying of the Vala"—"Völuspá inni skömmu." We may assume therefore, though in opposition to Sijmons and certain other critics, that it is a fragment of a lost and much older work, which dealt, like the greater Soothsaying, with the history of the gods.

Someone, as in Baldr's Dreams, is holding converse with a witch, called up perhaps from the dead. The unknown questioner desires to know the origin and kinship of all mythical beings. He asks first concerning the god's race, and learns that once, before the death of Baldr, the Æsir were twelve in number. Here a gap in the poem leaves their names unrecorded, but they may be conjectured from descriptions by Snorri and in Lokasenna of the full assembly in Ægir's halls. At these banquets were present Odin, Thor, Heimdal, Tyr, Vidar, Vali, Forseti, Ull, Hœnir, Bragi, and Loki, who, with Baldr, make the twelve.

Another passage is missing which should tell how the Wanes— Njörd, Frey, and Freyja—came among the other gods, and throughout there is such confusion and want of sequence that it is only possible to make the poem explicit by grouping the strophes with the help of familiar allusions.

The questioner would next learn whence came other powers beside the ruling gods, those tumultuous forces ever warring with them, the Jötuns; those wise women, the Valas, who could interpret dreams and foretell the future; and whence all wizards and witches and monsters like the great wolf Fenrir, and prodigies such as Odin's eight-footed steed Sleipnir? The answers to these questions are unfortunately often too dark to understand, or tell us only what is known from other sources. One awful being (st. 8), the mother of all witches, was born in mysterious fashion from a burning heart, which Loki, as fire-god, had devoured. She, it has been suggested, is the same as Golden-draught, who was burned and reburned in Odin's hall, and who was the cause of the first war between gods and Wanes (p. 183).

In alluding to Loki, who is half god, half giant, the questioner has turned once more to higher beings, and the birth of One is related, whose name is not mentioned, but who is easily recognised as Heimdal. The description agrees with what is told of him elsewhere, and belongs to his character as a god of nature. Heimdal, although he plays a considerable part in the Edda, is only half revealed to us, and his nature not clearly understood. He is seldom named by the skaldic poets; no sacrifices were offered to him, no temples built for his worship, he had no place in the hearts of men. Merely to ascribe a late origin to his myth is not sufficient explanation for this strange silence about a god so well known to the Edda. The myths which encircle him point back by their very contradictions to one who has lived through different ages in the changing thought and fancy of mankind. Their wonders are accepted only because they belong to the past. " Heimdal," says Snorri, " is called the White god. He is great and holy. Sometimes he is called Golden-tooth, for his teeth are of gold. His steed is Goldy-lock, and his dwelling place is Heaven-hill, by the bridge Bifröst. He is warder of the gods, and sits at the end of heaven guarding the bridge against the Mountain giants. He needs less sleep than a bird; he can see, by night as well as by day, a hundred miles around him. He hears grass growing on the earth and wool on the backs of sheep, besides all else that makes more sound. He owns the trumpet Gjallar-horn, whose blast is heard throughout the worlds." Thus shown as the dazzling god of light, he is un-

approachable; far seen, aloof, he sits on his mountain throne, guarding
Bifröst where the rainbow reaches heaven.   He is no less mysterious
in his birth, which Snorri also describes, quoting from some lost
"Song of Heimdal":—

> Child am I of mothers nine,
> of sisters nine the son.

These maidens, from their names in st. 12, are ocean waves, and
it is again as the god of light that he is born at the world's edge on the
horizon where the sky meets the earth and sea.   It is there at sunrise
that he drinks of the crimson splendour which is like the blood of
sacrifice offered to the gods.

Heimdal stands apart from other deities in the Edda.   He is less
human, except when, as Rig, he passes through the world of men and
becomes the kinsmen of all peoples.   His epithet of the " richest
ruler" belongs to him perhaps as owner of the wide and glorious
dwelling place of Heaven-hill.   The expression "weapon-famed" is
here translated "armed with glory," because it must be derived from
the sword of piercing sun rays which is usually the possession of the
Heaven god in mythology, but which Heimdal may well borrow as the
god of light.   In the above mentioned " Lay of Heimdal " his sword is
mentioned as being made of a " man's head," and the skaldic poets
use " Heimdal's sword " as a synonym for the head.   These obscure
allusions, for which even Snorri vouchsafes no explanation, suggest
that even in his day the traditions about Heimdal were already half
lost and forgotten.

All the revelations so far have been of the past; the Vala now
becomes prophetic.   She foretells the fearful signs and wonders in
nature, the "long dread winter" (p. 55) which shall herald the fulfilment of Weird with the Doom of the first ruling powers, the gods of
war, and the coming of the new Power, some say of Christianity, but
whose nature is here kept secret, like other hidden things—"the
Mightiest One's old mysteries," the runes which Odin knew alone, the
words which he whispered into Baldr's ear.

How then was this mythical fragment united to the less exalted
theme of Ottar's genealogy, which, if it were not for the myth in which
it is framed, should belong to the heroic lays?   Perhaps the author
of Hyndla's Lay had in his possession the old "Soothsaying," and
purposed to write a corresponding genealogy of earthly beings, enume-

rating those great Germanic heroes of legend and saga whom he deemed
worthy of immortality. He lingers with old-fashioned love for the list
of mighty names, feeling that they are in danger of perishing for ever
in these degenerate days when the power of the nobility is being seized
by the middle class *bóndi*. Now, while they are yet fresh in the
memories of men, let these names be recorded, and their worth attested
by association with those of the gods.

As the hero of his subject the writer takes Ottar the Simple, a
chieftain who is unknown to history, but who seems to have belonged
to the famous family of Hördaland. He is here identified with Od, the
human lover of Freyja, whose story is thus told by Snorri :—" Freyja
was wedded to a mortal called Ottar, and their daughter Hnoss, the
Treasure, is so beautiful that all things fair and costly are named after
her. But Ottar went far away, and Freyja followed him weeping, and
her tears were of red gold " (st. 32). Ottar of the poem has wagered
his inheritance with another unknown personage, Angantyr, that his
descent, could he only trace it, is the nobler. Freyja is willing to
help her favourite, and she takes him with her disguised as Golden-
bristle, the famous boar which belonged to Frey. They seek Hyndla,
who, like other valas or witches, dwells in a cave, and rides forth upon
a wolf at night. She is a giantess, and thus knows all the history of
mankind. But as such she must be propitiated by a goddess, and
Freyja promises to win her the favour of Odin, the War-father, who at
times can be so gracious ; Thor too, the enemy of giant-wives, shall be
appeased by sacrifice such as men offered to the gods.

Hyndla suspects the presence of Ottar, but Freyja denies it, and
in answer to questions of the latter she rehearses the generations of
kings while they ride through the night, and Ottar's heart must beat
with pride as she marshals forth the host of his dead forbears. It is
shown how he is allied to the most ancient and noble races, and heroes
who can trace their line back to the gods. To us all these great names
mean nothing, or merely call up shadowy figures in the land that lies
between history and romance. But recited in ancient days by the
skalds, before the warriors and women gathered in the hall, the famous
race names of Skjöldung, Skilfing, Odling, Yngling were full of deep
meaning, and expressed their ideal of glory in heroic deeds.

The Skjöldungs are ancient mythical figures who centre round the
birth cradle of the Germanic race. In the various Old English, Icelandic, and Danish sources, which do not always agree in their details,

is found the legend of an old culture hero, deemed perhaps a god in human form. He came as a child drifting over the sea in a boat, surrounded by treasures, with a sheaf of corn from which he took his name Skef, though the poem *Beowulf* has transferred the legend to his son Scyld. The boat approached a land called Skania, where Skef rescued a people in great misery, and taught them to cultivate their territory and defend it against the enemy. He died in old age, leaving Skjöld or Scyld to inherit the kingdom, and was sent forth once more over the sea in a boat no less richly endowed than when he came, " but no man," it is said, " knew who received the precious burden." From Skjöld came the Skjöldungs, or, as we learn from *Beowulf*, the Danes, whose home was Leira in the island of Seeland. Skef or Sceaf in Old English genealogies is the ancestor of the Angles and Saxons. With him we must identify Skilvir, also said to be the father of Skjöld, the progenitor of the Skilfings, another name for the Swedes.

But who are the Ynglings? Ing or Yng is also a great race-hero, and ancestor of the Swedes and Angles. In the poem Ynglinga-tal, the name Yngling and Skilfing is used interchangeably. Thus Yng must be identical with Skilvir, and Skilvir, as we have seen, is the same as Scef, or, according to *Beowulf*, Skjöld. All this confusion leads us back to one mythical founder of the Germanic race, from whom all the tribes claimed their descent, and whom they remembered as a culture hero, who had raised them from a state of savagery, and seemed to them in later days as the son of a god (see Rydberg, pp. 89, 90-95).

Then Hyndla turns to Ottar's immediate family, and those with which it is connected. The first great hero mentioned is Halfdan the Old (st. 18). He was the king of Denmark, and one of the patriarchs of the Germanic race, known to Saxo Grammaticus and to the author of *Beowulf*. His most famous achievement was the slaying of Sigtrygg, a mythical king. He sacrificed to the gods in order to obtain long life, but he was granted no more than " a man's life" of three hundred years, and the promise that no ignoble offspring should be born in his line—hence Ottar would desire to claim kinship with him (Skald-skaparmál).

The twelve berserk brothers of st. 23, sons of Arngrim and Eyfora, belong to Hervarar Saga, and their chieftain Angantyr is the principal figure in one of the finest of the Old Norse heroic poems. The word **berserk** had its origin in a superstitious belief that some men were "hamramr," or able to change their forms, and become bears or wolves, and were hence called berserks or were-wolves. Later on the name was given to those wild beings who from time to time were seized by fits of madness and rage, when they seemed possessed of more than human strength, and wrought fearful deeds in battle. The saga in question tells of a magic sword called Tyrfing which came into the hands of Angantyr. It had been forged by dwarfs, and stolen from them; therefore a curse followed it, and though it might serve its bearer well for a lifetime, it would at last bring him to death. The viking brothers ranged over land and sea, till in consequence of Angantyr's love for Ingibjörg they met in battle, and fell before, two warriors, Odd and Hjalmar, in the island of Samsey. Hervör, Angantyr's warlike daughter, had inherited the berserk spirit, and presently it came upon her. She armed herself like a warrior, and went forth to seek Tyrfing from her father's grave. Fearlessly she passed through the haunted land with its magic flickering flames until she stood on the howe, crying :—

> Hervard, Hjörvard,   Hrani, Angantyr !
> Wake where ye rest   the tree-roots under
> with helm and byrnie,   shield and harness,
> sword keen-whetted   and reddened spear !
> All are they come,   the sons of Arngrim,
> death-thirsting warriors,   to dust of earth ;
> and not one comes forth   of Eyfora's offspring
> in Munavagi   to speak with me :—

till at length, while the whole land was aflame with enchanted fires, the grave opened, and she won her heritage from the dead.

St. 25 scarcely requires explanation. With the mention of the famous but ill-starred Niflung and Völsung races, a note of warning comes into the poem. This great saga is so widely known and has been so oft repeated that it no longer belongs only to the people of the North, who told it first and best in written form. Jörmunrek married Svanhild, daughter of Sigurd; he caused his wife to be trampled to death by wild horses in consequence of a slander, and her brothers sought to avenge the deed. In the history of the Latin writer Jornandes he is Ermanric, a mighty king of the Goths in the fourth century, who was conquered in battle by the Huns. Again he is known in Saxo's chronicle as the Danish king, Jarmeric, and is mentioned in *Beowulf*

as Eormenric.   Under slightly different names, the same story of the
sister's death and the brother's vengeance is told in connection with
Ermanric and Jarmerik.   We have clearly one of the Germanic race
heroes, remembered by all the different tribes after their separation.
St. 29 alludes to another famous saga, and mentions the instigator of
one of the greatest legendary battles of the North.   Ivar was a
descendant of Angantyr (st. 28) ; he conquered and slew Hrörek, king
of Sweden, whose daughter, Aud the Deep-thoughted, he had married.
She fled with her little son Harald and married Radbard, king of
Russia ; their son was Randver.   Harald Battle-tusk lived to be king
over the Danes.   In his old age, desiring a glorious death, he challenged
Sigurd-ring, king of the Swedes, to meet with him at Bravellir.   There
took place a combat of world-wide renown, which is described by Saxo,
who delights in the slaughter and bloodshed like some old Viking.
Kings, princes, earls, nobles, chieftains from all Germanic tribes,
gathered upon the field ; thousands fell on either side, and the Swedes
were victorious.

After this passage followed the old fragmentary poem, placed
there, not perhaps by the author of Hyndla's Lay, but by some later
copyist who was ignorant of the old genealogies, and knew little of the
distinctions between gods and men.

The scene now returns to Freyja and Hyndla, whose ride is ended.
Hyndla would be left to sleep in peace once more, and bids Freyja hie
homewards on her wild night journey, with the darkness lit up only by
the flickering of enchanted fires like those which surrounded Hervör,
and ever haunt the places of the dead.   Freyja's mocking request to
pass the ale-cup to her boar is the acknowledgment of Ottar's presence ;
the dialogue between her and Hyndla grows dramatic and breathless,
ending with a curse from the witch and a blessing from the goddess
upon Ottar.

The rearrangement of strophes which is given in the translation
has been made with the help of a prose paraphrase in Örvar-Odds
Saga.   It agrees in most points with that suggested by Gering.   The
few recognised names have suggested the family groups.

BALDR'S DREAMS.

In Baldr's Dreams for the first time we meet face to face with the most sublime and beautiful figure in Old Norse mythology, one who is universally known, for the tenderness and pathos of his story appeal to modern sympathies; moreover, has ever proved a source of inspiration to modern critics, who make for darkness and mystery as the moth makes for the light. All endeavours have failed to unravel the secret of his personality, and to trace it to any one source in history or mythology.

This poem belongs to a closing chapter in the history of the gods. Baldr's death is the great tragedy which foreshadows their Doom. No facts are recorded of him in his lifetime; here and there in some passing allusion he enters a poem and flits across its pages like some gleaming ray of light, but only in his death does he become the most human and tender and best loved of all the gods. From the poetic Edda alone we learn little concerning him, and Snorri must be allowed to fill in the gaps with his own version of the story.

Baldr was the son of Odin and Frigg. Unlike Thor, he had no kinship with earth; both of his father and mother, he was born of heaven. "He was the best among the gods, and praised by all beings. He was so fair to behold and so bright that a glory streamed from him, and no white herb, even though it were the whitest of all herbs, could compare with the whiteness of Baldr's brow. He was the wisest of gods, the fairest spoken and the most pitiful, and yet of such nature that none might overrule his judgments. His home was in the heavens called Broad-beam, where nought unclean might enter."

Nothing further is told of Baldr's life, nor what part he played in the history of the gods; how he shared in their warring and striving, but not in their sinning; for of him "there is nought but good to tell." He must have had a love story which recounted the wooing of Nanna, his fair wife, who must perish with him; but now, in this poem, we hear that Baldr, while still youthful, has had evil dreams and forseen his fate. Perhaps, like some old Norse hero, his *fylgja* has stood before him—that shadowy spirit who follows each man, but is seen only at the sunset of life. All the gods gather in alarm and hold council, but none can tell, though all can guess, the meaning of Baldr's Dreams. Odin is sent down to Hel to seek tidings from a Vala, who, as one of the dead, has power to trace the workings of Weird before and behind. He rides thither by the same road which Hermod took afterwards and on the same steed, his own eight-footed Sleipnir, and stands calling on the Vala until she obeys the spell of the Master

Magician, and comes forth from the grave. He must have used incantations such as those "diabolical songs" which are said by Latin historians to have been sung by the heathen at night-time to call up their dead, and were so sternly prohibited by the Church.

The Vala is heard in speech with Odin. Her words are not the mere fortune-telling of a witch, but like the oracle of old she pronounces the doom of Baldr. The Weird motive now sounds in the poem, and continues like a grim undertone throughout as the Vala interprets one by one the visionary pictures of Baldr's dreams. He has first seen the interior of a great hall being prepared for the reception of an honoured guest; the benches are strewn, the mead cup is filled and overlaid with the bright shield, and all the place adorned as though for the coming of some king. But Baldr has guessed that this is Hel's abode, and is troubled. Now Odin learns the name of this expected king, and wrothfully asks who would dare thus to slay his son, the best loved among all the gods? He is answered that no dread Frost-giant or Mountain-giant, but one among themselves will shoot the fatal shaft. Who then shall avenge the deed before ever Baldr is laid on the bale-fire? The father's anger is appeased when he is told that the giantess Rind shall bear him a mighty child, who shall work vengeance on the author of the Woe.

The Vala is next questioned on the second vision which Baldr has seen—a mourning world, maidens weeping and in wild despair casting their veils to the winds. Why does she now break out in fierce indignant reproaches, and know that her tormentor is Odin? None living save a god could thus see into the future, and perhaps as a dweller in the underworld she resents the attempt which will be made to deprive Hel of its victim. Then Odin, with mocking fury and refusal to believe the prophecy of the Vala, bears the dread tidings home to Asgarth. But she has the last word, reminding him how even the gods must suffer Doom; for all their after efforts, the devices of the fond mother to save her son, are only a hopeless striving against Weird. Here Snorri takes up the story:—"The gods resolved to ask protection for Baldr against all harm, and Frigg took an oath from fire and water, from iron and all metals, from rocks and earth and trees, from poison and serpents that they would spare Baldr. When this was done and made known, it became the sport of Baldr and the gods to make him stand up at their meetings while some shot at him, some struck him, and some cast stones; but whatever they did he was unharmed, and they deemed it a glorious feat—save Loki, son of Leaf-isle, who was ill pleased.   He went in the likeness of a woman to Fen Halls, where Frigg dwelt, who asked what all the gods were doing at their assembly. The woman made answer that they were shooting at Baldr, but that nought harmed him.   Said Frigg—'Nor weapons nor trees will hurt Baldr, for I have taken an oath from them all.'   And the woman asked —'Have all things taken the oath to spare Baldr?'   Frigg answered —'There grows indeed, to the west of Valhöll, a tender shoot called the Mistletoe, which seemed too young to ask an oath from.'   Then all in a moment the woman vanished.   But Loki went and plucked the Mistletoe, and joined the gathering of the gods.   There was one, Höd, who stood without the circle, for he was blind.   Loki asked—'Why art thou not shooting at Baldr?' and he answered—'Because I cannot see where he stands, and moreover I am without weapon.' 'Thou must do as the others,' said Loki, 'and show honour to Baldr. Shoot now this wand; I will show thee where he stands.'   So Höd took the Mistletoe, and aimed as Loki showed him.   The shaft flew and pierced Baldr, who fell dead to the earth, and 'tis deemed the direst shot that ever was shot among gods and men.   When Baldr had fallen, speech failed the gods and likewise power in their hands to lift him.   Each looked at the other, and all were of one mind about him who had wrought the deed, but they could not seek revenge there, for it was a holy place of peace.   When the gods sought to speak there was only sound of weeping, and the one could not tell his sorrow to the other.   But the greatest sorrow was to Odin, for he best fore-knew what loss and woe had befallen the gods with the death of Baldr. When at length they had come to themselves again, Frigg asked who among them all desired to win her grace and favour, and would ride the Hel road and seek if haply he might find Baldr, and offer ransom to Hel that she should let him return home to Asgarth.   And Hermod, the Eager-hearted son of Odin, was chosen for the journey.   Then gliding Sleipnir, the steed of Odin, was brought forth, and Hermod mounted and rode swiftly away.   But the gods took the body of Baldr to send it floating out to sea.   His vessel, called Ring-horn, was the greatest of all ships, and when the gods sought to launch it forth and kindle the bale-fire thereon for Baldr, it could nowise be stirred.   So they sent to Jötunheim after the giantess, fire-shrivelled Hyrrök, who came riding on a wolf, using serpents for the reins.   When she had dismounted Odin called four berserks to mind the steed, but they could not hold it until they had felled it to the ground. Hyrrök went forward to the prow, and in one push she launched the boat with such force that sparks flew from the rollers, and the whole ground was shaken. Then was the Thunderer wroth! He seized his hammer, and would have broken her head if all the other gods had not asked mercy for her. Then they bore forth the dead form of Baldr and laid it in the vessel, and when his wife Nanna, Nep's daughter, beheld it her heart broke from sorrow, and she died. She too was laid on the bale-fire, and the flame was kindled. Thor stood by, and hallowed the pile with Mjöllnir. At his feet ran a dwarf called Lit, and Thor spurned it with his foot into the fire, and it was burned. All manner of folk came to the burning of Baldr. First came Odin, and with him Frigg and the valkyries and his ravens Hugin and Munin. Frey came driving in a car drawn by the boar called Golden-bristle or Fierce-fang, and Heimdal riding the steed Golden-lock. Freyja was there with her cats. Thither came, too, a host of Frost-giants and Mountain-giants. Then Odin laid on the bale-fire that ring called Draupnir, which is of such value that therefrom fall eight like rings every ninth night. And Baldr's steed was led to the bale-fire in all its trappings. Meanwhile Hermod rode nine whole nights through dales so dark and deep that he could see nought till he came to the loud roaring river Gjallar, and rode over the echoing Gjallar-bridge, which is thatched with shining gold. There the maiden called Modgud keeps watch. She asked Hermod his race and name, and told him how yesterday five phantom troops had ridden over the bridge, 'but under thee the bridge echoes full as loud, nor hast thou the hue of a dead man. Why art thou riding on the Hel-road?' He answered—'I must needs ride to Hel, and seek Baldr; hast thou seen aught of him on the Hel-road?' 'Baldr,' said she, 'has ridden over the Gjallar-bridge; downward and northward lies the way to Hel.' So Hermod rode on till he came to the Hel-gates. There he sprang from horseback, tightened his saddle-girths, and mounting again he spurred his steed so fiercely that it leapt high over the gates, and not so much as touched them with its heels. Then he rode onward to the hall, where he dismounted and entered. He saw there his brother Baldr sitting on the high seat, and he stayed the night. In the morning he besought Hel to let Baldr ride home with him, and told her how great mourning there was among the gods. Hel said that she would make trial whether Baldr was as much beloved as men said—'If all things, both quick and dead, in all the worlds, shall weep for Baldr, then shall he fare home to the gods, but if aught refuse, let Hel keep what she has.'   Then Hermod arose, and Baldr brought him forth from the hall, and gave him the ring Draupnir to bear to Odin as a token of remembrance, while Nanna sent a veil to Frigg and a golden veil to Fulla.   Then Hermod went his way home to Asgarth, and told them all the things which he had seen and heard."

The rest of Snorri's account and how Baldr could not be delivered is given with the Fragments (p. 273).

Other Icelandic sources of this myth are found in allusions of the skalds, and in the description of the bale-fire in Hús-drapa by Ulf Uggason.   Throughout there is little discrepancy and confusion; indeed, if a knowledge of Baldr had been confined to the North, he might have rested in peace.   But other nations claim to have known, and perhaps worshipped him; the Old English trace their descent from Bældæg, son of Wodan; in Germany they knew him as a hero, Phol (Mersburger Spruche); in Denmark strange rites were observed, with burning of rings at Baldershagi (Friþjofssaga).   In the latter country alone, however, do we find any legend corresponding to the above.   Saxo relates how Hotherus, a Swedish king, wooed and won Nanna, a Norwegian princess; but Balderus also loved her, and the two princes long fought for the maiden, until the latter was slain by a magic sword.   In this account Höd appears as the hero of the story, and is beloved by Nanna.   Baldr is the villain, and like other Old Norse gods he is degraded by Saxo to a demi-god.   He is invulnerable to all weapons except the sword which Hotherus wins from the wood-spirit, Miming.   In certain features the Danish story may be regarded as the older version; it is less exalted in tone, and nearer to folklore than to literature.   Loki's share in the deed, Hermod's ride to Hel, and the weeping for Baldr are probably late additions to the myth.

As to whether the sword or the mistletoe is the older weapon it is difficult to decide.   A fateful object with which the life of a hero is bound up is a common motive in mythology or fairy tale; sometimes it is a sword or a wand, sometimes a charmed drink, or even some beast or bird.   In Völuspá (st. 32) the mistletoe is described in this light, and if, as Frazer suggests, Baldr does indeed represent the tree spirit of an oak, then his life may be said to reside in the fair and slender plant which remains green in winter when the oak tree seems to die.

The dead Baldr has suffered yet more than the living.   A helpless victim, the prey of critics, he has been rent asunder, and his whole life story distributed in fragments to the different sources whence it came —nature myths, primitive worship, poetic fancy, legendary history, Christian influence, classical lore.   Theorists on all these topics have taken Baldr as their subject and encircled his name with hybrid myths, and drawn new pictures of his death scene.   Almost worthy of him is that of the glorious sun-god who perishes daily, or perhaps yearly, and with him his wife, the summer fruit and blossom ; or that in which he is seen as the incarnate spirit of nature's growth and life, which seems to die during the winter months, but which in the spring time will be born anew.   This interpretation of Baldr as a tree spirit, and of his death as the poet's description of a heathen rite, is fully discussed by Frazer in "The Golden Bough."   He shows how universal among nations was the offering of a human victim, not in sacrifice to some special deity, but in the performance of a magic drama by which men sought to assist nature through imitation of her work.   Savage and primitive peoples have often thought to make rain and sunshine by sprinkling water and lighting fires ; so too, in spring time, the death of the old tree spirit and the birth of the new might be enacted and furthered by human representatives.   It is true that many legends and customs may be interpreted in this light, but it does not serve to explain the Baldr myth.   There are no grounds, nor any details in his history, even with the ingenious use of the mistletoe, by which Baldr, as we know him, can be transformed into a tree spirit.

Another picture of ancient ceremonial is drawn by Kauffman.   In this scene Baldr is brought forth as the scapegoat : for men deemed it possible to expel, not merely the decaying spirit of vegetative life, but all the evils, physical and moral, which assailed them.   To serve this purpose a scapegoat was chosen to bear the ills of humanity.   In early days his person, reserved for a special end, was sacred and tabooed. No dishonour was attached to his vocation, and the higher the victim, who might be a king or even a god, the more efficacious was the sacrifice.   Subsequently the scapegoat was degraded, and became an object of shame, who was chosen from among criminals and outcasts, as in the Pharmakion at Athens, where a human victim was sacrificed as late as the fifth century.   May there not have been a time among the German nations when Baldr, the most innocent and lovable of all the gods, was sacrified in yearly ceremony for his kind and for humanity ?   Whatever the truth may be as to the origin of the myth,

I I

it is certainly as a scapegoat that he figures in the Edda. Weird was fast overtaking the old faulty war-gods, and the first victim was innocent Baldr.

Both these last theories recall acts of ancient ritual. We come now to another in which Baldr is the impersonation of an idea, the conception of a Christ in Old Norse religion, which arose from the need of humanity for a god divine in his beauty and goodness, but human in his suffering and death. This suggestion, however, demands too great a power of abstraction from an uncultured people; it only explains the final form of the Baldr myth as reinterpreted by a later age. Bugge was certainly of that opinion when he attempted to show that the death scene as given in the Edda is only a copy of the Christian sacrifice. Loki represents Lucifer, and Höd the blind Longinus as they were conceived in the traditions of the Middle Ages. Just as the eye is beginning to grow accustomed to this transformation scene, and to recognise familiar features and real correspondence, it changes anew, and Baldr, passing into Balderus, becomes Achilles; Höd or Hotherus is seen as Paris, and Nanna as Œnone. There is this truth in Bugge's theory, that the first conception of Baldr must have undergone gradual transformation with a nation's developing thought, and assumed in some degree the form and colour of external influences. But it is difficult to follow a change so sudden and complete.

The common sense theory which sifts fact from fiction has given us one other picture of Baldr. From the dim background of history he steps forth, some old king who seems more like a god when thus beheld in the twilight of past days. His name, which means a lord or prince, seems to confirm an explanation which always has the semblance of probability. But the hero chosen by a primitive race for such honours was usually a glorious conqueror or a benefactor of mankind, not the pathetic victim of a fruitless sacrifice. If the myth has its source in history, Saxo's more human love story must be the earlier version.

Let us return, however, to the first picture. Baldr stands invulnerable still. No hailing shower of commentary or weapon of research has destroyed the beauty and reality of the figure which Snorri and the Icelandic poets have drawn.

LOKI'S MOCKING.

"There is one," writes Snorri, "who is numbered among the gods, although some call him their reviler, and the shame both of gods and men. His name is Loki, or Lopt, the Rover of Air, son of the Jötun Fierce-beater. His mother is called Leaf-isle or Pine-needle, and his brothers are Byleipt and Hel-dazzler. Loki is beautiful and fair of face, but evil of mind and fickle in his ways. He is more versed in the art of cunning than others, and is crafty in all things. Oft he brings the gods into great plight, and delivers them oft by his wily counsel." This bright elusive figure, like a spark of the fire which he personifies, kindles with life and humour every tale into which he enters, appearing and reappearing in different forms, a god in his power, and a devil in his deeds. He well deserves a place among the portraits which art has drawn of the latter personality. No stormy power of evil like the Satan of *Paradise Lost*, he yet provokes war in heaven, and snares by his tempting the wives of gods. His rebellion is more dangerous to them than a wild assertion of the individual, for he is the undermining instrument of fate. Compared too with Mephistopheles, Loki, rich in human life and mirth and beauty, finds more victims among men than the cold seducer of the spirit. In all the more familiar myths of Snorri's Edda he appears a purely Scandinavian figure, of late origin and possibly moulded by Christian influence; but in the poems he may be traced back to some old Germanic fire god, perhaps called "Logi," flame, who lent his name and attributes to Loki, the "ender" or destroyer of the gods. However this may be, his double nature and the poetical contradictory myths which are told concerning him find explanation in his origin as a fire god. Fire is mighty, beneficent, life-restoring, swift, and beautiful to the eye; such character has Loki when, as Lodur, he bestows the gift of warmth and goodly hue on man, when he fetches Idun out of Jötunheim, and appears a god of wondrous beauty. But fire may also be cruel, treacherous, fierce, and destroying; and was it not Loki himself who enticed Idun out of Asgarth, who betrayed Freyja, mocked the gods at their banquet, worked the death of Baldr, and led the Hel hosts at the Doom? In all his mythical adventures Loki appears sometimes as the friend of the gods, and especially as the companion of Odin and Hœnir, and sometimes in alliance with the giants.   He commits some folly or crime, he bring the gods into danger, and then by his power and cunning he extricates them and is forgiven, until he works the evil which can never be atoned or remedied —the death of Baldr.   After this he must suffer punishment till Ragnarök.

"Loki's Mocking" is the best poem of its kind in the whole collection of the Edda.   Continually striving after more and more vivid representation, Old Norse art has at last attained its perfection in an inimitable dramatic poem, where the whole interest is centred in living personality.   The characters are drawn in masterly fashion with a neat, crisp touch; the dialogue is racy, humorous, forcible, and has a bitterness which flavours the whole.   Much skill is shown in the introduction of new speakers, with their ever varying tones, and quick repartees.   The author is never didactic; he has no end in view beyond this comedy of the fallen, discredited gods—or is it not rather their tragedy?   For although the collective poems of the Edda do not give us a complete history of the gods, and the earlier ones do not even suggest the somewhat ethical light in which it is here presented, this idea of tragedy is not a purely modern interpretation.   The poet of Völuspá regards the fall of the gods as the result of their warring, the retribution of Weird: the distinctive feature in the new world is its peacefulness.   The present poet has his own notion of the sequence of events.   This is clearly one of the latest, and the gods, as shown by him, are so degenerate that they can exist no more.   The banquet scene is a crisis in their history.   The Vala of the preceding poem had spoken the doom of Baldr.   In her solemn accents was heard the first note of warning, and Loki, with wild mocking words, pronounces judgment on the rest.

They are gathered for peaceful converse in the sea halls of Ægir, recalling with quiet satisfaction or intoxicated joy their old deeds of glory, when in bursts a fierce intruder, the fiery Loki, half demon in his spite and cunning, half god in his beauty and might.   Truths bitter and shameful he hurls at them, and they shrink condemned before his unwelcome revelation, and give him place at their banquet.   One by one he singles out the gods, and spares not the goddesses, and the sting of each accusation lies in its truth.   Bragi the poet, so ready in speech, is doubtless a boaster and a coward like the singer Hunferth in "Beowulf;" it is well known that Odin, the High One, has degraded himself by working magic, that Frigg is unfaithful, that Frey has parted with his sword to buy Gerd, that Thor was outwitted by Utgarth-Loki. Heimdal and Tyr he can taunt only with their sufferings; in Baldr he can find no stain, yet boasts that he himself was author of the crime whereby the god was slain. But Loki, though invincible in his words, cannot stand before Mjöllnir, and on the entrance of the Thunderer in god-like wrath, with a few parting gibes the hateful intruder takes flight. It is a wild picture of disillusionment, painted in lurid colours, which are intensified by recalling the gloomy scene which comes before, the tragedy of Baldr's death, and that which follows the extinction of the banquet lights, the punishment of Loki, and the fulfilment of Doom—for so events, as of a story already complete, seem to have shaped themselves in the poet's mind. It is a last gathering before the round table of the war-gods is dissolved. The very conception of a Baldr had been their condemnation, for it was the birth of a new ideal. Here the sceptic leaves them, stripped of all their old glory, shown as fickle, shadowy beings—the ever-changing gods of nature.

For it is in this light that the poem must be interpreted—as a much obscured picture of elemental forces. Loki figures throughout as the destructive fire-demon, from his strife with the peaceful hearth fire on entering to the last curse which he hurls upon Ægir. Most of his taunts and accusations may thus be explained, except in passages such as st. 17 and 52, where the myths of Idun and Skadj are unknown. Frey and Freyja, whose names are masculine and feminine forms of the same word (lord and lady), are in their origin different aspects of the same Sun deity; hence their close union as brother and sister and as husband and wife, but nothing further is known of some myth alluded to in st. 30, which must have grown up to explain it. Hence, too, the loss of Frey's sword in the sunbeam which he sent to Gerd, or earth (st. 42). Njörd also (st. 34) appears in the character of a peaceful sea god, "who," says Snorri, "dwells in Ship-home; he rules the way of the wind, and stills the sea and slakes the fire flame. He is not of Æsir race, but he was fostered in the land of Wanes, who gave him as hostage to the gods, and took in exchange one who is called Hœnir. Thus peace was made between the gods and Wanes." Loki, in st. 36, accuses Njörd of what is recounted of him in Ynglinga Saga, that before he came among the Æsir he was married to his sister, who bore him a son and daughter, Frey and Freyja. As such a union was not permitted among the Æsir, he now declares Frey to be the son of Skadi. His after history, how he was sent on by the gods as hostage into Jötunheim, and was kept a prisoner there during the long winter months like ocean itself when held in bondage by the frost, is told by Snorri, and given with the Fragments (p. 271). As sea god, too, Hymir's daughters, the glacier streams, poured themselves into his mouth (st. 34).

Drawn from some nature myth must be the allusions of st. 26. Odin, as heaven god, has a wife of like nature, Frigg; but, in less exalted character, he is also the husband of the Earth goddess, Jörd. Does Frigg allow herself to be wooed by Odin's brothers Vili and Vé, who are again different aspects of himself, as the cloud goddess, who is made the sport of the wind in all its moods? Frigg's unfaithfulness in Ynglinga Saga is told as traditional history of Odin, the race founder; it occurred during his banishment. Not he alone appears under varying forms as a nature god, but Frigg and Freyja have their shadowy image in Gefjon (st. 2), mentioned by Snorri as a "maiden who is served by such as die unwed." Here, like Frigg, she has fore-knowledge of fate, and like Freyja she owns the famous necklace (p. 131), which was won by Heimdal, "the fair youth" (st. 20), from Loki, who had stolen it.

Idun, the wife of Bragi, appears but this once in the poems. Snorri says—"She keeps in her casket those apples whereof the gods eat when they wax old, and which make them young again; thus they have given a great treasure into the keeping of Idun, which once was well nigh lost." These words recall one of the most famous incidents in the history of the gods, which involved the slaying of Thiazi (st. 50) and Njörd's periods of exile. Loki, when journeying with Odin and Hœnir, had once been made prisoner by the giant Thiazi, and was released only on promise of betraying Idun to the giants, who, like Freyja, was coveted by them as a summer goddess. He enticed her out of Asgarth by saying he had found apples as wondrous as her own. "Then there was wailing among the gods at the loss of Idun, and ere long they waxed grey-haired and old. They gathered in council, and each asked the other what he knew last concerning Idun, and it was found that she was last seen going forth from Asgarth with Loki." The latter, to save his life, donned Freyja's falcon plumes and flew into Jötunheim, and fetched back Idun in the form of a nut. Thiazi pursued him as an eagle, and, just missing him, flew into a fire which the gods had kindled outside the walls of Asgarth. His wings were burnt, and there he was slain. Skadi, his daughter, demanded vengeance, and would make peace only on two conditions—one, that the gods should make her laugh, which only Loki could do by acting the part of a buffoon; secondly, that she should choose a husband among them, and she chose Njörd (p. 271).

Even more famous than this occurrence was the binding of Fenrir by Tyr, the god who accompanied Thor in his quest after the cauldron. According to Snorri, "he is the best and bravest hearted of all the gods, who rules victory in battle." It appears from his name that he once owned a more distinguished place than that of war-god. Sanskrit *dyaus*, Greek *Zeus*, Latin *Jupiter*, Old High German *Ziu*, Old English *Tuesday*, Old Norse *Tyr*, are all derived from the same Germanic root *div*, to shine, which must originally have belonged to the Heaven god. Snorri relates how Loki had three terrible children by the giantess Sorrow-bringer—Fenrir, the World-serpent, and Hel. "All-father bade the gods bring them to him, and he cast the Serpent into the deep, where it lies encircling all lands, and grown so huge that it bites its own tail. Hel he cast into Mist-home; and the Wolf was reared at home. Tyr alone had courage to approach him with food. And when they beheld how he waxed mightier each day they remembered the prophecy, how it was foretold that he should work their woe. And after they had taken counsel together they forged a very strong fetter called Læding, and brought it to the Wolf and bade him try his strength upon it. Seeing that it was not over mighty, Fenrir let the gods bind him as they willed, and at his first struggle the fetter was broken. Thus he loosed himself from Læding.

"Then the gods forged another fetter, twice as strong, which they called Drómi, and bade the Wolf try his strength upon this, and told him that he would become famed for his might if a chain of such forging would not hold him. Fenrir knew well how strong was the fetter, but he knew likewise that he had waxed mightier since he broke Læding. Moreover, it came into his mind that one must needs risk somewhat for the sake of fame, and he allowed himself to be bound. When the gods said they were ready Fenrir shook himself, and loosened the fetter till it touched the ground; then he strove fiercely against it and spurned it off him, and broke it so that the pieces flew far and wide. Thus Fenrir freed himself from Drómi.

"Then were the gods filled with fear and deemed they would never be able to bind the Wolf, and All-father sent Skirnir, Frey's shining courier, down to the Underworld, where dwelt the Dark Elves or dwarfs, who forged for him the fetter called Gleipnir. Out of six things they wrought it—the footfalls of cats, the beards of women, the roots of mountains, the sinews of bears, the breath of fish, and the spittle of birds. It was soft and smooth as a silken band, yet strong and trusty withal."

The Wolf would consent to be bound only with this fetter on condition that one among the gods would lay a hand in his mouth. " And each god looked at the other, and weened that here was choice of two ills; but none made offer until Tyr put forth his right hand, and laid it in the Wolf's mouth." So they bound Fenrir, and watched him struggle, while the fetter grew tighter and sharper, " and they laughed, one and all, save Tyr alone, who lost his hand." But this attempt, as with Baldr, to stay the course of Weird is in vain, and the Wolf will remain bound only till Ragnarök.

St. 60 alludes to that luckless journey of Thor's into Jötunheim (p. xlviii.), when he was so many times outwitted by Utgarth-loki, who is here called Skrymir. On this occasion the giant had offered to carry the provisions of the gods with his own, and he bound them up so tightly that Thor could not loosen the knot.

This poem is a review of the whole life-history of the gods. It recalls all the main events which took place in their midst, it indicates the part played by each character; but the sceptical attitude of the writer can best be seen by comparing it with the dignity and pathos of the poem which follows Snorri's Fragments, Völuspá. The Fragments themselves have already been explained, where possible, by similar passages in the Poetic Edda.

THE SOOTHSAYING OF THE VALA.

In Völuspá the gods' history is reviewed once more from beginning to end, this time by one who sees it in its truest light—the artist. Just touched, as it seems, by later influence and new ideals, this poem cannot be taken as primitive, or as the work of one who held the mythical fancies as religious beliefs. The old gods have had their day, their story is complete; but once more it is told before it is forgotten, in an age when their nature and strivings are yet understood. Some poet, who has seen truth in the beauty of these old-world tales, has endeavoured to give them a unity which is still retained in spite of all after meddling with his work. It is seen in the thread which runs like a guiding principle throughout—the bond of Weird which weaves itself inch by inch out of the acts of gods and men. As we have shown, this poem is the conscious recognition of a principle which must exist in any mythology founded on a religion of nature. For this reason it needs to be read both first and last—first, because it sums up and interprets the other poems; and last, because without a previous knowledge of its myths the Vala's words can scarcely be understood. Even with such knowledge as we have already gathered some passages cannot be explained, owing to lost connections and forgotten incidents; others because their difficulty arises from the nature of mythology itself, with its rational and irrational ideas, its blendings of poetry and superstition, and the thoughts of one age with those of another. But, as the poet himself has seen, little beauty and no truth can be revealed in the detailed rehearsal of myths by which men have sought to represent the mysteries of life. He has given rather the spirit in which they tried to grasp them. The Old Norsemen turned a serious face towards life, and refused to regard it either as a playground or a home of rest; it was essentially a field of endeavour and of strife between man and nature, god and Jötun, powers of good and evil. All this is echoed in the struggle of the gods with Weird, the power and deep war-notes of the poem, the solemnity of tone which is relieved at times by a quiet rejoicing in the mere movement and activities of life. Peculiar, too, was the attitude of the Norseman towards the supernatural. Mysteries to him were not further mystified by speculation or emotion, but as such they were left and took their place among the factors of his daily life, where all else was tangible and definite to the eye. We can well imagine such an attitude of mind arising among men who had been brought to dwell in a land where nature is full of mystery, and who were forced to live a practical and strenuous life in conflict with powers only half understood. Loneliness and dim perils of ice and snow became a part of their every-day existence. Hence the atmosphere and setting of the poem—its background, dim and misty, grey and subdued in tone, lit only by aurora gleams of imagination; and its foreground, with the well-defined and vivid pictures.

Characteristic, too, is the figure of the Vala, so called probably,

though the point is much disputed, from the staff which she carried.*
She was a wandering prophetess, who, clad in her fur cap and her
dark robes, went from house to house, foretelling and divining hidden
things. The power of second sight which she claimed was common,
not only to such as she, but to many a good housewife in Icelandic
sagas. But while those so gifted knew only of trivial matters, interpreted dreams and omens, advised and warned, this Vala, addressing
all kindreds of the earth, reveals the fate and history of the world.
Like the witch in Baldr's Dreams, she has been called up from the
dead, and, like the Mighty Weaver, she is one of those primæval beings
who remember all things; and she recalls in visionary scenes, one by
one, the great events of time. Snorri has vainly attempted to bring
sequence and order into his corresponding description, and has invented
details which spoil the grandeur of that given by the Vala. For want
of better authority, however, we are often obliged to rely upon him for
explanations.

She tells first of the creation. In the beginning was chaos, when
as yet there was no heaven or earth—only, in the north, a region of
snow and ice; and, in the south, one of fire and heat, with a yawning
gap between, from which life arose in the form of Ymir, the stirring,
rustling, sounding Jötun, followed by others of his kind, born out of
the elements, and as yet hardly to be distinguished from them. Then
the gods were born, who forthwith made war upon these giant powers,
and, half subduing them, they ordered the universe with its worlds of
gods and elves, of dwarfs and giants, of men—the living in Midgarth,
the dead in Hel, all held in the sheltering embrace of a great World
Tree; but from whence sprang this Tree, or when and how it grew,
not even the giants could tell.

Sun, Moon, and stars were set in heaven, and when Sun turned
her face towards Earth, and shone upon its "threshold" stones,
it brought forth fruit, and its bare surface was overspread with
green. But as yet the paths of the heavenly bodies had not been
decreed. What did Sun do in her perplexity? How did she fling her
right hand over the rim of heaven? Did she appear to the spectator
to glide on towards the right, and linger in the northern heavens
without knowing the hall of her setting? Did she face round from the

---

* Zs f.d.a., vol. v., p. 42; Norsk. Hist. Tidsskr., vol. iv., p. 169; Golther, p. 652,
But cf Vigfusson, p. 721; Anz.f.d. Alt., xii, p. 49, note.

south, and marching back eastward, fling her own right hand over the horizon, and set in the east ? Or have we in st. 5 a description of the midnight sun dipping for a moment below the horizon, and then rising to put to shame Moon, who had not yet learned his secret influence over the destiny of man, and the stars, who knew not their courses? For the first time the gods gathered in council in their holy place by the Well of Weird to order this matter ; again they met to rescue the humble dwarf folk, who had been left half created as the maggots which crawled out of Ymir's flesh. They were given human form and a share in creative power, but all their work, the forging of secret treasures, they must do beneath the ground.

Then followed the greatest act of creation, concerning which the gods held no council, for it came to pass in the course of destiny. When Sun, obeying the law of her own being, had first shone upon the world, vegetative life was quickened in the earthy matter ; now the gods once faring on their homeward way bestowed, each after his own nature, gifts upon two barren trees, and human life was awakened, with individuality and a soul. Odin, as the Wind god, gave them breath, which has ever been held as the emblem of the spirit, or even as spirit itself. Hœnir, of whom little is known, except that he was wise (see below), gave an understanding mind. Loki (here called Lodur), the fire-god, gave warm blood and the bright hue of life, .

Meanwhile, what Snorri calls the "golden age" was passing, when the gods were building the fair homes mentioned by Grimnir, rejoicing in their work, in their play, and doubtless, too, in their love. It must have been then that Bragi wooed Idun with fluent tongue, that Baldr wedded Nanna, that Thor's heart was given to Sif the golden-haired, the most guileless among all the goddesses.

But soon this peaceful age was broken. The first shadow of Doom fell as three mighty maidens passed from Jötunheim, and sat them down beneath the tree Yggdrasil. These fair Norns, who wrote the past and present on their tables and laid down the future lots of men, are later forms of Weird, personified as a grim goddess of fate, and known to all Germanic races.

Then swiftly followed the first war among kindred races of the gods, the Æsir and the Wanes. From the last more cultured tribe there came a witch called Golden-draught among the warlike Æsir. Two things she taught this simple folk—the lust for gold, and the use of magic. The last was deemed an unpardonable sin among Germanic

nations, and was punished by burning. In like manner the Æsir sought
to destroy Golden-draught by burning her in Odin's hall; but in vain,
for as many times as they burned her she was born anew (p. liv.).
War broke out and the Wanes demanded were-gild, and a council of
peace was held; but the War-father arose, and hurling his spear gave
the signal for strife to rage anew. It ended in the storming and
destruction of Asgarth by the Wanes. Here a gap in the poem or a
timely clouding of the Vala's vision hides the shame and defeat of the
gods. In Ynglinga Saga (iv.) it is told as legendary history that after
a while both sides became weary of a war in which victory fell now to
the one and now to the other, and in which the countries of both
were spoiled. So they held a peace meeting, and made a truce and
exchanged chieftains. The Wanes sent their noblest, Njörd, with his
children Frey and Freyja; and the Æsir sent Hœnir, who was deemed
well fitted to be a ruler, and with him they sent also one of great
understanding, Mimir, in exchange for Kvasir, the wisest among the
Wanes. Hœnir was made a chief in Wane-home. When the people
found that he could give no counsel without Mimir, but said on all
occasions—"Let others decide," they thought themselves cheated by
the Æsir, and cut off Mimir's head and sent it to Odin. He smeared
it with herbs, and sang rune-songs and gave it power of speech,
through which he learned many secret things. According to Snorri,
Kvasir was a wondrous being fashioned by all the gods, from whose
blood the Song-mead was brewed (p. xxviii.). In both accounts the
details are evidently of late invention. This war between strength and
valour on the one side, art and skill on the other, is like a shadowy
recollection of a time in history, when the barbaric children of the
North were dazzled by Roman gold and Roman civilisation. But such
a strife, with the first weakening of the war powers, was inevitable in
the story of the gods.*

Immediately following this incident, it would seem from the allusion of the Vala (st. 25), took place an event which Snorri recounts—
a fierce struggle with the Jötuns, and a crafty attempt on their part
to win Freyja, the summer-goddess, who had just been brought to
Asgarth. The gods were in need of a builder to raise anew the walls
of their dismantled city, which by the last war had been left open to

* For the war between the gods and Wanes, see article by Dt. and Hl.; Beit., vol.
xviii, p. 542.

the inroads of Frost and Mountain-giants. A craftsman appeared and offered to do the work in three half years, but asked as his payment Freyja, and with her the Sun and Moon. At the evil counsel of Loki, and seemingly in the absence of Thor, they agreed to his demands if he could finish the work in a single winter, before the first day of summer, otherwise his reward would be forfeited. He worked night and day with the help of his giant horse Svadilfari, and the walls were well nigh complete when it still wanted three days before the summer. Then the gods took counsel, and questioned one another "who had thus planned to send Freyja as bride into Jötunheim, who had filled all the sky and heaven with darkness by taking thence the sun and moon?" It is this scene which the poem describes, but it tells nothing of what is learned from Snorri that "the gods knew, one and all, that he must have counselled this, who ever counsels ill, Loki, the son of Leaf-isle." Then they laid hands upon him, and made him swear to deliver them out of their plight; and he did this by changing himself into a mare, and enticing Svadilfari away into the woods. "And when the craftsman saw that he could not finish the work he flew into a Jötun-rage, and the gods knew now for certain that it was one of the Mountain-giants who had come among them; and oaths were disregarded and Thor was called, who came even as swiftly. Then was Mjöllnir raised aloft, and the craftsman received his wage; but he returned not into Jötunheim with the Sun and Moon, for at the first blow his skull was broken into pieces, and he was sent down to Mist-hel beneath." Once more a scene of shame is veiled, for the gods had broken faith with the Jötuns in trying to undo their own folly.

When the Vala resumes, a new part of the poem has begun, and her words become more mysterious. She is revealing now no longer old tidings heard or things remembered, but secret knowledge which she has won at night time when she "sat out" enchanting and holding commune with the spirits of nature. On some such occasion, it seems that Odin has come to consult with her, but when this occurred or whether she is rehearsing a past incident is not made clear.

She proves first her power to foretell the future by showing that her knowledge penetrates to the holiest secrets of the gods. She knows of their pledges—Heimdal's hearing, Odin's eye, and Baldr's life. Heimdal can hear grass growing in the earth, and wool on the back of sheep. Is it his ear which he has hidden in the sacred well beneath Yggdrasil to obtain this wonderful power which he needs in his watch against the Mountain-giants? And why has Odin pledged his eye to Mimir? This last question can be answered only by tracing back the history of Mimir. In German tradition he is a wise teacher and wonderful smith, who instructed Siegfried and Weland; according to Snorri, he is Hœnir's companion, whom the Wanes beheaded, and who became the friend and counsellor of Odin; in the Poetic Edda he is also closely associated with the god, whose wisdom, as we have seen, is not the natural attribute of his divinity, but is drawn from all sources. Giants, Valas from Hel, ravens in the air instruct him, but his friend of friends is Mimir, the Deep-thinker, with whom he takes counsel at the Doom. Mimir is a giant in the older Edda, and guardian of a sacred well of Wisdom, or rather, at an earlier date, that well itself, from whose source or head flowed the moisture used in the writing of the runes (p. xxxi.), and in whose waters Odin has pledged his eye to gain insight into hidden things. A further interpretation, which Müllenhoff suggests, belongs to a still older stratum of thought —a nature myth of the sun drawing precious moisture from the sea, and in return casting its own reflection, its second eye, into the deep. Sun and sea, thus mutually dependent together, give nourishment to the world, as Odin and Mimir together bestow their wisdom.

In st. 32 is mentioned the third and yet more mysterious pledge, Baldr's life and fate, which are bound up with the mistletoe (p. lxiv.). But the description of the Vala is now growing more and more visualised, and she herself can scarce interpret the floating pictures which represent now some future, now some present scene. She is looking into all the different worlds—Earth, where the Valkyries are speeding to the battlefields of men; Asgarth, where beside Valhöll the fateful mistletoe is already high upgrown; the cave where she foresees the torment of Loki; Hel, where evil men are suffering the penalty of their misdeeds; Jötunheim, with its feasting-hall of giants; dark dwarf-land, where no sun nor moon can penetrate, lit only by the glowing forge fires of these active beings; and again eastward into Jötunheim, where Sköll was fostered, the dark wolf-son of Fenrir, who follows the fleeing Sun goddess across the heavens until he clutches her in the west, and stains all the sky at sunset with crimson like the blood of men (p. xvi.).

All these grim sights have in them something fearful and ill-omened; the shadow of fate is growing darker, the Weird motive is heard more and more clearly. Now the true "spaedom" of the Vala begins; she has turned to the future, and foretells the Doom of the gods. But she grows less visionary; the scene is a twilight glimpse of dawn; she can only see dimly, and she is listening—to the crowing of the cocks in Giant-land, in Asgarth, and in Hel, and following the long expected signals of alarm she hears a rumbling through all Jötun-heim as the giant-enemies of the gods bestir themselves for battle; the clashing of weapons in Valhöll as the War-sons of Odin awake and pour forth through the five hundred doorways, while the gods are gathering at the doomstead and holding speech together; in Hel, the rending of chains—Fenrir has broken loose, Loki is free. She hears the gleeful song of the giants' warder answered by Heimdal with the roaring blast of Gjalla-horn, which sounds through all the worlds. In the earth, too, among men, she hears wars and rumours of wars, crashing of shields and swords; from below comes the groaning of the imprisoned dwarfs; and throughout, at intervals, waxing louder and wilder, the deep baying of the Hel-hound, Garm. Amid this tumult she catches another sound, more fearful still, the shivering and rustling of the great Ash, the Tree of Fate, as it quivers, but does not fall—and yet one other sound, a voice in the storm, the murmur of words: Odin is holding speech with Mimir.

Now light falls; once more the Vala can see; the foes are gathering from all quarters on the great battlefield, which measures a hundred miles each way. From the east come Frost and Mountain-giants; from the south come Fire-giants; from the north the Hel-hosts, and Loki; from the west must come the gods, led by Odin, with all his Chosen warriors.

In single combats the last battle is depicted. Weird is triumphant. A second time must the Heaven-goddess weep, when the War-father is devoured by Fenrir, though vengeance quickly follows, and the Wolf falls before Vidar; Frey, who has parted with the sword which waged itself, is destroyed by the Fire-giant Surt; Thor meets once more with the World Serpent, and still glorious in defeat, he slays and is slain. Thus the war-gods perish, and fire consumes the world.

Throughout this passage the tone of the poem has changed. Solemn and meditative at first, or rippling blithely on through each fresh disclosure of life, it has grown abrupt and stormy with the strivings of Weird to fulfil itself. Now again it changes to a tone of peaceful exultation, which heralds the restitution of all things. There is nothing visionary now, or mystic, in the scene. It is a calm, fresh morning after the night of storm; all nature is at rest; life is resumed. Seldom do we find in old poetry so realistic a description—the green earth is still bathed with moisture; the rushing of waterfalls is heard; the living eagles, in contrast to the pale-beaked monster of st. 50, seek their wonted food in mountain pools. The gods are come again, but not all, for the rule of the war-gods is at an end, and their home of battle will henceforth be the dwelling-place of peace. It is a continuation of a former existence, without labour and without strife; old sports are renewed, old achievements are not forgotten, old mysteries are disclosed. Powers of evil depart, and there comes a new god. But here fresh mysteries appear, and must wait for solution by a later poet who seeks, like the present one, to explain existent myths in the light of a higher creed.

THE ELDER EDDA

COMMONLY CALLED SÆMUND'S EDDA

EDITED AND TRANSLATED BY OLIVE BRAY

PART I

B

Page 2

Page 3

Óþinn ok Frigg sátu í Hliþskjálfu ok sá um heima alla. Óþinn mælti: 'Sér þu Agnar fóstra þinn, hvar hann elr börn viþ gýgi í hellinum? En Geirröþr fóstri minn er konungr ok sitr nú at landi.' Frigg segir: 'Hann er matníþingr sá, at hann kvelr gesti sína, ef honum þykkja ofmargir koma.' Óþinn segir, at þat er in mesta lygi; þau veþja um þetta mál. Frigg sendi eskimey sína Fullu til Geirröþar. Hon baþ konung varaz, at eigi fyrgörþi hánum fjölkunnigr maþr sá er þar var kominn í land, ok sagþi þat mark á, at engi hundr var svá ólmr at á hann mundi hlaupa. En þat var enn mesti hégómi, at Geirröþr konungr væri eigi matgóþr; ok þó lætr hann handtaka þann mann er eigi vildu hundar á ráþa. Sá var í feldi blám ok nefndiz Grimnir ok sagþi ekki fleira frá sér, þótt hann væri at spurþr. Konungr lét hann pína til sagna ok setja milli elda tveggja, ok sat hann þar átta nætr. Geirröþr konungr átti þá son tíu vetra gamlan ok hét Agnarr eptir bróþur hans. Agnarr gekk at Grimni ok gaf hánum horn fullt at drekka ok sagþi, at konungr görþi illa, er hann lét pína hann saklausan. Grimnir drakk af; þá var eldrinn svá kominn, at feldrinn brann af Grimni. Hann kvaþ:

1.   Heitr est, hripuþr!   ok heldr til mikill;
         göngumk firr, funi!
     loþi sviþnar,   þót á lopt berak,
         brinnumk feldr fyrir.

2.   Átta nætr   satk milli elda hér,
         svát mér manngi mat né bauþ,
     nema einn Agnarr,   es einn skal ráþa
         Geirröþar sunr Gotna landi.

3.   Heill skaltu Agnarr!   alls þik heilan biþr
         Veratýr vesa;
     eins drykkjar   þú skalt aldregi
         betri gjöld geta.

Odin and Frigg were sitting once on Window-shelf, gazing out over all the world. Said Odin :—" Seest thou Agnar, thy fosterling, how he begets children with a giantess in a cave ? But Geirröd, my fosterling, is a king, and rules over the realm." " He is such a meat-grudger," answered Frigg, " that he starves his guests when he deems that too many are come into his halls." Odin swore that this was the greatest lie, and they wagered on the matter. Frigg sent her hand-maiden Fulla to Geirröd to bid the king beware lest an enchanter, who had come into the land, should bewitch him, and she gave them this sign whereby he might be known : no dog, however fierce, would assail him. Men had lied greatly in saying that Geirröd was not hospitable, but for all that he caused a certain guest to be seized, whom the dogs would not attack. He came clad in a blue mantle, calling himself Grimnir, the Masked One, and would tell nought beside, however much they asked him. Then the king ordered him to be tortured till he should speak, and they set him in the midst between two fires, and eight nights he sat there. Geirröd's son, who was ten years old, and named Agnar after the king's brother, went up to Grimnir and gave him to drink out of a brimming horn, saying that the king had done ill thus to torture him without cause ; and Grimnir drank. At length, when the fire had waxed so nigh that his mantle burned upon him, he spake :—

1. Fierce art thou, fire !   and far too great ;
        flame, get thee further away !
 my cloak is scorched   though I hold it high ;
        my mantle burns before me.

2. Eight nights have I sat   betwixt the fires,
        while no man offered me food,
    save only Agnar,   the son of Geirröd,
        who alone shall rule the realm.

3. Blest be thou, Agnar   the God of all beings
        shall call a blessing upon thee :
    for one such draught   thou shalt never more
        so fair a guerdon win.

2.—Rule the realm *or* land of the Goths, *a name used in a general sense for warriors or a nation.*

4. Land es heilagt   es ek liggja sé
    ásum ok ölfum nær :
    enn í þrúþheimi   skal Þórr vesa,
    unz of rjúfask regin.

5. Ýdalir heita   þars Ullr hefr
    sér of görva sali ;
    Alfheim Frey   gáfu í árdaga
    tívar at tannfé.

6. Bœr's enn þriþi,   es blíþ regin
    silfri þökþu sali :
    Válaskjalf heitir   es vélti sér
    áss í árdaga.

7. Sökkvabekkr heitir enn fjórþi,   enn þar svalar knegu
    unnir glymja yfir :
    þar þau Óþinn ok Sága   drekka of alla daga
    glöþ ór gollnum kerum.

8. Glaþsheimr heitir enn fimti   þars en gollbjarta
    Valhöll víþ of þrumir ;
    en þar Hróptr   kýss hverjan dag
    vápndauþa vera.

9. Mjök es auþkent   þeims til Óþins koma
    salkynni at sea :
    sköptum's rann rept,   skjöldum's salr þakiþr,
    brynjum of bekki straït.

10. Mjök es auþkent   þeims til Óþins koma
    salkynni at sea :
    vargr hangir   fyr vestan dyrr
    ok drúpir örn yfir.

(The Twelve Homes of the Gods.)

4. Holy is the land   which yonder lies
      near the world of gods and elves :
   in the Home of Strength   shall the Thunderer dwell,
      even till the Powers perish.

5. Yew-dale is called   the realm where Ull
      hath set him a hall on high ;
   and Elf-home that   which the gods gave Frey
      as tooth-fee in days of yore.

6. A third home is there   whose hall is thatched
      with silver by blessed Powers ;
   Vala-shelf   that seat is named,
      which was founded in former days.

7. The fourth is Falling-brook ;   there, for ever,
      the chill waves are rushing over ;
   while day by day   drink Odin and Saga,
      glad-hearted, from golden cups.

8. The fifth is called Glad-home,   and gold-bright Valhöll,
      spacious, lies in its midst :
   there Odin shall choose   his own each day
    . of the warriors fallen in war.

9. 'Tis easily known   by all who come
      to visit Odin's folk ;
   with shafts 'tis raftered,   with shields 'tis roofed,
      with byrnies the benches are strewn.

10. 'Tis easily known   by all who come
      to visit Odin's folk ;
   there hangs a wolf   'fore the western door,
      and an eagle hovers over.

5.—Frey, Elf-home, *see Introd. to Skm. and Ls. st. 43.* Tooth-fee, *gift to a child at teething.*   7.—"*Falling-brook*": Sökkvabekkr *has usually been rendered* Sinking-bench ; *Detter suggests the above.* 8.—Odin, *here called* Hropt : *See Introd.*

11. Þrymheimr heitir enn sétti,   es Þjazi bjó,
      sa enn ámátki jötunn ;
    en nú Skaþi byggvir,   skír brúþr goþa,
      fornar toptir föþur.

12. Breiþablik 'rú en sjaundu,   en þar Baldr hefr
      sér of görva sali :
    á því landi   es ek liggja veit
      fǽsta feiknstafi.

13. Himinbjörg 'ru en áttu,   en þar Heimdall kveþa
      . . . valda veum :
    þar vörþr goþa   drekkr í vǽru ranni
      glaþr enn góþa mjöþ.

14. Folkvangr 's enn niundi,   en þar Freyja rǽþr
      sessa kostum í sal :
    hálfan val   hón kýss hverjan dag
      en hálfan Óþinn á.

15. Glitnir 's enn tiundi,   hann es golli studdr
      ok silfri þakþr et sama :
    en þar Forseti   byggvir flestan dag
      ok svǽfir allar sakar.

16. Noatún 'ru en elliftu,   en þar Njörþr hefr
      sér of görva sali :
    manna þengill   enn meinsvani
      hátimbruþum hörgi rǽþr.

17. Hrísi vex   ok hávu grasi
      Víþars land Viþi :
    en þar mögr   of lǽzk af mars baki
      frǿkn at hefna föþur.

11. The sixth is Sound-home,   where Thiazi bode,
         that fearful Jötun of yore ;
     now Skadi dwells,   fair bride of gods,
         in her father's former home.

12. The seventh is Broad-gleam ;   there hath Baldr
         set him a hall on high,
     away in the land   where I ween are found
         the fewest tokens of ill.

13. The eighth is Heaven-hill ;   world-bright Heimdal
         rules o'er its holy fanes :
     in that peaceful hall   the watchman of gods
         glad-hearted the good mead quaffs.

14. The ninth is Folk-field ;   Freyja rules there
         choice of seats in the hall :
     one half the dead   she chooses each day
         but half the War-father owns.

15. The tenth is Glistener   pillared with gold,
         and eke with silver roofed ;
     there Forseti dwells   nigh the long day through,
         the Judge, and soothes all strife.

16. The eleventh is Noatun ;   Njörd in that haven
         hath built him a hall by the sea ;
     a prince of men,   ever faultless found,
         he holds the high built fanes.

17. With brushwood grows,   and with grasses high,
         Wood-home, Vidar's land ;
     from his steed that son   of Odin shall show him
         strong to avenge his sire.

11.—*Thiazi, Skadi, see Ls. st. 50 and Introd.* Jötun *or giant*; J *in Icelandic is pronounced like* Y *; so also Freyja, Njörd.* 14.—*Freyja seems here to stand for Frigg, wife of Odin, who shared the slain with him.* 16.—*Njörd in that haven; the suggested meaning for* Noatún *is "Ship-haven," see Fragments from Sn.E. and Saga-book, iv., 191, 192.* 17.—*Vidar, see Vm. st. 53 : Vsp. st. 54.*   C

18. (21) Þýtr Þund,   unir Þjóþvitnis
              fiskr flóþi í :
          árstraumr   þykkir ofmikill
              valglaumi at vaþa.

19. (23) Fimm hundruþ golfa   ok of fjórum tögum
              hykk Bilskirni meþ bugum ;
          ranna þeira   es ek rept vita
              míns veitk mest magar.

20. (22) Valgrind heitir   es stendr velli á
              heilög fyr helgum durum ;
          forn's sú grind,   en þat faïr vitu,
              hvé's í lás of lokin.

21. (24) Fimm hundruþ dura   ok of fjórum tögum
              hykk á Valhöllu vesa ;
          átta hundruþ einherja   ganga ór einum durum,
              þás þeir fara viþ Vitni at vega.

22. (18) Andhrimnir   lætr í Eldhrimni
              Sæhrimni soþinn,
          fleska bazt :   en þat faïr vitu,
              viþ hvat einherjar alask.

23. (19) Gera ok Freka   seþr gunntamiþr
              hróþugr Herjaföþr :
          en viþ vín eitt   vápngöfugr
              Óþinn æ lifir.

18.—*The rearrangement of strophes, which is not an attempt at restoration, but made for the sake of clearness, is indicated by figures in parenthesis corresponding to the strophe numbering of* **R**.

(The Sky-road to Valhöll.)

18. The Thunder-flood roars,   while sports the fish
       of the mighty Wolf therein;
    o'erwhelming seems   the flow of that stream
       for the host of slain to wade.

19. Halls five hundred   and forty more
       hath the Lightning-abode in its bendings,
    of all the high roofed   houses I know,
       highest is that of the Thunderer.

(Valhöll.)

20. Death-barrier stands,   the sacred gate,
       on the plain 'fore the sacred doors;
    old is the lattice   and few have learned
       how it is closed on the latch.

21. Doors five hundred,   and forty more
       I ween may be found in Valhöll;
    and eight hundred Chosen   pass through each one
       when they fare to fight with the Wolf.

22. There Sooty-face boils   in Sooty-flame
       the boar called Sooty-black;
    'tis the best of fare,   which few have heard
       is the chosen warriors' food.

23. Glorying, the battle-wont   Father of Hosts
       feeds Ravener and Greed, his wolves;
    but on wine alone   ever Odin lives,
       the Weapon-famed god of war.

18.—Thunder-flood.—*The river name* Thund *may thus be connected with Icl.* þunor *by the suffix* þ *(V), or, meaning* Swollen, *with Icl.* þindan *(B).* The fish of the mighty Wolf *is according to G. the sun, or prey of the wolf of darkness, st. 39: she shines in the heavens till swallowed by Fenrir; see Vm. 46. Cf. Dt. Hl. who translate the Wolf's flood or stream which flowed from his jaws, and connect the passage with the storming of Asgarth by the Wanes mentioned in Vsp. 24.*   21.—*See Vsp. st. 43.*   23, 24.—Wolves, ravens: *these particulars are taken from Sn.E., who had evidently other sources than Grm. for his description.*

24. (20)   Huginn ok Muninn   fljúga hverjan dag
           jörmungrund yfir :
           oumk of Hugin   at hann aptr né komi,
           þó seumk meirr of Munin.

25.   Heiþrún heitir geit   es stendr höllu á [Herjaföþrs]
           ok bítr at Léráþs limum ;
           skapker fylla   hón skal ens skíra mjaþar,
           knáat sú veig vanask.

26.   Hjörtr heitir Eikþyrnir   es stendr höllu á [Herjaföþrs]
           ok bítr af Léráþs limum ;
           en af hans hornum   drýpr í Hvergelmi,
           þaþan eigu vötn öll vega.

27.   Síþ ok Víþ,   Sékin ok Ækin,
           Svöl ok Gunnþró,   Fjörm ok Fimbulþul,
               Rín ok Rinnandi,
           Gipul ok Göpul,   Gömul ok Geirvimul,
               þér hverfa of hodd goþa ;
           Þyn ok Vín,   Þöll ok Höll,
               Gráþ ok Gunnþorin.

28.   Vín á heitir,   önnur Vegsvinn,
               þriþja Þjóþnuma ;
           Nyt ok Nöt,   Nönn ok Hrönn,
           Slíþ ok Hríþ,   Sylgr ok Ylgr,
           Víþ ok Ván,   Vönd ok Strönd,
           Gjöll ok Leiptr,   þér falla gumnum nér,
               en falla til Heljar heþan.

29.   Körmt ok Örmt   ok Kerlaugar tvér,
               þær skal Þórr vaþa
           dag hverjan,   es hann dǿma ferr
               at aski Yggdrasils ;
           þvít ásbrú   brinnr öll loga,
               heilög vötn hloa.

_____

27, 28.—*Interpolations* B, Mh, S, J.

24. Ravens, Hugin and Munin,   of Thought and Memory
    wing the wide world each day:
I tremble for Thought,   lest he come not again,
    yet for Memory more I fear.

(The Waters of the World.)

25. Sky-bright o'er Valhöll   stands, the goat,
    who gnaws the Shelterer's boughs;
she fills a bowl   with the shining mead:
    'Tis a draught which runs not dry.

26. Oak-thorn o'er Valhöll   stands, the hart,
    who gnaws the Shelterer's boughs;
run drops from his horns   into Roaring-kettle
    whence flow all floods in the world.

*   *   *   *

29. Kormt and Ormt   and the Bath-tubs twain,
    these must the Thunderer wade,
when he fares each day   to his throne of doom
    under Yggdrasil's ash;
thence Bifröst burns,   the bridge of the gods,
    and the mighty waters well.

27, 28.—*The names contained in these strophes do not all bear interpretation and seem to belong to existing, not mythical, rivers, some of which were to be found in Britain.*

30. Glaþr ok Gyllir,   Gler ok Skeiþbrimir,
        Silfrintoppr ok Sinir,
     Gísl ok Falhófnir,   Golltoppr ok Léttfeti,
        þeim ríþa æsir joum
     dag hverjan,   es dœma fara
        at aski Yggdrasils.

31. Þriar rœtr   standa á þria vega
        und aski Yggdrasils:
     Hel býr und einni,   annarri hrímþursar,
        þriþju menskir menn.

31A. *Örn sitr   á asks limum*
         es vel kveþa mart vita;
      öglir einn   hönum augna í milli
         Veþrfölnir vakir.

32. Ratatoskr heitir íkorni   es rinna skal
        at aski Yggdrasils;
     arnar orþ   hann skal ofan bera
        ok segja Níþhöggvi niþr.

33. Hirtir 'u auk fjórir   þeirs af hæfingar á
        gaghalsir gnaga:
     Daïnn ok Dvalinn, ...
        Duneyrr ok Dyraþrór.

31A.—*Not found in the MSS., but reconstructed from the prose of* **Sn. E** *by G.S.Mk,*
Mh.

*   *   *   *   *

30. Glad One, Goldy,   Gleamer, Race-giant,
     Silvery-lock and Sinewy,
Shiner, Pale-hoof,   Gold-lock, Lightfoot,
     these are the steeds which the gods ride,
when they fare each day   to their thrones of doom
     under Yggdrasil's ash.

(The World Tree's torments.)

31. There are three roots stretching   three divers ways
     from under Yggdrasil's ash:
'neath the first dwells Hel,   'neath the second Frost giants,
     and human kind 'neath the third.

31A. An eagle sits   in the boughs of the ash,
     knowing much of many things;
and a hawk is perched,   Storm-pale, aloft
     betwixt that eagle's eyes.

32. Ratatosk is the squirrel   with gnawing tooth
     which runs in Yggdrasil's ash:
he bears the eagle's   words from above
     and to Fierce-stinger tells below.

33. There are four harts too,   who with heads thrown back
     gnaw the topmost boughs of the tree:
Däinn the Dead One.   Dvalin the Dallier,
     Duneyr and Dyrathror.

31.—Yggdrasil's ash, *the World Tree; see Vsp. st. 2, 19; Hav. st. 137.* Human
kind.—*These are the dead folk whose dwelling is in the underworld (see Vsp. st. 52), not,
as Snorri suggests, the living. We are repeatedly told that* Yggdrasil *springs from under
the earth.* (Dt. Hl.) Hel, *see Bdr. st. 1.*

34. Ormar fleiri liggja   und aski Yggdrasils,
    an of hyggi hverr ósviþra apa:
    Goinn ok Moinn.   þeir'u Grafvitnis synir,
    Grábakr ok Grafvölluþr,
    Ofnir ok Svafnir   hykk at æ skyli
    meiþs kvistu má.

35. Askr Yggdrasils   drýgir erfiþi
    meira an menn viti:
    hjörtr bítr ofan,   en á hliþu fúnar,
    skerþir Níþhöggr neþan.

36. Hrist ok Mist   vilk at mér horn beri,
    Skeggjöld ok Skögul;
    Hildr ok Þrúþr,   Hlökk ok Herfjötur,
    Göll ok Geirönul,
    Randgríþ ok Ráþgriþ   ok Reginleif,
    þǽr bera einherjum öl.

37. Árvakr ok Alsviþr   þeir skulu upp heþan
    svangir sól draga;
    en und þeira bógum   fálu blíþ regin,
    ǽsir, ísarn kól.

38. Svalinn heitir,   hann stendr sólu fyrir,
    Skjöldr skínanda goþi:
    björg ok brim   veitk at brinna skulu,
    ef hann fellr í frá.

39. Sköll heitir ulfr   es fylgir enu skírleita
    goþi til Varnar-viþar,
    en annarr Hati,   Hróþvitnis sunr,
    skal fyr heiþa brúþi himins.

39.—Varnar-viþar *Dt. Hl.*, Ísarnviþar S, G, varna viþar **R A**.

34. More serpents lie under   Yggdrasil's ash
    than a witless fool would ween—
Goin and Moin,   the offspring of Grave-monster,
    Grey-back and Grave-haunting worm,
Weaver and Soother,   I ween they must ever
    rend the twigs of the tree.

35. Yggdrasil's ash   suffers anguish more
    than mortal has ever known,
on high gnaw harts,   it rots at the side,
    and Fierce-stinger rends it beneath.

(Then cries he from the fire-torment.)

36. Would that Hrist and Mist   would bear me a horn!
    my Valkyries, Axe and Spear-point,
Bond and War-fetter,   Battle and Might,
    Shrieker and Spear-fierce in strife;
Shield-fierce, Counsel-fierce,   Strength-maiden—all
    who bear ale to the Chosen in War.

(Sun and Earth.)

37. Early-woke, All-fleet,   hence must these horses
    wearily draw up the sun,
but under their withers   the gods, gracious Powers,
    an iron-coolness have hid.

38. There is one called the Cooler   who stands 'fore the Sun,
    a shield from the shining goddess:
the mountains I ween,   and the stormy sea
    will flame if he fall from thence.

39. Sköll is the wolf called   who hunts the bright sun-goddess
    even to the Sheltering grove;
a second fares, Moon-hater,   offspring of Fenrir
    in front of that fair bride of heaven.

35.—Fierce-stinger, *the dragon of the underworld ; see Vsp. st. 39.* 36.—Valkyries, *or war maidens of Odin ; see Vsp. st. 31.* 39.—Sköll, Moon-hater, *wolves of
darkness ; see Vsp. st. 40.* Fenrir, *the great Wolf who swallows Odin ; see Vsp. st. 53.*

D

40.   Ór Ymis holdi   vas jörþ of sköpuþ,
            en ór sveita sœr,
      björg ór beinum,   baþmr ór hári
            en ór hausi himinn.

41. (40)   En ór hans bröum   görþu blíþ regin
            miþgarþ manna sunum,
      en ór hans heila   vöru þau en harþmóþgu
            ský öll of sköpuþ.

42. (41)   Ullar hylli   hefr ok allra goþa
            hverrs tekr fyrstr á funa ;
      þvít opnir heimar   verþa of ása sunum,
            þás hefja af hvera.

43. (42)   Ívalda synir   gengu í árdaga
            Skíþblaþni at skapa,
      skipa bazt   skírum Frey,
            nýtum Njarþar bur.

44. (43)   Askr Yggdrasils   hann es œztr viþa,
            enn Skíþblaþnir skipa,
      Óþinn ása,   en joa Sleipnir,
      Bifröst brua,   en Bragi skalda,
      Hábrók hauka,   en hunda Garmr.

40, 41.—*One strophe* **R**.

40.   From the flesh of Ymir   the world was formed,
              from his blood the billows of the sea,
      the hills from his bones,   the trees from his hair,
              the sphere of heaven from his skull.

41. (40)   Out of his brows   the blithe Powers made
              Midgarth for sons of men,
      and out of his brains   were the angry clouds
              all shaped above in the sky.

(The Kettle is taken off the fire in Geirröd's hall.)

42. (41)   The favour of Ull   and of all the Powers
              to him touching first the fire!
      For gods can enter   the homes of men
              when the kettle is raised from the hearth.

(The Treasures of the World.)

43. (42)   Went the Wielder's sons   of old to build
              Skidbladnir the wooden bladed,
      best of all ships,   for the bright god Frey,
              ever bountiful son of Niörd.

44. (43)   Yggdrasil's ash,   'tis the best of trees,
              but Skidbladnir of ships,
      Odin of gods,   Sleipnir of steeds,
      Bifröst of bridges,   Bragi of skalds,
      Habrok of hawks   and Garm of hounds.

40.—Ymir, *a Jötun, the first born of beings ; see Vm. st. 21, 29.*   41.—Midgarth : *In Old English poems also the earth is called* Middle-garth.   42.—*So understood by the Copenhagen edition (1848). When the kettle is taken off the gods can see Odin through the roof opening, come to his rescue, and then hold a triumphal feast ; see st. 45 (G. J. L.). Dt. Hl. explain it in connection with the strophe·following. The house was set open to guests at meal-time, and he who thus first invited a god and kindled the friendly hearth fire was regarded as one of the benefactors of the race.*   43.—The Wielder's sons *are rival forgers of the* Sparkler's *race; see Vsp. st. 37.*   44.—Skidbladnir, *see Saga-book, iv., 192, 193.*

45. (44) Svipum hefk nú ypt   fyr sigtíva sunum,
              viþ þat skal vilbjörg vaka :
          öllum ásum   þat skal inn koma
          Ægis bekki á
          Ægis drekku at.

46. (50) Ölr est, Geirröþr !   hefr þú ofdrukkit,
              . . . .
          miklu'st hnugginn,   es þú'st mínu gengi
          öllum einherjum ok Óþins hylli.

47. (51) Fjölþ þér sagþak,   en þú fátt of mant :
              of þik véla vinir ;
          mæki liggja   ek sé míns vinar
          allan í dreyra drifinn.

48. (52) Eggmóþan val   nú mun Yggr hafa,
              þitt veitk líf of liþit ;
          úfar'u dísir   nú knátt Óþin sea,
          nálgask þú mik, ef megir !

49. (45) Hétumk Grímr   hétumk Gangleri,
              Herjan ok Hjalmberi,
          þekkr ok Þriþi,   þuþr ok Uþr,
          Helblindi ok Hár,

50. (46) Saþr ok Svipall   ok Sanngetall,
              Herteitr ok Hnikarr,
          Bíleygr, Báleygr   Bölverkr, Fjölnir,
          Grímr ok Grimnir,   Glapsviþr, Fjölsviþr,
(47)   Síþhöttr, Síþskeggr,   Sigföþr, Hnikuþr,
          Alföþr, Valföþr,   Atríþr, Farmatýr :
          einu nafni   hétumk aldrigi,
              síz meþ folkum fórk.

_____

46.—*This strophe, as the alliteration shows, is in* fornyrþislag, *but imperfect ;*
H. G. S.

(Grimnir reveals himself as Odin.)

45. (44) Now my face have I shown   to the war-god's sons,
therewith shall help awake,
and the gods shall gather,   all glad, to the bench
in Ægir's feasting hall.

46. (50) Dulled with ale art thou, Geirröd,   too much hast thou drunk,
of great treasure art thou deprived,
bereft of my help,   and of all chosen warriors,
even the favour of Odin.

47. (51) Much have I told thee,   but little thou mindest,
by tricks thou hast been betrayed :
ere long shall I see   thy sword, good friend,
lying all bathed in blood.

48. (52) Thy days are run out,   the Dread War-father owns
him who is slain by the sword :
the spirits are hostile,   behold now ! 'tis Odin ;
more nigh shalt thou come if thou canst.

(He makes known his names.)

49. They have called me Hood-winker,   called me Wanderer,
Helm-bearer, Lord of the Host,
Well-comer, Third Highest, Wave, and Slender,
High One, Dazzler of Hel.

50. They have called me Soothsayer,   True and Fickle,
On-driver, Eager in War,
Flashing-eyed, Flaming-eyed,   Bale-worker, Shape-shifter,
Veiled One, Masked One,   Wile-wise and Much-wise,
Broad-hat, Long-beard,   War-father, On-thruster,
All-father, Death-father,   On-rider, Freight-wafter—
ne'er was I called   by one name alone
since I passed through the people of men.

45.—Ægir's feasting hall, *see Ls.*

51. (48) Grimnir hétumk   at Geirröþar,
       en Jalkr at Ásmundar,
en þá Kjalarr,   es ek kjalka dró,
Þrór þingum at,   Viþurr at vígum,
Óski ok Ómi,   Jafnhár, Biflindi,
       Göndlir ok Hárbarþr meþ goþum.

52. (49) Sviþurr ok Sviþrir   es ek hét at Sökkmímis
       ok dulþak enn aldna jötun,
þas ek Miþvitnis   vask ens mæra burar
       orþinn einbani.

53. (53) Óþinn nú heitik,   Yggr áþan hétk,
       hétumk Þundr fyr þat,
Vakr ok Skilfingr,   Váfuþr ok Hróptatýr,
       Gautr ok Jalkr meþ goþum,
(54) Ofnir ok Svafnir,   es hykk at orþnir sé
       allir af einum mér.

Geirröþr konungr sat ok hafþi sverþ um kné sér ok brugþit til miþs. En er hann heyrþi at Óþinn var þar kominn, þá stóþ hann upp ok vildi taka Óþin frá eldinum. Sverþit slapp ór hendi hánum ok vissu hjöltin niþr. Konungr drap fœti ok steyptiz áfram, en sverþit stóþ í gögnum hann, ok fekk hann bana. Óþinn hvarf þá, en Agnarr var þar konungr lengi síþan.

51.—Viþurr at vígum **A**, *not found in* **R**.

51.   They called me Grimnir,   the Masked one, at Geirröd's,
            Jalk was I named at Osmund's,
        Keeler once,   when I drew the sledge,
        Thror in council,   in strife the Stormer,
        Wish-giver, Wind-roar,   Tree-rocker, Equal-ranked,
            Grey-beard and Wizard of gods.

52.   They called me Sage   and Wise when I duped
            the old Jötun who dwells 'neath the earth,
        and slew single-handed   the glorious son
            of that monster who owned the Mead.

53.   They call me now Odin,   but erewhile the Dread One,
            Thund was I called before that,
        Watcher and Shaker,   Wafter and Counseller,
            Maker and Jalk among gods,
        Weaver and Soother,   names which I deem
            come all from Myself alone.

King Geirröd was sitting by with a half-drawn sword across his knees. When he knew that Odin was there, he rose up desiring to remove the god from the fire. But as he did so the sword slipped out of his hand point upwards, while losing his feet he fell forward upon it, and was pierced through and slain. Then Odin vanished, and Agnar was left to rule long time as king.

51.—Tree-rocker, *Odin as Wind god. Another meaning suggested for* Biflindi *is* Shield-shaker.   52.—The old Jötun, Suttung, *who owned the Song-mead; see Hav. st. 102.*

ALVÍSSMÁL.

Alvíss kvaþ:

1. ' Bekki breiþa   nú skal brúþr meþ mér,
    heim í sinni snuask ;
  hratat of mǽgi   mun hverjum þykkja,
    heima skalat hvílþ nema.'

þórr kvaþ:

2. ' Hvat's þat fira ?   hví 'stu svá fölr umb nasar ?
    vastu í nótt meþ naï ?
  þursa líki   þykkjumk á þér vesa,
    estat þú til brúþar borinn.'

Alvíssmál.—*In* **B**, *No. 11. Cited in* **Sn.E.**

SUNSHINE IN THE HALL

THE WISDOM OF ALL-WISE.

All-wise.

1. Ere long shall a bride   deck the bench beside me,
        we will hasten home together:
    swift in my wooing   shall I seem to all beings,
        but at home none shall hinder my peace.

Thor.

2. What being art thou   so pale of hue?
        Hast dwelt to-night with the dead?
    A likeness to giants   I trow hangs o'er thee;
        thou wast not born for a bride!

E

Alvíss kvaþ:

3. 'Alvíss ek heiti,   býk fyr jörþ neþan,
        ák und steini staþ;
    vagna vers   emk á vit kominn:
        bregþi engi föstu heiti firar.'

Þórr kvaþ:

4. 'Ek mun bregþa,   þvít ek brúþar á
        flest of ráþ sem faþir;
    vaskak heima,   þás þér heitit vas,
        sá einn es gjöfir meþ goþum.'

Alvíss kvaþ:

5. 'Hvat's þat rekka   es í ráþum telsk
        fljóþs ens fagrgloa?
    fjarrafleina þik   munu faïr kunna:
        hverr hefr baugum þik borit?'

Þórr kvaþ:

6. 'Vingþórr heitik,   ek hef víþa ratat,
        sunr emk Síþgrana;
    at ósátt minni   skaltu þat et unga man hafa
        ok þat gjaforþ geta.'

Alvíss kvaþ:

7. 'Sáttir þínar   es vilk snimma hafa
        ok þat gjaforþ geta;
    eiga viljak   heldr an án vesa
        þat et mjallhvíta man.'

Þórr kvaþ:

8. 'Meyjar ástum   muna þér verþa,
        vísi gestr! of varit,
    ef ór heimi kannt   hverjum at segja
        allt þats viljak vita.

4.—Gjöfir, **R**, *B. Hl.*   Gjöf's, *G. H.* at fá einn þér gjaforþ, *Gv. S.*

All-wise.

3. I am All-wise who dwell   far under the Earth,
    I hide in a rock for my home;
    I look for the Thunderer,   Lord of the goat-wain:
    let none break a firm-sworn vow.

Thor.

4. I will break it, who rule   o'er the bride as father;
    he alone among gods is the giver:
    I was far from home   when that fair maid of mine
    was promised thee ever as bride.

All-wise.

5. What hero is this,   who holds in his power
    that fair glowing maiden as gift?
    Like a far-straying arrow,   none knows who thou art,
    nor whence all the wealth which thou wearest.

Thor.

6. Winged-thunder am I,   wide have I wandered,
    son of Sigrani Long-bearded:
    ne'er with my will   shalt thou win the young maiden
    and get thee a wife among gods.

All-wise.

7. Thy good-will then   must I speedily gain
    and win me a wife among gods:
    I would liefer hold   in my arms than lack
    that snow-white maiden as mine.

Thor.

8. The maiden's love   thou shalt not lack,
    stranger, who seemest wise!
    if thou canst tell   out of every world
    all that I long to learn.

3.—The goat-wain, *Thor's chariot; see Hym. st. 7, 38, Introd. þrk.*   6.—Sigrani,
a name for Odin in his form of an old man with a long beard.

9. 'Seg mer þat, Alvíss!   öll of rök fira
        vörumk, dvergr! at vitir :
    hvé sú jörþ heitir   es liggr fyr alda sunum,
        heimi hverjum í ? '

Alvíss kvaþ :

10. ' Jörþ heitir meþ mönnum,   en meþ ásum fold,
        kalla vega vanir,
    ígrœn jötnar,   alfar groandi,
        kalla aur uppregin."

Þórr kvaþ :

11. ' Seg mer þat, Alvíss!   öll of rök fira
        vörumk, dvergr ! at vitir :
    hvé sá himinn heitir   enn Ymi kendi
        heimi hverjum í ? '

Alvíss kvaþ :

12. ' Himinn heitir meþ mönnum,   en hlýrnir meþ goþum,
        kalla vindofni vanir,
    uppheim jötnar,   alfar fagra ræfr,
        dvergar drjúpan sal.'

Þórr kvaþ :

13. ' Seg mer þat, Alvíss!   öll of rök fira
        vörumk, dvergr ! at vitir :
    hversu máni heitir,   sás menn sea,
        heimi hverjum í ? '

Alvíss kvaþ :

14. ' Máni heitir meþ mönnum,   en mýlinn meþ goþum,
        kalla hvél helju í,
    skyndi jötnar,   en skin dvergar,
        kalla alfar ártala.'

11.—Enn Ymi kendi, *S's suggestion for the unknown* erakendi *of* **R**   14.—Mýlinn
R, mylinn, *MSS. of* **Sn. E.**, *G. S. H., Hl.*

9. Tell me this, All-wise,   since thou art learned
        in the ways of all beings, I ween :—
    how is Earth, which lies spread   before sons of men,
        named by the wights of all worlds.

All-wise.

10. Earth 'tis named among men,   but Field among gods,
        Wanes call it ever the Way;
    Jötuns, Fair Green,   elves, the Grower,
        high Powers call it Clay.

Thor.

11. Tell me this, All-wise,   since thou art learned
        in the ways of all beings I ween :—
    how is Heaven, which once   was born of Ymir
        named by the wights of all worlds?

All-wise.

12. Heaven 'tis named among men,   Time-teller among gods,
        Wanes call it Weaver of Wind,
    Jötuns, Overworld,   elves, the Fair Roof,
        dwarfs, the Dripping Hall.

Thor.

13. Tell me this, All-wise,   since thou art learned
        in the ways of all beings, I ween :—
    how is the Moon   which men behold
        named by the wights of all worlds?

All-wise.

14. Moon 'tis named among men,   the Ball among gods,
        but the Whirling Wheel in Hel,
    of Jötuns, the Hastener,   of dwarfs, the Shimmerer,
        'tis Year-teller called of elves.

11.—Born of Ymir, *see Grm. st. 40; Vm. st. 21 and Introd.*

þórr kvaþ:

15. 'Seg mer þat, Alvíss!   öll of rök fira
    vörumk, dvergr! at vitir :
  hvé sú sól heitir,   es sea alda synir,
    heimi hverjum í ? '

Alvíss kvaþ:

16. 'Sól heitir meþ mönnum,   en sunna meþ goþum,
    kalla dvergar Dvalins leika,
  eygló jötnar,   alfar fagra hvél,
    alskír ása synir.'

þórr kvaþ :

17. 'Seg mer þat, Alvíss!   öll of rök fira
    vörumk, dvergr! at vitir :
  hvé þau ský heita,   es skúrum blandask,
    heimi hverjum í ? '

Alvíss kvaþ :

18. 'Ský heita meþ mönnum,   en skúrván meþ goþum,
    kalla vindflot vanir,
  úrván jötnar   alfar veþrmegin,
    kalla í helju hjalm huliþs.'

þórr kvaþ :

19. 'Seg mer þat, Alvíss!   öll of rök fira
    vörumk, dvergr! at vitir :
  hvé sá vindr heitir,   es víþast ferr,
    heimi hverjum í ? '

Thor.

15. Tell me this, All-wise,   since thou art learned
      in the ways of all beings, I ween :—
   how is Sol which the sons   of men behold
      named by the wights of all worlds ?

All-wise.

16. Sol 'tis named among men,   but Sun among gods,
      dwarfs call it Dallier's playmate,
   Ever-glowing, the Jötuns,   Fair wheel, the elves,
      All-shine, the children of gods.

Thor.

17. Tell me this, All-wise,   since thou art learned
      in the ways of all beings, I ween :—
   how are Clouds of the sky,   that with showers are mingled,
      named by the wights of all worlds ?

All-wise.

18. They are clouds among men,   Shower-promise to gods,
      Wind-floater called of Wanes,
   Rain-omen of Jötuns,   Storm-might of elves,
      Helm of the Hidden in Hel.

Thor.

19. Tell me this, All-wise,   since thou art learned
      in the ways of all beings, I ween :
   how is the Wind   which wanders wide
      named by the wights of all worlds ?

14.—Ball, *a doubtful word.* G. V. *suggest* Fire. Hastener, *because pursued by a wolf; see Grm. st. 39.*

16.—Dallier's playmate. *The sun makes sport of dwarfs who are caught above ground at dawn; st. 35.*

Alvíss kvaþ:

20. 'Vindr heitir meþ mönnum,   en váfuþr meþ goþum,
      kalla gneggjuþ ginnregin,
    œpi jötnar,   alfar dynfara,
      kalla í helju hviþuþ.'

Þorr kvaþ:

21. 'Seg mer þat, Alvíss!   öll of rök fira
      vörumk, dvergr! at vitir:
    hvé þat logn heitir,   es liggja skal,
      heimi hverjum í?'

Alvíss kvaþ:

22. 'Logn heitir meþ mönnum,   en lǽgi meþ goþum,
      kalla vindslot vanir,
    ofhlý jötnar,   alfar dagsefa,
      kalla dvergar dags veru.'

Þórr kvaþ:

23. 'Seg mer þat, Alvíss!   öll of rök fira
      vörumk, dvergr! at vitir:
    hvé sá marr heitir,   es menn roa,
      heimi hverjum í?'

Alvíss kvaþ:

24. 'Sǽr heitir meþ mönnum,   en sílǽgja meþ goþum,
      kalla vág vanir,
    álheim jötnar,   alfar lágastaf,
      kalla dvergar djúpan mar.'

Þórr kvaþ:

25. 'Seg mer þat, Alvíss!   öll of rök fira
      vörumk, dvergr! at vitir:
    hvé sá eldr heitir,   es brinnr fyr alda sunum,
      heimi hverjum í?'

24.—Sílǽgja, *G. J.;* síl-ægja, *C.;* silegja, **R**, *B.*

All-wise.

20. Wind 'tis named among men,   but Waverer of gods,
    the wise Powers call it Whinnier,
Jötuns, the Howler,   elves, Roaring Rider,
    in Hel 'tis called Swooping Storm.

Thor.

21. Tell me this, All-wise,   since thou art learned
    in the ways of all beings, I ween :—
how is the Calm,   ever wont to rest,
    named by the wights of all worlds ?

All-wise.

22. Calm 'tis named among men,   Sea-rest among gods,
    Wanes ever call it Wind-lull,
Jötuns, the Swelterer,   elves, Day-soother,
    dwarfs, the Refuge of Day.

Thor.

23. Tell me this, All-wise,   since thou art learned
    in the ways of all beings, I ween :—
how is the Sea   which is sailed of men,
    named by the wights of all worlds ?

All-wise.

24. Sea 'tis named among men,   Wide Ocean of gods,
    Wanes call it flowing Wave,
Jötuns, Eel-home,   elves, the Water-stave,
    by dwarfs 'tis called the Deep.

Thor.

25. Tell me this, All-wise,   since thou art learned
    in the ways of all beings, I ween :
how is Fire, which burns   before men's sons,
    named by the wights of all worlds ?

20.—Waverer, *one of Odin's names as Wind-god.*   24.—Wide Ocean, *others
suggest* Silent Water.

F

Alvíss kvaþ:

26. ' Eldr heitir meþ mönnum,   en meþ ásum funi,
      kalla vág vanir,
    freka jötnar,   en forbrenni dvergar,
      kalla í helju hröþuþ.'

Þórr kvaþ:

27. ' Seg mer þat, Alvíss !   öll of rök fira
      vörumk, dvergr ! at vitir :
    hvé sá viþr heitir,   es vex fyr alda sunum,
      heimi hverjum í ?'

Alvíss kvaþ:

28. ' Viþr heitir meþ mönnum,   en vallar fax meþ goþum,
      kalla hlíþþang halir,
    eldi jötnar,   alfar fagrlima,
      kalla vönd vanir.'

Þórr kvaþ:

29. ' Seg mer þat, Alvíss !   öll of rök fira
      vörumk, dvergr ! at vitir :
    hvé sú nótt heitir,   en Nörvi kenda,
      heimi hverjum í ?'

Alvíss kvaþ:

30. ' Nótt heitir meþ mönnum,   en njól méþ goþum,
      kalla grímu ginnregin,
    óljós jötnar,   alfar svefngaman,
      kalla dvergar draumnjörun.'

Þórr kvaþ:

31. ' Seg mer þat, Alvíss !   öll of rök fira
      vörumk, dvergr ! at vitir :
    hvé þat sáþ heitir,   es sá alda synir,
      heimi hverjum í ?'

26.—Vág, *Mb. H. J.;* vag, **R,** *B. Gv. Hl.;* végin, *S. G.*   Freka, *Gv. S. G.;*
frekan, **R,**   28.—Fax, *so most authorities for* far, **R.**

All-wise.

26. Fire 'tis named among men,   but Flame among gods,
    Wanes call it leaping Wave,
Jötuns, the Ravener,   Hel-folk, the Racer,
    dwarfs, the Burning Bane.

Thor.

27. Tell me this, All-wise,   since thou art learned
    in the ways of all beings, I ween:
how is Wood which waxes   before men's sons
    named by the wights of all worlds?

All-wise.

28. Wood 'tis named among men,   Wold-locks among gods,
    by heroes Sea-weed of the hills,
Jötuns, Life-feeder,   elves, the Fair-limbed,
    Waves ever call it Wand.

Thor.

29. Tell me this, All-wise,   since thou art learned
    in the ways of all beings, I ween:
how is Night who is born,   the daughter of Nörr,
    named by the wights of all worlds?

All-wise.

30. She is Night among men,   but Mist among gods,
    the high Powers call her Hood,
the Jötuns, Unlight,   elves, the Sleep-joy,
    dwarfs, the Goddess of Dreams.

Thor.

31. Tell me this, All-wise,   since thou art learned
    in the ways of all beings, I ween:—
how is Seed which is sown   by the sons of men
    named by the wights of all worlds?

28.—Heroes, *the dead warriors in Hel, Icelandic* halir, *is used elsewhere for the dead folk (See Vm. st. 43) and has probably the same meaning here.*

Alvíss kvap:

32. ' Bygg heitir meþ mönnum,   en barr meþ goþum,
        kalla vöxt vanir,
    æti jötnar,   alfar lágastaf,
        kalla í helju hnipinn.'

þórr kvap:

33. ' Seg mer þat, Alvíss !   öll of rök fira
        vörumk, dvergr ! at vitir :
    hvé þat öl heitir,   es drekka alda synir,
        heimi hverjum í ?'

Alvíss kvaþ:

34. ' Öl heitir meþ mönnum,   en meþ ásum bjórr,
        kalla veig vanir,
    hreina lög jötnar,   en í helju mjöþ,
        kalla sumbl Suttungs synir.'

þórr kvaþ:

35. ' Í einu brjósti   ek sák aldrigi
        fleiri forna stafi ;
    tálum miklum   ek kveþ tældan þik :
        uppi est, dvergr ! of dagaþr,
        nú skínn sól í sali.'

All-wise.

32.   'Tis named Barley among men,   but Bear among gods,
    Wanes call it Growth of the ground,
Jötuns, Food-stuff,   elves, the Sap-staff,
    Hel-dwellers, Drooping Head.

Thor.

33.   Tell me this, All-wise,   since thou art learned
    in the ways of all beings, I ween:—
how is Ale which sons   of men drink oft
    named by the wights of all worlds?

All-wise.

34.   Ale 'tis named among men,   but Beer among gods,
    the Stirring Draught of Wanes,
of Jötuns, Clear-flowing,   of Hel-folk, Mead,
    by the Sons of Suttung, Feast.

Thor.

35.   Not e'er have I found   in the bosom of one
    more learning of olden lore;
but with wiles art thou duped,   thus dallying here,
    while dawn is upon thee, dwarf!
    Behold! Sun shines in the hall.

(All-wise the dwarf is turned into stone.)

32.—Bear *is an old word for* barley, *and cognate with the Icelandic* barr.

VAFÞRÚÞNISMÁL.

Óþinn kvaþ:

1. ‘Ráþ mér nú, Frigg!   alls mik fara týþir
      at vitja Vafþrúþnis;
    forvitni mikla   kveþk mér á fornum stöfum
      viþ enn alsvinna jötun.’

Frigg kvaþ:

2. ‘Heima letja   mundak Herjaföþr
      í görþum goþa;
    þvít engi jötun   hugþak jafnramman
      sem Vafþrúþni vesa.’

Vafþrúþnismál.—*In* **R,** *No. 3, st. 20 to the end in* **A,** *cited in* **Sn. E.**

THE WORDS OF THE MIGHTY WEAVER.

Odin.

1. Now counsel me, Frigg   for I fain would seek
     the Mighty Weaver of words.
   I yearn to strive   with that all-wise giant
     in learning of olden lore.

Frigg.

2. Nay, Father of Hosts !   I fain would keep thee
     at home in the garth of the gods ;
   no giant I deem   so dread and wise
     as that Mighty Weaver of words.

Óþinn kvaþ:

3. ' Fjölþ ek fór,   fjölþ freistaþak,
    fjölþ of reyndak regin;
    hitt viljak vita   hvé Vafþrúþnis
    salakynni sé.'

Frigg kvaþ:

4. ' Heill þú farir!   heill aptr komir!
    heill þu á sinnum sér!
    æþi þér dugi,   hvars skalt, Aldaföþr!
    orþum mæla jötun.'

5.   Fór þá Óþinn   at freista orþspeki
    þess ens alsvinna jötuns:
    at höllu hann kvam   ok átti Hýms faþir,
    inn gekk Yggr þegar.

Óþinn kvaþ:

6. ' Heill þú, Vafþrúþnir!   nú'mk í höll kominn,
    á þik sjalfan at sea;
    hitt viljak fyrst vita,   ef þú fróþr sér
    eþa alsviþr, jötunn!'

Vafþrúþnir kvaþ:

7. ' Hvat's þat manna   es í mínum sal
    verpumk orþi á?
    út né kömr   órum höllum frá
    nema þú enn snotrari sér.'

Óþinn kvaþ:

8. ' Gagnráþr heitik,   nú'mk af göngu kominn
    þyrstr til þinna sala;
    laþar þurfi—hef ek lengi farit—
    ok andfanga, jötunn!'

5.—Hýms, *J for* Ims **R A** *where the alliteration fails.*   8.—Gagnráþr, **R A**, *emended to the more usual* gangráþr *by R. G.*

Odin.

3. Far have I fared   much have I ventured,
        oft have I proved the Powers;
    this now must I know   how the house-folk fare
        in the Mighty Weaver's home.

Frigg.

4. Then safely go,   come safely again,
        and safely wend thy way:
    may thy wit avail thee,   Father of beings,
        when thou weavest words with the giant!

*   *   *   *   *

5. Then Odin went   to prove with words
        the wisdom of the all-wise giant:
    he reached the hall   of the Jötun race;
        the Dread One entered forthwith.

Odin.

6. Hail, Mighty Weaver!   here in this hall
        I have come thyself to see;
    and first will try   if thou art in truth
        all-wise and all-knowing, Giant.

Weaver.

7. What man is here,   who dares in my hall
        to throw his words at me thus?
    thou shalt ne'er come forth   again from our courts
        if thou be not the wiser of twain.

Odin.

8. Riddle-reader I am called,   I come from my roaming
        thirsty here to thy halls,
    in need of welcome   and kindly greeting,
        long way have I wandered, Giant.

Vafþrúþnir kvaþ:

9. ' Hví þu þá, Gagnráþr!   mælisk af golfi fyrir ?
   farþu í sess í sal !
   þá skal freista,   hvaþarr fleira viti,
   gestr eþa enn gamli þulr.'

Óþinn kvaþ:

10. ' Óauþugr maþr,   es til auþugs kömr,
    mǽli þarft eþa þegi !
    ofrmǽlgi mikil   hykk at illa geti
    hveims viþ kaldrifjaþan kömr.'

Vafþrúþnir kvaþ:

11. ' Seg mér, Gagnráþr!   alls þu á golfi vill
    þíns of freista frama :
    hvé sá hestr heitir   es hverjan dregr
    dag of dróttmögu ? '

Óþinn kvaþ:

12. ' Skinfaxi heitir   es enn skíra dregr
    dag of dróttmögu ;
    hesta baztr   þykkir meþ Hreiþgotum,
    ey lýsir mön af mari.'

Vafþrúþnir kvaþ:

13. ' Seg þat, Gagnráþr!   alls þu á golfi vill
    þíns of freista frama :
    hvé sá jór heitir   es austan dregr
    nótt of nýt regin ? '

Weaver.

9. Why speak, Riddle-reader,   standing thus?
        take here thy seat in the hall;
    and soon shall be seen   who knows the more,
        stranger or ancient sage.

Odin.

10. Let the penniless wretch   in the house of the rich
        speak needful words or none:
    prating, I ween,   works ill for him
        who comes to the cold in heart.

I.

(The Proving of Riddle-reader.)

Weaver.

11. Say, Riddle-reader!   since on the floor
        thou fain wouldst show thy skill,
    how the Steed is called   which draws each Day
        over the children of men.

Odin.

12. 'Tis Shining-Mane   who draws bright Day
        over the children of men;
    they hold him best   of steeds in the host;
        streams light from his mane evermore.

Weaver.

13. Say, Riddle-reader!   since on the floor
        thou fain wouldst show thy skill,
    how the Steed is called   who forth from the east
        draws Night o'er the blessed Powers.

Óþinn kvaþ:

14. 'Hrímfaxi heitir   es hverja dregr
    nótt of nýt regin;
  méldropa   fellir morgin hvern,
    þaþan kömr dögg of dali.'

Vafþrúþnir kvaþ:

15. 'Seg þat, Gagnráþr!   alls þu á golfi vill
    þíns of freista frama:
  hvé sú á heitir   es deilir meþ jötna sunum
    grund auk meþ goþum?'

Óþinn kvaþ:

16. 'Ifing heitir á   es deilir meþ jötna sunum
    grund auk meþ goþum;
  opin rinna   hón skal of aldrdaga,
    verþrat íss á á.'

Vafþrúþnir kvaþ:

17. 'Seg þat, Gagnráþr!   alls þu á golfi vill
    þíns of freista frama:
  hvé sá völlr heitir   es finnask vígi at
    Surtr ok en svásu goþ?'

Óþinn kvaþ:

18. 'Vígríþr heitir völlr   es finnask vígi at
    Surtr ok en svásu goþ;
  hundraþ rasta   hann's á hverjan veg,
    sá's þeim völlr vitaþr.'

Vafþrúþnir kvaþ:

19. 'Fróþr est, gestr!   farþu á bekk jötuns,
    ok mælumsk í sessi saman!
  höfþi veþja   vit skulum höllu í,
    gestr! of geþspeki.'

Odin.

14. 'Tis Rimy-Mane who draws evermore
  each Night o'er the blessed Powers;
he lets fall drops from his bit each dawning;
  thence comes dew in the dales.

Weaver.

15. Say, Riddle-reader! since on the floor
  thou fain wouldst show thy skill,
how the River is called which parts the realm
  of the Jötun race from the gods.

Odin.

16. That River is Ifing which parts the realm
  of the Jötun race from the gods;
free shall it flow while life days last;
  never ice shall come o'er that stream.

Weaver.

17. Say, Riddle-reader! since on the floor
  thou fain wouldst show thy skill,
how the Field is called where in strife shall meet
  dark Surt and the gracious gods.

Odin.

18. War-path is the Field where in strife shall meet
  dark Surt and the gracious gods:
a hundred miles it measures each way;
  'tis the Field marked out by Fate.

Weaver.

19. Wise art thou, stranger, but come now and sit
  by my side on the Jötun's seat;
let us talk and wager on wisdom of mind
  our two heads here in the hall.

(Odin seats himself by the giant.)

16.—Ifing *is probably the river mentioned in Arbl., st. 2.* 17.—Surt, *a fire giant;
see st. 50 and Vsp. st. 52, 53, Ls. st. 42.*

Óþinn kvaþ:

20. 'Seg þat et eina,   ef þitt œþi dugir
         ok þú, Vafþrúþnir ! vitir:
      hvaþan jörþ of kvam   eþa upphiminn
         fyrst, enn fróþi jötunn ? '

Vafþrúþnir kvaþ:

21. 'Ór Ymis holdi   vas jörþ of sköpuþ
         en ór beinum björg,
      himinn ór hausi   ens hrímkalda jötuns,
         en ór sveita sǽr,'

Óþinn kvaþ:

22. 'Seg þat annat,   ef þitt œþi dugir
         ok þú, Vafþrúþnir ! vitir:
      hvaþan máni of kvam,   sás ferr menn yfir,
         eþa sól et sama ? '

Vafþrúþnir kvaþ:

23, 'Mundilferi heitir   hann es Mána faþir
         ok svá Sólar et sama ;
      himin hverfa   þau skulu hverjan dag
         öldum at ártali.'

Óþinn kvaþ:

24. 'Seg þat et þriþja,   alls þik svinnan kveþa,
         ef þú, Vafþrúþnir ! vitir:
      hvaþan dagr of kvam,   sás ferr drótt yfir,
         eþa nótt meþ niþum ? '

II.

(The Proving of the Mighty Weaver.)

Odin.

20. Answer well the first,   if thou hast the wit,
    and knowest, Mighty Weaver,—
· from whence the Earth   and the heavens on high,
    wise Giant, came once to be.

Weaver.

21. From the flesh of Ymir   the world was formed,
    from his bones were mountains made,
and Heaven from the skull   of that frost-cold giant,
    from his blood the billows of the sea.

Odin.

22. Answer well the second,   if thou hast the wit,
    and knowest, Mighty Weaver,—
whence Moon hath come   who fares over men,
    and whence Sun hath had her source.

Weaver.

23. The Mover of the Handle   is father of Moon,
    and the father eke of Sun,
round the heavens   they roll each day
    for measuring of years to men.

Odin.

24. Answer well the third   if thou hast the wit,
    and knowest, Mighty Weaver,—
whence Day arose   to pass o'er the race,
    and Night with her waning Moons.

21.—Ymir, *the first-born of Jötuns; see st. 29, Grm. st. 40, Vsp. st. 3.* 22.—
Moon, sun, *see Grm. st. 31.* 23.—Mover of the handle. *This mysterious being Mundilferi is not mentioned elsewhere. Rydberg traces a belief that the heavens were turned by a gigantic world mill. (Teutonic Mythology, p. 397).*

Vafþrúþnir kvaþ:

25. 'Dellingr heitir,   hann es Dags faþir,
    en Nótt vas Nörvi borin ;
    ný ok niþ   skópu nýt regin
    öldum at ártali.'

Óþinn kvaþ:

26. 'Seg þat et fjórþa,   alls þik fróþan kveþa,
    ef þú, Vafþrúþnir ! vitir:
    hvaþan vetr of kvam   eþa varmt sumar
    fyrst meþ fróþ regin ?'

Vafþrúþnir kvaþ:

27. 'Vindsvalr heitir,   hann es Vetrar faþir,
    en Svósuþr Sumars;'
    [Vindsvals faþir   var Vásuþr of heitinn,
    öll es su ætt til ötul.]

Óþinn kvaþ:

28. 'Seg þat et fimta,   alls þik fróþan kveþa,
    ef þú, Vafþrúþnir ! vitir:
    hverr ása elztr   eþa Ymis niþja
    yrþi í árdaga ?'

Vafþrúþnir kvaþ:

29. 'Örófi vetra,   áþr væri jörþ sköpuþ,
    þá vas Bergelmir borinn ;
    Þrúþgelmir   vas þess faþir,
    en Aurgelmir afi.'

Óþinn kvaþ:

30. 'Seg þat et sétta,   alls þik svinnan kveþa,
    ef þú, Vafþrúþnir ! vitir:
    hvaþan Aurgelmir   kvam meþ jötna sunum
    fyrst, enn fróþi jötunn ?'

27.—*The gap in* **R** *thus supplied by B., who paraphrases the prose of Sn.E.*

Weaver.

25.   There is one called Dawning,   the father of Day,
          but Night was born of Nörr;
     new and waning moons   the wise Powers wrought
          for measuring of years to men.

Odin.

26.   Answer well the fourth,   if thou hast the wit,
          and knowest, Mighty Weaver,—
     whence Winter came   and warm Summer first
          the wise Powers once among.

Weaver.

27.   There is One called Sweetsouth,   father of Summer,
          but Wind-cool is winter's sire,
     the son was he   of Sorrow-seed;
          all fierce and dread is that race.

Odin.

28.   Answer well the fifth,   if thou hast the wit,
          and knowest, Mighty Weaver :—
     who was born of gods   or of Jötun brood,
          the eldest in days of yore?

Weaver.

29.   Untold winters   ere Earth was fashioned
          roaring Bergelm was born;
     his father was Thrudgelm   of Mighty Voice,
          loud-sounding Ymir his grandsire.

Odin.

30.   Answer well the sixth,   if thou hast the wit,
          and knowest, Mighty Weaver,—
     whence came Ymir,   loud-sounding Jötun,
          the first of thy race, wise Giant.

25.—Nörr, *see Alv. st.* **29.**   29.—*In this passage* Ymir *is called* Aurgelmir; "gelmir" *in all these names seems to signify the roaring, rushing sound of the elemental powers in chaos.*

H

Vafþrúþnir kvaþ:

31. 'Ór Élivágum   stukku eitrdropar,
        svá óx unz ór varþ jötunn;
    [þar órar ǽttir   kvámu allar saman,
        því's þat ǽ allt til atalt.']

Óþinn kvaþ:

32. 'Seg þat et sjaunda,   alls þik svinnan kveþa,
        ef þú, Vafþrúþnir! vitir:
    hvé sá börn of gat   enn aldni jötunn,
        es hann hafþit gýgjar gaman?'

Vafþrúþnir kvaþ:

33. 'Und hendi vaxa   kváþu hrímþursi
        mey ok mög saman;
    fótr viþ fǿti   gat ens fróþa jötuns
        sexhöfþaþan sun.'

Óþinn kvaþ:

34. 'Seg þat et átta,   alls þik svinnan kveþa,
        ef þú, Vafþrúþnir! vitir:
    hvat fyrst of mant   eþa fremst of veizt?
        þú 'st alsviþr, jötunn!'

Vafþrúþnir kvaþ:

35. 'Órófi vetra   áþr væri jörþ of sköpuþ,
        þá vas Bergelmir borinn;
    þat ek fyrst of man,   es sa enn fróþi jötunn
        á vas lúþr of lagiþr.'

Óþinn kvaþ:

36. 'Seg þat et niunda,   alls þik svinnan kveþa,
        ef þú, Vafþrúþnir! vitir:
    hvaþan vindr of kömr   sás ferr vág yfir?
        ǽ menn hann sjalfan of sea.'

31, lines 3, 4.—*Missing in* **R A**. *Supplied from* **r** *by* **B. Gv. L. C. J. G. S.**

Weaver.

31. From Stormy-billow   sprang poison-drops,
     which waxed into Jötun form,
and from him are come   the whole of our kin ;
     all fierce and dread is that race.

Odin.

32. Answer well the seventh,   if thou hast the wit,
     and knowest, Mighty Weaver,—
how that ancient Being   begot his children
     who knew not joy of a giantess.

Weaver.

33. 'Tis said that under   the Frost-giant's arm
     grew a boy and girl together;
foot with foot begot   of that first wise giant,
     and a six-headed son was born.

Odin.

34. Answer well the eighth,   if thou hast the wit,
     and knowest, Mighty Weaver,—
what mindst thou of old,   and didst earliest know ?
     since I ween thou art all wise, giant !

Weaver.

35. Untold winters   ere Earth was shaped,
     roaring Bergelm was born ;
I mind me first   when that most wise giant
     of old in a cradle was laid.

Odin.

36. Answer well the ninth,   if thou hast the wit,
     and knowest, Mighty Weaver,—
whence comes the Wind   which fares o'er the waves,
     but which never man hath seen.

31.—Stormy-billow, *a mythical river between* Asgard *and* Jötunheim ; *see Hym.*
st. 5, Sn.E. c. 5.   35.—Cradle. *Icelandic* luþr *has various meanings*—meal-bin
box, boat, ark ; *see Introd.*

Vafþrúþnir kvaþ:

37. ' Hræsvelgr heitir   en sitr á himins enda,
     jötunn í arnar ham;
     af hans vǽngjum   kveþa vind koma
     alla menn yfir.'

Óþinn kvaþ:

38. ' Seg þat et tiunda,   alls þú tíva rök
     öll, Vafþrúþnir! vitir:
     hvaþan Njörþr of kvam   meþ ása sunum—
     hofum ok hörgum   hann rǽþr hundmörgum—
     ok vasat hann ásum alinn?'

Vafþrúþnir kvaþ:

39. ' Í Vanaheimi   skópu hann vís regin
     ok seldu at gíslingu goþum;
     í aldar rök   hann mun aptr koma
     heim meþ vísum Vönum.'

Óþinn kvaþ:

40. ' Seg þat et ellifta,   *alls þik svinnan kveþa,*
     ef þú, Vafþrúþnir! vitir:
     hverir'u ýtar   es Óþins túnum í
     höggvask hverjan dag?'

Vafþrúþnir kvaþ:

41. ' Allir einherjar   Óþins túnum í
     höggvask hverjan dag;
     val þeir kjósa   ok ríþa vígi frá,
     sitja meirr of sáttir saman.'

40.—*In* **R A** *the strophe runs* Segþu þat ellifta,   hvar ýta túnum í, *followed by* 41 *ll. 2, 3, 4, which are again repeated in* 41, *emended to agree with* 24, 34, 36, **G. H. S.**

Weaver.

37. Corpse-swallower sits   at the end of heaven,
          a Jötun in eagle form;
      from his wings, they say,   comes the wind which fares
          over all the dwellers of Earth.

Odin.

38. Answer well the tenth,   since all tidings of gods
          thou knowest, Mighty Weaver,—
      whence Niörd first came   mid the Æsir kin—
      courts and altars   he owns in hundreds—
          who was not reared in their race.

Weaver.

39. In Wane-home once   the wise Powers made him
          and gave him as hostage to gods;
      in the story of time   he shall yet come home
          to the wise foreseeing Wanes.

Odin.

40. Answer well the eleventh,   since they call thee wise,
          if thou knowest, Mighty Weaver—
      who are the beings   who thus do battle
          in the dwellings of Odin each day?

Weaver.

41. All the Chosen Warriors   are waging war
          in the dwellings of Odin each day:
      they choose the slain,   ride home from the strife,
          then at peace sit again together.

37.—Corpse-swallower *is perhaps identical with the raven of Vsp. 47.*   38, 39.—
Æsir, Wanes. *These are the two races of the gods; for their war, see Vsp. st. 21-24 and
Introd. to Vsp.*   41.—Chosen Warriors, *see Grm. st. 21.*

Óþinn kvaþ:

42. ' Seg þat et tolfta,   hví þú tíva rök
    öll, Vafþrúþnir! vitir:
    frá jötna rúnum   ok allra goþa
    segir þu et sannasta,
    enn alsvinni jötunn!'

Vafþrúþnir kvaþ:

43. ' Frá jötna rúnum   ok allra goþa
    ek kann segja satt,
    þvít hvern hefk   heim of komit:
    niu kvamk heima   fyr Niflhel neþan,
    hinig deyja [ór helju] halir.'

Óþinn kvaþ:

44. ' Fjölþ ek fór,   fjölþ ek freistaþak,
    fjölþ of reyndak regin:
    hvat lifir manna,   þás enn mæra líþr
    fimbulvetr meþ firum?'

Vafþrúþnir kvaþ:

45. ' Líf ok Lífþrasir,   en þau leynask munu
    í holti Hoddmimis;
    morgindöggvar   þau sér at mat hafa
    en þaþan af aldir alask.'

Óþinn kvaþ:

46. ' Fjölþ ek fór,   fjölþ ek freistaþak,
    fjölþ of reyndak regin:
    hvaþan kömr sól   á enn slétta himin
    þás þessi hefr Fenrir farit?'

Odin.

42. Answer well the twelfth,   how all the story
    of the Powers thou knowest, Weaver.—
    Canst thou truly tell me   the secrets of Jötuns
    and all the gods, wise giant ?

Weaver.

43. Most truly I can   tell thee the secrets
    of Jötuns and all the gods ;
    since I have been   into every world,
    even nine worlds   to Mist-Hel beneath
    whither die the dead from Hel.

Odin.

44. Far have I fared,   much have I ventured,
    oft have I proved the Powers :
    what beings shall live   when the long Dread Winter
    comes o'er the people of earth ?

Weaver.

45. Life and Life-craver,   who hidden shall lie
    in the boughs of Yggdrasil's Ash :
    morning dews   they shall have as meat ;
    thence shall come new kindreds of men.

Odin.

46. Far have I fared,   much have I ventured,
    oft have I proved the Powers :
    whence comes a new Sun   in the clear heaven again
    when the Wolf has swallowed the old.

43.—Nine Worlds. *Nine was a mystic number ; Háv. 137, Skm. 21, 39, &c. In Alv. are mentioned worlds of Æsir, Wanes, giants, dwarfs, elves, men, and the dead in Hel, but nine are never enumerated ; Cf. Vsp. 2.*   44.—Dread Winter *or* Fimbul-vetr *is the sign of the coming doom of the gods (st. 51) mentioned by Snorri ; see also Hdl. st. 16.*   45.—Yggdrasil *is suggested by* Hodd-mimir's wood; *Cf. Mimameid Fj. st. 14 18, and Introd. Háv., which is clearly the World tree.*   46.—The Wolf, *Fenrir.*

Vafþrúþnir kvaþ :

47. ' Eina dóttur   berr Alfröþull,
          áþr henni Fenrir fari ;
       sú skal ríþa,   þás regin deyja
          móþur brautir mær.'

Óþinn kvaþ :

48. ' Fjölþ ek fór,   fjölþ ek freistaþak,
          fjölþ of reyndak regin :
       hverjar 'u meyjar   es líþa mar yfir,
          fróþgeþjaþar fara ? '

Vafþrúþnir kvaþ :

49. ' Þriar þjóþir   falla þorp yfir
          meyja Mögþrasis,
       hamingjur einar   þærs í heimi 'rú,
          þó þær meþ jötnum alask.'

Óþinn kvaþ :

50. ' Fjölþ ek fór,   fjölþ ek freistaþak,
          fjölþ of reyndak regin :
       hverir ráþa æsir   eignum goþa,
          þás sloknar Surta logi ? '

Vafþrúþnir kvaþ :

51. ' Víþarr ok Váli   byggva vé goþa,
          þás sloknar Surta logi ;
       Móþi ok Magni   skulu Mjöllni hafa
          Vingnis at vígþroti.'

49.—þjóþir, *Hl. G. H. J.*. þjóþár, **R A.**

Weaver.

47. One daughter alone   shall that Elf-beam bear
        before she is swallowed by the Wolf;
    and the maid shall ride   on the mother's path
        after the Powers have perished.

Odin.

48. Far have I fared,   much have I ventured,
        oft have I proved the Powers:
    who are those maidens   who pass o'er the sea
        wandering, wise in mind?

Weaver.

49. There fly three troops   of Mögthrasir's maidens
        and hover o'er homes of men;
    the only guardian   spirits on earth,
        and they are of Jötuns born.

Odin.

50. Far have I fared,   much have I ventured,
        oft have I proved the Powers:
    who shall afterwards hold   the wealth of the gods
        when the fire of dark Surt is slaked?

Weaver.

51. In the fanes of the gods   shall dwell Vidar and Vali
        when the fire of dark Surt is slaked;
    to Modi and Magni   shall Mjöllnir be given
        when to Thor comes the end of strife.

49.—*Mögthrasir is unknown. The interpretation " Son-craver" suggested by G. is
doubtful.*   51.—*Vidar, see Grm. 17, Vsp. 54, and Vali, both sons of Odin; see Bdr. st.
11. Modi, see Hym. st. 35, and Magni, see Hrbl. st. 9; both sons of Thor. Mjöllnir,
Thor's hammer; see Þrk. and Introd. To Thor comes the end: he is slain by the
World-serpent, Vsp. st. 56. He is here called Vingnir; see Alv., st. 6.*

Óþinn kvaþ:

52. 'Fjölþ ek fór,   fjölþ ek freistaþak,
        fjölþ of reyndak regin:
    hvat verþr Óþni   at aldrlagi,
        þás of rjúfask regin?'

Vafþrúþnir kvaþ:

53. 'Ulfr gleypa   mun Aldaföþr,
        þess mun Víþarr vreka;
    kalda kjapta   hann klyfja mun
        vitnis vígi at.'

Óþinn kvaþ:

54. 'Fjölþ ek fór,   fjölþ ek freistaþak,
        fjölþ of reyndak regin:
    hvat mælti Óþinn,   áþr á bál stigi,
        sjalfr í eyra syni?'

Vafþrúþnir kvaþ:

55. 'Ey manni þat veit,   hvat þu í árdaga
        sagþir í eyra syni:
    feigum munni   mæltak mína forna stafi
        auk of ragna rök.
    Nú viþ Óþin   deildak orþspeki,
        þú'st æ vísastr vera.'

Odin.

52. Far have I fared,   much have I ventured,
         oft have I proved the Powers:
    what foe shall bring,   at the Doom of gods,
         to Odin the end of life?

Weaver.

53. Fenrir shall swallow   the Father of men,
         but this shall Vidar avenge:
    with his sword he shall cleave   the ice-cold jaws
         of the mighty monster in strife.

Odin.

54. Far have I fared,   much have I ventured,
         oft have I proved the Powers:
    what spake Odin's self   in the ear of his son,
         when Baldr was laid on the bale fire?

Weaver.

55. That no man knows,   what Thou didst speak
         of old in the ear of thy son.
    Thus with fated lips   have I uttered old lore
         and told the great Doom of the Powers;
    for I have striven in word-skill   with Odin's self;
         thou art ever the wisest of all.

54.—*See Bdr., st. No. 10.*

HÁVAMÁL.

1. Gáttir allar,
   áþr gangi fram,
       umb skoþask skyli,
       umb skygnask skyli ;
   þvít óvist es,
   hvar óvinir
       sitja á fleti fyrir.

Hávamál.—*In* **R** *No. 2 ; cited in* **Sn. E.**

THE WORDS OF ODIN
THE HIGH ONE.

(Wisdom for Wanderers and
Counsel to Guests.)

1. At every door-way,
   ere one enters,
       one should spy round,
       one should pry round,
   for uncertain is the witting
   that there be no foeman sitting,
       within, before one on the floor.

The High One, *a name for Odin; see Grm. st. 49.*

2. Gefendr heilir!   gestr's inn kominn ;
        hvar skal sitja sjá ?
   mjök es bráþr   sás á bröndum skal
        síns of freista frama.

3. Elds es þörf   þeims inn es kominn
        auk á kné kalinn ;
   matar ok váþa   es manni þörf
        þeims hefr of fjall farit.

4. Vatns es þörf   þeims til verþar kömr,
        þerru ok þjóþlaþar,
   góþs of œþis   ef sér geta mætti
        orþ, ok endrþögu.

5. Vits es þörf   þeims víþa ratar,
        dǽlt es heima hvat ;
   at augabragþi   verþr sás etki kann
        auk meþ snotrum sitr.

6. At hyggjandi sinni   skylit maþr hrœsinn vesa,
        heldr gǽtinn at geþi ;
   þás horskr ok þögull   kömr heimisgarþa til,
        sjaldan verþr víti vörum.
   þvít óbrigþra vin   fǽr maþr aldrigi,
        an manvit mikit.

7. Enn vari gestr,   es til verþar kömr,
        þunnu hljóþi þegir,
   eyrum hlýþir,   en augum skoþar :
        svá nýsisk fróþra hverr fyrir.

8. Hinn es sæll   es sér of getr
        lof ok líknstafi ;
   ódǽlla er viþ þat   es maþr eiga skal
        annars brjóstum í.

2.—á bröndum, **R** ; á brautum, *paper MSS. and K. D. M.*

2. Hail, ye Givers !   a guest is come ;
        say ! where shall he sit within ?
    Much pressed is he   who fain on the hearth
        would seek for warmth and weal.

3. He hath need of fire,   who now is come,
        numbed with cold to the knee ;
    food and clothing   the wanderer craves
        who has fared o'er the rimy fell.

4. He craves for water,   who comes for refreshment,
        drying and friendly bidding,
    marks of good will,   fair fame if 'tis won,
        and welcome once and again.

5. He hath need of his wits   who wanders wide,
        aught simple will serve at home ;
    but a gazing-stock   is the fool who sits
        mid the wise, and nothing knows.

6. Let no man glory   in the greatness of his mind,
        but rather keep watch o'er his wits.
    Cautious and silent   let him enter a dwelling ;
        to the heedful comes seldom harm,
    for none can find   a more faithful friend
        than his wealth of mother wit.

7. Let the wary stranger   who seeks refreshment
        keep silent with sharpened hearing ;
    with his ears let him listen,   and look with his eyes ;
        thus each wise man spies out the way.

8. Happy is he   who wins for himself
        fair fame and kindly words ;
    but uneasy is that   which a man doth own
        while it lies in another's breast.

9.   Sá es sæll   es sjalfir of á
        lof ok vit meþan lifir,
     þvít ill ráþ   hefr maþr opt þegit
        annars brjóstum ór.

10.   Byrþi betri   berrat maþr brautu at,
        an sé manvit mikit;
     auþi betra   þykkir þat í ókunnum staþ,
        slíkt es válaþs vera.

11.   Byrþi betri   berrat maþr brautu at,
        an sé manvit mikit;
     vegnest verra   vegra hann velli at,
        an sé ofdrykkja öls.

12. (11)   Esa svá gott,   sem gott kveþa,
        öl alda sunum,
     þvít færa veit,   es fleira drekkr,
        síns til geþs gumi.

13. (12)   Óminnis hegri heitir   sás of ölþrum þrumir,
        hann stelr geþi guma;
     þess fugls fjöþrum   ek fjötraþr vask
        í garþi Gunnlaþar.

14. (13)   Ölr ek varþ,   varþ ofrölvi
        at ens fróþa Fjalars;
     því's ölþr bazt,   at aptr of heimtir
        hverr sitt geþ gumi.

15. (14)   Þagalt ok hugalt   skyli þjóþans barn
        ok vígdjarft vesa;
     glaþr ok reifr   skyli gumna hverr
        unz sinn bíþr bana.

12.—*The strophe numbering of* **R** *is marked in brackets.*

9. Happy is he   who hath in himself
      praise and wisdom in life;
for oft doth a man   ill counsel get
      when 'tis born in another's breast.

10. A better burden   can no man bear
      on the way than his mother wit:
'tis the refuge of the poor,   and richer it seems
      than wealth in a world untried.

11. A better burden   can no man bear
      on the way than his mother wit:
and no worse provision   can he carry with him
      than too deep a draught of ale.

12. Less good than they say   for the sons of men
      is the drinking oft of ale:
for the more they drink,   the less can they think
      and keep a watch o'er their wits.

13. A bird of Unmindfulness   flutters o'er ale feasts,
      wiling away men's wits:
with the feathers of that fowl   I was fettered once
      in the garths of Gunnlod below.

14. Drunk was I then,   I was over drunk
      in that crafty Jötun's court.
But best is an ale feast   when man is able
      to call back his wits at once.

15. Silent and thoughtful   and bold in strife
      the prince's bairn should be.
Joyous and generous   let each man show him
      until he shall suffer death.

13.—Gunnlod; *st. 104.*   14.—That crafty Jötun, Suttung; *st. 102. The name Fjalar in the text also belongs to Thor's famous opponent; see Hrbl. st. 26. Possibly it is here used in a general sense for any Jötun.*

K

16. (15)   Ósnjallr maþr   hyggsk munu ey lifa,
              ef viþ víg varask,
           en elli gefr   hánum engi friþ,
              þót hánum geirar gefi.

17. (16)   Kópir afglapi,   es til kynnis kömr,
              þylsk hann umb eþa þrumir;
           alt es senn,   ef hann sylg of getr,
              uppi's þá geþ guma.

18 (17)   Sá einn veit   es víþa ratar
              auk hefr fjölþ of farit,
           hverju geþi   stýrir gumna hverr
              . sás vitandi 's vits.

19. (18)   Haldit maþr á keri,   drekki þó at hófi mjöþ,
              mæli þarft eþa þegi;
           ókynnis þess   vár þik engi maþr,
              at þú gangir snimma at sofa.

20. (19)   Gráþugr halr,   nema geþs viti,
              etr sér aldrtrega;
           opt fær hlægis,   es meþ horskum kömr,
              manni heimskum magi.

21. (20)   Hjarþir þat vitu,   nær þær heim skulu,
              ok ganga þá af grasi;
           en ósviþr maþr   kann ævagi
              síns of mál maga.

22. (21)   Vesall maþr   ok illa skapi
              hlær at hvívetna;
           hitki hann veit,   es hann vita þyrfti,
              at hann esa vamma vanr.

23. (22)   Ósviþr maþr   vakir of allar nætr
              ok hyggr   at hvívetna;
           þá es móþr   es at morni kömr,
              allt es víl sem vas.

16. A coward believes   he will ever live
    if he keep him safe from strife:
but old age leaves him   not long in peace
    though spears may spare his life.

17. A fool will gape   when he goes to a friend,
    and mumble only, or mope;
but pass him the ale cup   and all in a moment
    the mind of that man is shown.

18. He knows alone   who has wandered wide,
    and far has fared on the way,
what manner of mind   a man doth own
    who is wise of head and heart.

19. Keep not the mead cup   but drink thy measure;
    speak needful words or none:
none shall upbraid thee   for lack of breeding
    if soon thou seek'st thy rest.

20. A greedy man,   if he be not mindful,
    eats to his own life's hurt:
oft the belly of the fool   will bring him to scorn
    when he seeks the circle of the wise.

21. Herds know the hour   of their going home
    and turn them again from the grass;
but never is found   a foolish man
    who knows the measure of his maw.

22. The miserable man   and evil minded
    makes of all things mockery,
and knows not that   which he best should know,
    that he is not free from faults.

23. The unwise man   is awake all night,
    and ponders everything over;
when morning comes   he is weary in mind,
    and all is a burden as ever.

24. (23) Ósnotr maþr   hyggr sér alla vesa
              viþhlǽjendr vini ;
         hitki hann fiþr,   þót of hann fár lesi,
              ef meþ snotrum sitr.

25. (24) Ósnotr maþr   hyggr sér alla vesa
              viþhlǽjendr vini ;
         þá þat fiþr,   es at þingi kömr,
              at á formǽlendr fá.

26. (25) Ósnotr maþr   þykkisk allt vita,
              ef á ser í vá veru ;
         hitki hann veit,   hvat hann skal viþ kveþa,
              ef hans freista firar.

27. (26) Ósnotr maþr,   es meþ aldir kömr,
              þat es bazt at þegi ;
         engi þat veit,   at hann etki kann,
              nema hann mǽli til mart.
         Veita maþr   hinns vǽtki veit,
              þót hann mǽli til mart.

28. (27) Fróþr sá þykkisk   es fregna kann
              ok segja et sama ;
         eyvitu leyna   megu ýta synir
              þvís gengr of guma.

29. (28) Œrna mǽlir   sás ǽva þegir
              staþlausu stafi ;
         hraþmǽlt tunga,   nema haldendr eigi,
              opt sér ógott of gelr.

30. (29) At augabragþi   skala maþr annan hafa,
              þót til kynnis komi ;
         margr fróþr þykkisk   ef freginn esat,
              ok naï þurrfjallr þruma.

31. (30) Fróþr þykkisk   sás flótta tekr
              gestr at gest háþinn ;
         veita görla   sás of verþi glissir
              þót meþ grömum glami.

24. The unwise man   weens all who smile
        and flatter him are his friends,
    nor notes how oft   they speak him ill
        when he sits in the circle of the wise.

25. The unwise man   weens all who smile
        and flatter him are his friends;
    but when he shall come   into court he shall find
        there are few to defend his cause.

26. The unwise man   thinks all to know,
        while he sits in a sheltered nook;
    but he knows not one thing,   what he shall answer,
        if men shall put him to proof.

27. For the unwise man   'tis best to be mute
        when he comes amid the crowd,
    for none is aware   of his lack of wit
        if he wastes not too many words;
    for he who lacks wit   shall never learn
        though his words flow ne'er so fast.

28. Wise he is deemed   who can question well,
        and also answer back:
    the sons of men   can no secret make
        of the tidings told in their midst.

29. Too many unstable   words are spoken
        by him who ne'er holds his peace;
    the hasty tongue   sings its own mishap
        if it be not bridled in.

30. Let no man be held   as a laughing-stock,
        though he come as guest for a meal:
    wise enough seem many   while they sit dry-skinned
        and are not put to proof.

31. A guest thinks him witty   who mocks at a guest
        and runs from his wrath away;
    but none can be sure   who jests at a meal
        that he makes not fun among foes.

32. (31) Gumnar margir   erusk gagnhollir,
       en at virþi vrekask;
   aldar róg   þat mun æ vesa,
       órir gestr viþ gest.

33. (32) Árliga verþar   skyli maþr opt fá,
       nema til kynnis komi:
   sitr ok snópir,   lætr sem solginn sé,
       ok kann fregna at föu.

34. (33) Afhvarf mikit   es til ills vinar
       þót á brautu bui,
   en til góþs vinar   liggja gagnvegir,
       þót sé firr farinn.

35. (34) Ganga skal,   skala gestr vesa
       ey í einum staþ;
   ljúfr verþr leiþr,   ef lengi sitr
       annars fletjum á.

36. (35) Bú es betra,   þót lítit sé,
       halr es heima hverr;
   þót tvær geitr eigi   ok taugreptan sal,
       þat's þó betra an bœn.

37. (36) Bú es betra,   þót lítit sé,
       halr es heima hverr;
   blóþugt's hjarta   þeims biþja skal
       sér í mál hvert matar.

38. (37) Vápnum sínum   skala maþr velli á
       feti ganga framarr,
   þvít óvist's at vita,   nær verþr á vegum úti
       geirs of þörf guma.

39. (38) Fannkak mildan mann   eþa svá matargóþan,
       at værit þiggja þegit,
   eþa síns fear   svági *gjöflan*,
       at leiþ sé laun ef þegi.

33.—Nema, **R**, *Dt. Hl.; né án*, B. Gv. S. G.   39.—Gjöflan, *G. B. Gv. Mk.*

32. Oft, though their hearts   lean towards one another,
     friends are divided at table;
ever the source   of strife 'twill be,
     that guest will anger guest.

33. A man should take always   his meals betimes
     unless he visit a friend,
or he sits and mopes,   and half famished seems,
     and can ask or answer nought.

34. Long is the round   to a false friend leading,
     e'en if he dwell on the way;
but though far off fared,   to a faithful friend
     straight are the roads and short.

35. A guest must depart   again on his way,
     nor stay in the same place ever;
if he bide too long   on another's bench
     the loved one soon becomes loathed.

36. One's own house is best,   though small it may be;
     each man is master at home;
though he have but two goats   and a bark-thatched hut
     'tis better than craving a boon.

37. One's own house is best,   though small it may be,
     each man is master at home;
with a bleeding heart   will he beg, who must,
     his meat at every meal.

38. Let a man never stir   on his road a step
     without his weapons of war;
for unsure is the knowing   when need shall arise
     of a spear on the way without.

39. I found none so noble   or free with his food,
     who was not gladdened with a gift,
nor one who gave   of his gifts such store
     but he loved reward, could he win it.

40. (39) Fear síns   es fengit hefr
      skylit maþr þörf þola ;
   opt sparir leiþum   þats hefr ljúfum hugat,
      mart gengr verr an varer.

41. (40) Vápnum ok váþum   skulu vinir gleþjask,
      þat's á sjölfum sýnst ;
   viþrgefendr [ok endrgefendr]   erusk vinir lengst,
      ef þat bíþr at verþa vel.

42. (41) Vin sínum   skal maþr vinr vesa
      ok gjalda gjöf viþ gjöf,
   hlátr viþ hlátri   skyli hölþar taka,
      en lausung viþ lygi.

43. (42) Vin sínum   skal maþr vinr vesa,
      þeim ok þess vin,
   en óvinar síns   skyli engi maþr
      vinar vinr vesa.

44. (43) Veiztu, ef vin átt   þanns þú vel truir,
      ok vill af hánum gott geta,
   geþi skalt viþ þann blanda   ok gjöfum skipta,
      fara at finna opt.

45. (44) Ef átt annan   þanns þú illa truir,
      vill af hánum þó gott geta,
   fagrt skalt viþ þann mǽla,   en flátt hyggja
      ok gjalda lausung viþ lygi.

46. (45) Þat's enn of þann   es þú illa truir,
      ok þér's grunr at hans geþi :
   hlǽja skalt viþ þeim   ok of hug mǽla,
      glík skulu gjöld gjöfum.

47. (46) Ungr vask forþum,   fór ek einn saman,
      þá varþk villr vega ;
   auþugr þóttumk   es ek annan fann :
      maþr es manns gaman.

40. Let no man stint him   and suffer need
     of the wealth he has won in life;
oft is saved for a foe   what was meant for a friend,
     and much goes worse than one weens.

41. With raiment and arms   shall friends gladden each other,
     so has one proved oneself;
for friends last longest,   if fate be fair,
     who give and give again.

42. To his friend a man   should bear him as friend,
     and gift for gift bestow,
laughter for laughter   let him exchange,
     but leasing pay for a lie.

43. To his friend a man   should bear him as friend,
     to him and a friend of his;
but let him beware   that he be not the friend
     of one who is friend to his foe.

44. Hast thou a friend   whom thou trustest well,
     from whom thou cravest good?
Share thy mind with him,   gifts exchange with him,
     fare to find him oft.

45. But hast thou one   whom thou trustest ill
     yet from whom thou cravest good?
Thou shalt speak him fair,   but falsely think,
     and leasing pay for a lie.

46. Yet further of him   whom thou trusted ill,
     and whose mind thou dost misdoubt;
thou shalt laugh with him   but withhold thy thought,
     for gift with like gift should be paid.

47. Young was I once,   I walked alone,
     and bewildered seemed in the way;
then I found me another   and rich I thought me,
     for man is the joy of man.

L

48. (47) Mildir, frœknir   menn bazt lifa,
       sjaldan sút ala,
en ósnjallr maþr   uggir hotvetna,
       sýtir æ glöggr viþ gjöfum.

49. (48) Váþir mínar   gaf ek velli at
       tveim trémönnum ;
rekkar þat þóttusk   es þeir ript höfþu :
       neiss es nökkviþr halr.

50. (49) Hrörnar þöll   sús stendr þorpi á,
       hlýrat börkr né barr ;
svá es maþr   sás manngi ann,
       hvat skal hann lengi lifa ?

51. (50) Eldi heitari   brinnr meþ illum vinum
       friþr fimm daga,
en þá sloknar,   es enn sétti kömr,
       ok versnar vinskapr allr.

52. (51) Mikit eitt   skala manni gefa,
       opt kaupir í litlu lof ;
meþ hölfum hleifi   ok meþ höllu keri
       fengumk félaga.

53. (52) Lítilla sanda   lítilla sæva :
       lítil eru geþ guma ;
þvít allir menn   urþut jafnspakir,
       hölf es öld hvár.

54. (53) Meþalsnotr   skyli manna hverr,
       æva til snotr sé ;
þeim era fyrþa   fegrst at lifa,
       es vel mart vitu.

53.—Hvár, *B's emendation, Dt. Hl. L.;* hvar, **R,** *H. G. J. S.*   54.—Era, *Dt. Hl.;* er, **R,** *G. H.*

48. Most blest is he   who lives free and bold
            and nurses never a grief,
     for the fearful man   is dismayed by aught,
            and the mean one mourns over giving.

49. My garments once   I gave in the field
            to two land-marks made as men ;
     heroes they seemed   when once they were clothed ;
            'tis the naked who suffer shame !

50. The pine tree wastes   which is perched on the hill,
            nor bark nor needles shelter it ;
     such is the man   whom none doth love ;
            for what should he longer live ?

51. Fiercer than fire   among ill friends
            for five days love will burn ;
     but anon 'tis quenched,   when the sixth day comes,
            and all friendship soon is spoiled.

52. Not great things alone   must one give to another,
            praise oft is earned for nought ;
     with half a loaf   and a tilted bowl
            I have found me many a friend.

53. Little the sand   if little the seas,
            little are minds of men,
     for ne'er in the world   were all equally wise,
            'tis shared by the fools and the sage.

54. Wise in measure   let each man be ;
            but let him not wax too wise ;
     for never the happiest   of men is he
            who knows much of many things.

49.—Two land-marks, *so V. explains* two tree-men.   50.—*On the hill or in the* open. *Icelandic* þorp *has this meaning, beside the more common one of* hamlet ; *G. The context makes it quite clear that an unsheltered spot is intended, but as the Norwegian pine flourishes on the hill and dies out among houses, we may perhaps infer that the poem did not originate in Norway.*   51.—Five days, *the old week before the Christian week of seven days.*   53.—*Many useless suggestions have been made to explain this strophe, which is perhaps only a general reflection on the vanity of human nature.*

55. (54) Meþalsnotr   skyli manna hverr,
           æva til snotr sé;
           þvít snotrs manns hjarta   verþr sjaldan glatt,
           ef sá's alsnotr es á.

56. (55) Meþalsnotr   skyli manna hverr,
           æva til snotr sé;
           örlög sín   viti engi fyrir,
           þeim's sorgalausastr sefi.

57. (56) Brandr af brandi   brenn unz brunninn es,
           funi kveykisk af funa;
           maþr af manni   verþr at máli kuþr,
           en til dœlskr af dul.

58. (57) Ár skal rísa   sás annars vill
           fé eþa fjör hafa;
           liggjandi ulfr   sjaldan lær of getr
           né sofandi maþr sigr.

59. (58) Ár skal rísa   sás á yrkjendr fá
           ok ganga síns verka á vit;
           mart of dvelr   þanns of morgin sefr,
           halfr es auþr und hvötum.

60. (59) Þurra skíþa   ok þakinna næfra,
           þess kann maþr mjöt,
           þess viþar   es vinnask megi
           mál ok misseri.

61. (60) Þveginn ok mettr   ríþi maþr þingi at,
           þót sét væðr til vel;
           skúa ok bróka   skammisk engi maþr,
           né hests in heldr,
           þót hann hafit goþan.

57, line 3.—**R**, *Dt. Hl. J.*, maþr manni verþr af máli kuþr, *Mh.* **G. H. S.**

55. Wise in measure   should each man be ;
        but let him not wax too wise ;
    seldom a heart   will sing with joy
        if the owner be all too wise.

56. Wise in measure   should each man be,
        but ne'er let him wax too wise :
    who looks not forward   to learn his fate
        unburdened heart will bear.

57. Brand kindles from brand   until it be burned,
        spark is kindled from spark,
    man unfolds him   by speech with man,
        but grows over secret through silence.

58. He must rise betimes   who fain of another
        or life or wealth would win ;
    scarce falls the prey   to sleeping wolves,
        or to slumberers victory in strife.

59. He must rise betimes   who hath few to serve him,
        and see to his work himself ;
    who sleeps at morning   is hindered much,
        to the keen is wealth half-won.

60. Of dry logs saved   and roof-bark stored
        a man can know the measure,
    of fire-wood too   which should last him out
        quarter and half years to come.

61. Fed and washed   should one ride to court
        though in garments none too new ;
    thou shalt not shame thee   for shoes or breeks,
        nor yet for a sorry steed.

62. (61)   Snapir ok gnapir,   es til sævar kömr,
                örn á aldinn mar;
            svá es maþr   es meþr mörgum kömr
            ok á formælendr fá.

63. (62)   Fregna ok segja   skal fróþra hverr,
                sás vill heitinn horskr;
            einn vita,   né annarr skal,
                þjóþ veit, ef þrír 'ú.

64. (63)   Ríki sitt   skyli ráþsnotra hverr
                í hófi hafa;
            þá þat fiþr   es meþ frœknum kömr,
                at engi's einna hvatastr.

65. (64)   [Gætinn ok geyminn   skyli gumna hverr
                ok varr at vintrausti]
            orþa þeira,   es maþr öþrum segir,
                opt hann gjöld of getr.

66. (65)   Mikilsti snimma   kvamk í marga staþi,
                en til síþ í suma;
            öl vas drukkit,   sumt vas ólagat:
                sjaldan hittir leiþr í liþ.

67. (66)   Hér ok hvar   mundi mér heim of boþit,
                ef þyrftak at málungi mat
            eþa tvau lær hengi   at ens tryggva vinar,
                þars hafþak eitt etit.

68. (67)   Eldr es baztr   meþ ýta sunum
                auk sólar sýn,
            heilyndi sitt   ef maþr hafa naïr,
                án viþ löst at lifa.

65, lines 1 and 2.—*A blank in* **R** *is thus supplied by the paper MSS., B. C. T. S.*

62. Like an eagle swooping   over old ocean,
    snatching after his prey,
so comes a man   into court who finds
    there are few to defend his cause.

63. Each man who is wise   and would wise be called
    must ask and answer aright.
Let one know thy secret,   but never a second,—
    if three a thousand shall know.

64. A wise counselled man   will be mild in bearing
    and use his might in measure,
lest when he come   his fierce foes among
    he find others fiercer than he.

65. Each man should be watchful   and wary in speech,
    and slow to put faith in a friend.
For the words which one   to another speaks
    he may win reward of ill.

66. At many a feast   I was far too late,
    and much too soon at some;
drunk was the ale   or yet unserved:
    never hits he the joint who is hated.

67. Here and there to a home   I had haply been asked
    had I needed no meat at my meals,
or were two hams left hanging   in the house of that friend
    where I had partaken of one.

68. Most dear is fire   to the sons of men,
    most sweet the sight of the sun;
good is health   if one can but keep it,
    and to live a life without shame.

62.—*The meaning of this strophe is somewhat obscure, but perhaps the idea is that the eagle, wont to seek his food in the quiet mountain pools, is baffled in face of the stormy sea; see Vsp. 59.* 66.—Hits the joint; *or, as we should say,* hits the nail on the head.

69. (68)   Esat maþr alls vesall,   þót sé illa heill ;
            sumr's af sunum sæll,
      sumr af frændum,   sumr af fé œrnu,
      sumr af verkum vel.

70. (69)   Betra's lifþum   an sé ólifþum,
            ey getr kvikr kú ;
      eld sák upp brinna   auþgum manni fyrir,
      en úti vas dauþr fyr durum.

71. (70)   Haltr ríþr hrossi,   hjörþ rekr handarvanr,
            daufr vegr ok dugir ;
      blindr es betri   an brendr sé,
            nýtr mangi nás.

72. (71)   Sunr es betri,   þót sé síþ of alinn
            ept genginn guma ;
      sjaldan bautarsteinar   standa brautu nær,
            nema reisi niþr at niþ.

73. (72)   Tveir'u einherjar,   tunga's höfuþs bani ;
            erumk í heþin hverjan   handar væni.
      Nótt verþr feginn   sás nesti truir,
            skammar'u skips rár
            hverf es haustgríma ;
      fjölþ of viþrir   á fimm dögum,
            en meira á mánaþi.

74. (73)   Veita maþr   hinns vætki veit :
            margr verþr af öþrum api ;
      maþr es auþugr,   annarr óauþugr,
            skylit þann vætkis vá.

70.—An sé ólifþum, R's emendation, B. Gv. Mh G. G. H. S. J.; ok sællifþum, R,
Dt. Hl. Mb. L.   73.—Einherjar, Mh. G. H. S.; eins herjar, R, Dt. Hl.   74.—Af
öþrum, R. K. D. Mk. B. M.; aflöþrum R; af löþrum Hl.; af auþi um, H. G. S.;
af aurum, Gv. V. J.

69. Not reft of all   is he who is ill,
        for some are blest in their bairns,
    some in their kin   and some in their wealth,
        and some in working well.

70. More blest are the living   than the lifeless,
        'tis the living who comes by the cow;
    I saw the hearth-fire burn   in the rich man's hall
        and himself lying dead at the door.

71. The lame can ride horse,   the handless drive cattle,
        the deaf one can fight and prevail,
    'tis happier for the blind   than for him on the bale-fire,
        for no man hath care for a corpse.

72. Best have a son   though he be late born
        and before him the father be dead:
    seldom are stones   on the wayside raised
        save by kinsmen to kinsmen.

73. Two are hosts against one,   the tongue is the head's bane,
        'neath a rough hide a hand may be hid;
    he is glad at night fall   who knows of his lodging,
        short is the ship's berth,
        and changeful the autumn night,
    much veers the wind   ere the fifth day
        and blows round yet more in a month.

74. He that learns nought   will never know
        how one is the fool of another,
    for if one be rich   another is poor
        and for that should bear no blame.

72.—Stones, *Icelandic* bautarsteinar *were monumental stones set upon the high road, many thousands of which are preserved, some with runic inscriptions.* 73.—*This agrees with the Icelandic proverb:* A man's hand may oft be found beneath a wolf-skin; *but others understand:* There is chance of a fist from under a cloak.

75. (74) Deyr fé,   deyja frǽndr,
       deyr sjalfr et sama,
en orþstírr   deyr aldrigi
    hveims sér góþan getr.

76. (75) Deyr fé,   deyja frǽndr,
       deyr sjalfr et sama ;
ek veit einn   at aldri deyr :
    dómr of dauþan hvern.

77. (76) Fullar grindr   sák fyr Fitjungs sunum,
       nú bera vánarvöl ;
svá es auþr   sem augabragþ,
    hann es valtastr vina.

78. (77) Ósnotr maþr,   ef eignask getr
       fé eþa fljóþs munugþ,
metnaþr þroask,   en manvit aldri,
    fram gengr hann drjúgt í dul.

79. (78) Þat's þá reynt,   es at rúnum spyrr,
       enum reginkunnum :
þeims görþu ginnregin,
    ok fáþi fimbulþulr,
       þá hefr bazt ef þegir.

80. (79) At kveldi skal dag leyfa,   konu es brend es,
    mǽki es reyndr es,   mey es gefin es,
  ís es yfir kömr,   öl es drukkit es.

81. (80) Í vindi skal viþ höggva,   veþri á sjó roa,
    myrkri viþ man spjalla,   mörg 'ru dags augu ;
  á skip skal skriþar orka,   en á skjöld til hlífar,
    mǽki höggs,   en mey til kossa.

75. Cattle die   and kinsmen die,
        thyself too soon must die,
     but one thing never,   I ween, will die,—
        fair fame of one who has earned.

76. Cattle die   and kinsmen die,
        thyself too soon must die,
     but one thing never,   I ween, will die,—
        the doom on each one dead.

77. Full-stocked folds   had the Fatling's sons,
        who bear now a beggar's staff:
     brief is wealth,   as the winking of an eye,
        most faithless ever of friends.

78. If haply a fool   should find for himself
        wealth or a woman's love,
     pride waxes in him   but wisdom never
        and onward he fares in his folly.

79. All will prove true   that thou askest of runes—
        those that are come from the gods,
     which the high Powers wrought,   and which Odin painted:
        then silence is surely best.

(Maxims for All Men.)

80. Praise day at even,   a wife when dead,
     a weapon when tried,   a maid when married,
     ice when 'tis crossed,   and ale when 'tis drunk.

81. Hew wood in wind,   sail the seas in a breeze,
     woo a maid in the dark,   —for day's eyes are many,—
     work a ship for its gliding,   a shield for its shelter,
     a sword for its striking,   a maid for her kiss;

79.—Runes, *st. 139, 141.*

82. (81) Viþ eld skal öl drekka,   en á ísi skríþa,
magran mar kaupa,   en mæki saurgan,
heima hest feita,   en hund á búi.

83. (82) Meyjar orþum   skyli manngi trua,
né þvís kveþr kona;
þvít á hverfanda hvéli   vöru þeim hjörtu sköpuþ
ok brigþ í brjóst of lagiþ.

84. (83) Brestanda boga,   brinnanda loga,
gínanda ulfi,   galandi kráku,
rýtanda svíni,   rótlausum viþi,
vaxanda vági,   vellanda katli,

85. (84) fljúganda fleini,   fallandi báru,
ísi einnættum,   ormi hringlegnum,
brúþar beþmálum   eþa brotnu sverþi,
bjarnar leiki   eþa barni konungs,

86. (85) sjúkum kalfii,   sjalfráþa þræli,
völu vilmæli,   val nýfeldum—
(86) bróþurbana sínum,   þót á brautu mœti,
húsi halfbrunnu,   hesti alskjótum—
þá's jór ónýtr,   ef einn fótr brotnar:—
verþit maþr svá tryggr,   at þessu truï öllu.

87. (85) Akri ársánum   trui engi maþr
né til snimma syni:
veþr ræþr akri,   en vit syni,
hætt es þeira hvárt.

88. (87) Svá's friþr kvenna   es flátt hyggja,
sem aki jó óbryddum   á ísi hálum,
teitum, tvévetrum,   ok sé tamr illa,
eþa í byr óþum   beiti stjórnlausu,
eþa skyli haltr henda   hrein í þáfjalli.

82. Drink ale by the fire,   but slide on the ice;
    buy a steed when 'tis lanky,   a sword when 'tis rusty;
    feed thy horse neath a roof,   and thy hound in the yard.

83. The speech of a maiden   should no man trust
    nor the words which a woman says;
    for their hearts were shaped   on a whirling wheel
    and falsehood fixed in their breasts.

84. Breaking bow,   or flaring flame,
    ravening wolf,   or croaking raven,
    routing swine,   or rootless tree,
    waxing wave,   or seething cauldron,

85. flying arrows,   or falling billow,
    ice of a night time,   coiling adder,
    woman's bed-talk,   or broken blade,
    play of bears   or a prince's child,

86. sickly calf   or self-willed thrall,
    witches flattery,   new-slain foe,
    brother's slayer   though seen on the highway,
    half burned house,   or horse too swift—
    useless were it   with one leg broken—
    be never so trustful   as these to trust.

87. Let none put faith   in the first sown fruit
    nor yet in his son too soon;
    whim rules the child   and weather the field,
    each is open to chance.

88. Like the love of women   whose thoughts are lies
    is the driving un-roughshod   o'er slippery ice
    of a two year old,   ill-tamed and gay;
    or in a wild wind steering   a helmless ship,
    or the lame catching reindeer   in the rime-thawed fell.

89. (88)   Bert ek nú mæli   þvít ek bæþi veit,
           brigþr es karla hugr konum;
         þá vér fegrst mælum,   es vér flást hyggjum,
           þat tælir horska hugi.

90. (89)   Fagrt skal mæla   ok fé bjóþa
             sás vill fljóþs ást fá,
           líki leyfa   ens ljósa mans :
             sá fær es friar.

91. (90)   Ástar firna   skyli engi maþr
             annan aldrigi;
           opt fá á horskan,   es á heimskan né fá,
             lostfagrir litir.

92. (91)   Eyvitar firna   es maþr annan skal
             þess's of margan gengr guma;
           heimska ór horskum   görir hölþa sunu
             sá enn mátki munr.

93. (92)   Hugr einn þat veit,   es býr hjarta nær,
             einn's hann sér of sefa;
           öng es sótt verri   hveim snotrum manni
             an sér öngu at una.

94. (93)   Þat ek þá reynda,   es ek í reyri sat
             ok vættak míns munar;
           hold ok hjarta   vörumk en horska mær,
             þeygi at heldr hana hefik.

95. (94)   Billings mey   ek fann beþjum á
             sólhvita sofa;
           jarls ynþi   þóttumk etki vesa,
             nema viþ þat lík at lifa.

(Lessons for Lovers.)

89. Now plainly I speak,   since both I have seen;
          unfaithful is man to maid;
      we speak them fairest   when thoughts are falsest
          and wile the wisest of hearts.

90.—Let him speak soft words   and offer wealth
          who longs for a woman's love,
      praise the shape   of the shining maid—
          he wins who thus doth woo.

91.—Never a whit   should one blame another
          whom love hath brought into bonds:
      oft a witching form   will fetch the wise
          which holds not the heart of fools.

92. Never a whit   should one blame another
          for a folly which many befalls;
      the might of love   makes sons of men
          into fools who once were wise.

93. The mind knows alone   what is nearest the heart
          and sees where the soul is turned:
      no sickness seems   to the wise so sore
          as in nought to know content.

(Odin's Love Quests.)

94. This once I felt   when I sat without
          in the reeds, and looked for my love;
      body and soul of me   was that sweet maiden
          yet never I won her as wife.

95. Billing's daughter   I found on her bed,
          fairer than sunlight sleeping,
      and the sweets of lordship   seemed to me nought
          save I lived with that lovely form.

89.—Odin *has had many love adventures in disguise; see* Hrbl. *st. 16, 18 30.*
95.—Billing, *a dwarf.*

96. (95) 'Auk nær aptni   skaltu, Óþinn ! koma,
          ef þú vill þér mæla man ;
       allt eru ósköp,   nema einir viti
          slíkan löst saman.'

97. (96) Aptr ek hvarf   ok unna þóttumk,
          vísum vilja frá ;
       hitt ek hugþa,   at ek hafa mynda
          geþ hennar allt ok gaman.

98. (97) Svá kvam ek næst,   at en nýta vas
          vígdrótt öll of vakin ;
       meþ brinnöndum ljósum   ok bornum viþi—
          svá var mér vílstígr vitaþr.

99. (98) Auk nær morni,   es ek vas enn of kominn,
          þá vas saldrótt of sofin ;
       grey eitt fannk þá   ennar góþu konu
          bundit beþjum á.

100. (99) Mörg es góþ mær,   ef görva kannar,
          hugbrigþ viþ hali :
       þá ek þat reynda,   es et ráþspaka
          teygþak á flærþir fljóþ ;
       háþungar hverrar   leitaþi mer et horska man,
          ok hafþak þess vætki vífs.

101. (100) Heima glaþr gumi   ok viþ gesti reifr
          sviþr skal of sik vesa ;
       minnugr ok málugr,   ef hann vill margfróþr vesa,
          opt skal góþs geta ;
 (101) fimbulfambi heitir   sás fátt kann segja,
          þat's ósnotrs aþal.

96. 'Yet nearer evening   come thou, Odin,
     if thou wilt woo a maiden:
all were undone   save two knew alone
     such a secret deed of shame.'

97. So away I turned   from my wise intent,
     and deemed my joy assured,
for all her liking   and all her love
     I weened that I yet should win.

98. When I came ere long   the war troop bold
     were watching and waking all:
with burning brands   and torches borne
     they showed me my sorrowful way.

99. Yet nearer morning   I went, once more,—
     the housefolk slept in the hall,
but soon I found   a barking dog
     tied fast to that fair maid's couch.

100. Many a sweet maid   when one knows her mind
     is fickle found towards men:
I proved it well   when that prudent lass
     I sought to lead astray:
shrewd maid, she sought me   with every insult
     and I won therewith no wife.

(Odin's Quest after the Song Mead.)

101. In thy home be joyous   and generous to guests
     discreet shalt thou be in thy bearing,
mindful and talkative,   wouldst thou gain wisdom,
     oft making mention of good.
he is 'Simpleton' named   who has nought to say,
     for such is the fashion of fools.

N

102. (102) Enn aldna jötun sóttak,   nu emk aptr of kominn,
            fátt gatk þegjandi þar;
            mörgum orþum   mǽltak í minn frama
            í Suttungs sölum.

103. (104) Rata munn   létumk rúms of fá
            auk of grjót gnaga,
            yfir ok undir   stóþumk jötna vegir,
            svá hǽttak höfþi til.

104. (103) Gunnlöþ göfumk   gollnum stóli á
            drykk ens dýra mjaþar;
            ill iþgjöld   létk hana eptir hafa
            síns ens heila hugar,
            síns ens svára sefa.

105.   Vel keypts litar   hefk vel notit,
            fás es fróþum vant;
            þvít Óþrörir   es nú upp kominn
            á alda vés jaþar.

106.   Ifi 'rumk á,   at vǽrak enn kominn
            jötna görþum ór,
            ef Gunnlaþar né nytak,   ennar góþu konu,
            þeirars lögþumk arm yfir.

107.   Ens hindra dags   gengu hrímþursar
            [Háva ráþs at fregna]
            Háva höllu í;
            at Bölverki spurþu,   ef vǽri meþ böndum kominn
            eþa hefþi Suttungr of soit.

107, line 2.—*Mh. Gv. Mk. G. S. J. agree that this line is an interpolation, as it spoils both sense and metre.*

102. I sought that old Jötun,   now safe am I back,
    little served my silence there;
but whispering many   soft speeches I won
    my desire in Suttung's halls.

103. I bored me a road there   with Rati's tusk
    and made room to pass through the rock;
while the ways of the Jötuns   stretched over and under
    I dared my life for a draught.

104. 'Twas Gunnlod who gave me   on a golden throne
    a draught of the glorious mead,
but with poor reward   did I pay her back
    for her true and troubled heart.

105. In a wily disguise   I worked my will;
    little is lacking to the wise,
for the Soul-stirrer now,   sweet Mead of Song,
    is brought to men's earthly abode.

106. I misdoubt me if ever   again I had come
    from the realms of the Jötun race,
had I not served me   of Gunnlod, sweet woman,
    her whom I held in mine arms.

107. Came forth, next day,   the dread Frost Giants,
    and entered the High One's hall:
they asked—was the Baleworker   back mid the Powers,
    or had Suttung slain him below?

102.—*Suttung, a giant of the underworld,*   *For Snorri's version of this story, see Introd. and cf. Grm. st. 52.*   103.—*Rati or the* Gnawer, *a tool.*   105.—*The Soul-stirrer, st. 139. One of Odin's characters is that of Song-giver to man; see st. 141, 759, Introd. and Hdl. st. 3.*   107.—Baleworker, *the name which Odin had given himself in disguise.*

108.   Baugeiþ Óþinn   hykk at unnit hafi,
        hvat skal hans trygþum trua?
        Suttung svikvinn   hann lét sumbli frá
        ok grǿtta Gunnlöþu.

109.   Mál's at þylja   þular stóli á:
        Urþar brunni at
        sák ok þagþak,   sák ok hugþak,
        hlýddak á manna mál.

110.   of rúnar heyrþak dǿma,   né of ráþum þögþu
        Háva höllu at,
        Háva höllu í;
        heyrþak segja svá.

111. (110) Ráþumk þér, Loddfáfnir!   en þú ráþ nemir,
        njóta mundu, ef nemr,
        þér munu góþ, ef getr:
        nótt þú rísat   nema á njósn sér
        eþa leitir þér innan út staþar.

112. (111) Ráþumk þér, Loddfáfnir!   en þú ráþ nemir,
        njóta mundu, ef nemr,
        þér munu góþ, ef getr:
        fjölkunnigri konu   skalta í faþmi sofa,
        svát hón lyki þík liþum.

113. (111) Hón svá görir,   at þú gaïr eigi
        þings né þjóþans máls;
        mat þú villat   né mannskis gaman,
        ferr þú sorgafullr at sofa.

109.—Manna mál, **R** *Dt. Hl. J.;* háva mál, *Ml. S. G. H. Mk.*

108. A ring-oath Odin   I trow had taken—
     how shall one trust his troth?
  'twas he who stole   the mead from Suttung,
     and Gunnlod caused to weep.

(The Counselling of the Stray-Singer.)

109. 'Tis time to speak   from the Sage's Seat;
     hard by the Well of Weird
  I saw and was silent,   I saw and pondered,
     I listened to the speech of men.

110. Of runes they spoke,   and the reading of runes
     was little withheld from their lips:
  at the High One's hall,   in the High One's hall,
     I thus heard the High One say:—

111. I counsel thee, Stray-Singer,   accept my counsels,
     they will be thy boon if thou obey'st them,
     they will work thy weal if thou win'st them:
  rise never at night time   except thou art spying
     or seekest a spot without.

112. I counsel thee, Stray-Singer,   accept my counsels,
     they will be thy boon if thou obey'st them,
     they will work thy weal if thou win'st them:
  thou shalt never sleep   in the arms of a sorceress,
     lest she should lock thy limbs;

113. So shall she charm   that thou shalt not heed
     the council or words of the king,
  nor care for thy food   or the joys of mankind,
     but fall into sorrowful sleep.

108.—Stray-Singer, *the meaning of* Loddfáfnir *is not yet fully decided; see Introd-*
109.—Well of Weird, *the most sacred spot in the world, where the gods meet in council under Yggdrasil; see Grm. st. 30, Vsp. st. 19.*

114. (112)　Ráþumk þér, Loddfáfnir!　　en þú ráþ nemir,
　　　　　　　njóta mundu, ef nemr,
　　　　　　　þér munu góþ, ef getr:
　　　　annars konu　　　teyg þér aldrigi
　　　　　eyrarúnu at.

115. (113)　Ráþumk þér, Loddfáfnir!　　en þú ráþ nemir,
　　　　　　　njóta mundu, ef nemr,
　　　　　　　þér munu góþ, ef getr:
　　　　á fjalli eþa firþi　　　ef þik fara tíþir,
　　　　　fásktu at virþi vel.

116. (114)　Ráþumk þér, Loddfáfnir!　　en þú ráþ nemir,
　　　　　　　njóta mundu, ef nemr,
　　　　　　　þér munu góþ, ef getr:
　　　　illan mann　　　láttu aldrigi
　　　　　óhöpp at þér vita,
　　　　þvít af illum manni　　　fǽr þú aldrigi
　　　　　gjöld ens góþa hugar.

117. (115)　Ofarla bíta　　　ek sá einum hal
　　　　　orþ illrar konu:
　　　　fláráþ tunga　　　varþ hánum at fjörlagi,
　　　　　ok þeygi of sanna sök.

118. (116)　Ráþumk þér, Loddfáfnir!　　en þú ráþ nemir,
　　　　　　　njóta mundu, ef nemr,
　　　　　　　þér munu góþ, ef getr:
　　　　veiztu ef vin átt　　　þanns þú vel truir,
　　　　　farþu at finna opt,
　　　　þvít hrísi vex　　　ok hávu grasi
　　　　　vegr es vǽtki tröþr.

119. (117)　Ráþumk þér, Loddfáfnir!　　en þú ráþ nemir,
　　　　　　　njóta mundu, ef nemr,
　　　　　　　þér munu góþ, ef getr:
　　　　góþan mann　　　teyg þér at gamanrúnum
　　　　　ok nem líknargaldr meþan lifir.

114. I counsel thee, Stray-Singer,   accept my counsels,
      they will be thy boon if thou obey'st them,
      they will work thy weal if thou win'st them:
seek not ever   to draw to thyself
      in love-whispering another's wife.

115. I counsel thee, Stray-Singer,   accept my counsels,
      they will be thy boon if thou obey'st them,
      they will work thy weal if thou win'st them:
should thou long to fare   over fell and firth
      provide thee well with food.

116. I counsel thee, Stray-Singer,   accept my counsels,
      they will be thy boon if thou obey'st them,
      they will work thy weal if thou win'st them:
tell not ever   an evil man
      if misfortunes thee befall,
from such ill friend   thou needst never seek
      return for thy trustful mind.

117. Wounded to death,   have I seen a man
      by the words of an evil woman;
a lying tongue   had bereft him of life,
      and all without reason of right.

118. I counsel thee, Stray-Singer,   accept my counsels,
      they will be thy boon if thou obey'st them,
      they will work thy weal if thou win'st them:
hast thou a friend   whom thou trustest well,
      fare thou to find him oft;
for with brushwood grows   and with grasses high
      the path where no foot doth pass.

119. I counsel thee, Stray-Singer,   accept my counsels,
      they will be thy boon if thou obey'st them,
      they will work thy weal if thou win'st them:
in sweet converse call   the righteous to thy side,
      learn a healing song while thou livest.

120. (118) Ráþumk þér, Loddfáfnir !　　en þú ráþ nemir,
　　　　　　njóta mundu, ef nemr,
　　　　　　þér munu góþ, ef getr :
　　　vin þínum　　　ves þú aldrigi
　　　fyrri at flaumslitum ;
　　　sorg etr hjarta,　　　ef þú segja né naïr
　　　einhverjum allan hug.

121. (119) Ráþumk þér, Loddfáfnir !　　en þú ráþ nemir,
　　　　　　njóta mundu, ef nemr,
　　　　　　þér munu góþ, ef getr :
　　　orþum skipta　　　þú skalt aldrigi
　　　viþ ósvinna apa ;

122. (119) þvít af illum manni　　　mundu aldrigi
　　　　　　góþs laun of geta,
　　　en góþr maþr　　　mun þik görva mega
　　　　　líknfastan at lofi.

123. (120) Sifjum's þá blandat,　　　hverrs segja ræþr
　　　　　　einum allan hug :
　　　allt es betra　　　an sé brigþum at vesa,
　　　esat vinr es vilt eitt segir.

124. (121) Ráþumk þér, Loddfáfnir !　　en þú ráþ nemir,
　　　　　　njóta mundu, ef nemr,
　　　　　　þér munu góþ, ef getr :
　　　þrimr orþum senna　　　skalta þér viþ verra mann ;
　　　opt enn betri bilar,
　　　þas enn verri vegr.

125. (122) Ráþumk þér, Loddfáfnir !　　en þú ráþ nemir,
　　　　　　njóta mundu, ef nemr,
　　　　　　þér munu góþ, ef getr :
　　　skósmiþr þú vesir　　　né skeptismiþr,
　　　　nema þér sjölfum sér :
　　　skór's skapaþr illa　　　eþa skapt sé rangt,
　　　　þá's þér böls beþit.

120. I counsel thee, Stray-Singer,   accept my counsels,
          they will be thy boon if thou obey'st them,
          they will work thy weal if thou win'st them:
      be never the first   with friend of thine
          to break the bond of fellowship;
      care shall gnaw thy heart   if thou canst not tell
          all thy mind to another.

121. I counsel thee, Stray-Singer,   accept my counsels,
          they will be thy boon if thou obey'st them,
          they will work thy weal if thou win'st them:
      never in speech   with a foolish knave
          shouldst thou waste a single word.

122. From the lips of such   thou needst not look
          for reward of thine own good will;
      but a righteous man   by praise will render thee
          firm in favour and love.

123. There is mingling in friendship   when man can utter
          all his whole mind to another;
      there is nought so vile   as a fickle tongue;
          no friend is he who but flatters.

124. I counsel thee, Stray-Singer,   accept my counsels,
          they will be thy boon if thou obey'st them,
          they will work thy weal if thou win'st them:
      strive not in three words   with a man worse than thee;
          oft the worst lays the best one low.

125. I counsel thee, Stray-Singer,   accept my counsels,
          they will be thy boon if thou obey'st them,
          they will work thy weal if thou win'st them:
      be not a shoemaker   nor yet a shaft maker
          save for thyself alone:
      let the shoe be misshapen,   or crooked the shaft,
          and a curse on thy head will be called.

O

126. (123) Ráþumk þér, Loddfáfnir! en þú ráþ nemir,
njóta mundu, ef nemr,
þér munu góþ, ef getr:
hvars böl kannt, kveþu þer bölvi at
ok gefat fiöndum friþ.

127. (124) Ráþumk þér, Loddfáfnir! en þú ráþ nemir,
njóta mundu, ef nemr,
þér munu góþ, ef getr:
illu feginn ves þú aldrigi,
en lát þer at góþu getit.

128. (125) Ráþumk þér, Loddfáfnir! en þú ráþ nemir,
njóta mundu, ef nemr,
þér munu góþ, ef getr:
upp líta skalattu í orrostu—
gjalti glíkir verþa gumna synir—
síþr þitt of heilli halir.

129. (126) Ráþumk þér, Loddfáfnir! en þú ráþ nemir,
njóta mundu, ef nemr,
þér munu góþ, ef getr:
ef vill þér góþa konu kveþja at gamanrúnum
ok fá fögnuþ af,
fögru skalt heita ok láta fast vesa;
leiþisk manngi gótt, ef getr.

130. (127) Ráþumk þér, Loddfáfnir! en þú ráþ nemir,
njóta mundu, ef nemr,
þér munu góþ, ef getr:
varan biþk þik vesa ok eigi ofvaran;
ves viþ öl varastr ok viþ annars konu
ok viþ þat et þriþja, at þik þjófar né leiki.

131. (128) Ráþumk þér, Loddfáfnir! en þú ráþ nemir,
njóta mundu, ef nemr,
þér munu góþ, ef getr:
at háþi né hlátri hafþu aldrigi
gest né ganganda;

126.   I counsel thee, Stray-Singer,   accept my counsels,
          they will be thy boon if thou obey'st them,
          they will work thy weal if thou win'st them :
    when in peril thou seest thee,   confess thee in peril,
          nor ever give peace to thy foes.

127.   I counsel thee, Stray-Singer,   accept my counsels,
          they will be thy boon if thou obey'st them,
          they will work thy weal if thou win'st them :
    rejoice not ever   at tidings of ill,
          but glad let thy soul be in good.

128.   I counsel thee, Stray-Singer,   accept my counsels,
          they will be thy boon if thou obey'st them :
          they will work thy weal if thou win'st them :
    look not up in battle   when men are as beasts,
          lest the wights bewitch thee with spells.

129.   I counsel thee, Stray-Singer,   accept my counsels,
          they will be thy boon if thou obey'st them,
          they will work thy weal if thou win'st them :
    wouldst thou win joy   of a gentle maiden,
          and lure to whispering of love,
    thou shalt make fair promise,   and let it be fast,—
          none will scorn their weal who can win it.

130.   I counsel thee, Stray-Singer,   accept my counsels,
          they will be thy boon if thou obey'st them,
          they will work thy weal if thou win'st them :
    I pray thee be wary,   yet not too wary,
          be wariest of all with ale,
    with another's wife,   and a third thing eke,
          that knaves outwit thee never.

131.   I counsel thee, Stray-Singer,   accept my counsels,
          they will be thy boon if thou obey'st them,
          they will work thy weal if thou win'st them :
    hold not in scorn,   nor mock in thy halls
          a guest or wandering wight.

132. opt vitu ógörla   þeirs sitja inni fyrir,
     hvers þeir'u kyns es koma.
     Esat maþr svá góþr,   at galli né fylgi,
     né svá illr, at einugi dugi.

133. Ráþumk þér, Loddfáfnir!   en þú ráþ nemir,
     njóta mundu, ef nemr,
     þér munu góþ, ef getr:
     at hárum þul   hlǽþu aldrigi,
     opt's gott þats gamlir kveþa;
     opt ór skörpum belg   skilin orþ koma
     þeims hangir meþ hám
     ok skollir meþ skrám
     ok váfir meþ vilmögum.

131. Ráþumk þér, Loddfáfnir!   en þú ráþ nemir,
     njóta mundu, ef nemr,
     þér munu góþ, ef getr:
     gest né geyja   ne á grind hrökkvir,
     get þú váluþum vel.

135. Ramt's þat tré   es ríþa skal
     öllum at upploki:
     baug þú gef,   eþa þat biþja mun
     þér lǽs hvers á liþu.

136. Ráþumk þér, Loddfáfnir!   en þú ráþ nemir,
     njóta mundu, ef nemr,
     þér munu góþ, ef getr:
     hvars öl drëkkr,   kjóstu þér jarþarmegin—
     [þvít jörþ tekr viþ ölþri,   en aldr viþ sóttum,
     eik viþ abbindi,   ax viþ fjölkyngi,
     viþ haulvi hýrogi,   heiptum skal mána kveþja,
     beiti viþ bitsóttum,   en viþ bölvi rúnar—]
     fold skal viþ flóþi taka.

136.—Viþ haulvi hýrogi, *V.'s emendation, S.;* haull viþ hýrogi, **R**; höll viþ hýrógi, *J. G. H. Gv.*

132. They know but unsurely   who sit within
        what manner of man is come :
   none is found so good   but some fault attends him,
        or so ill but he serves for somewhat.

133. I counsel thee, Stray-Singer,   accept my counsels,
        they will be thy boon if thou obey'st them,
        they will work thy weal if thou win'st them :
   hold never in scorn   the hoary singer ;
        oft the counsel of the old is good ;
   come words of wisdom   from the withered lips
        of him left to hang among hides,
        to rock with the rennets
        and swing with the skins.

134. I counsel thee, Stray-Singer,   accept my counsels,
        they will be thy boon if thou obey'st them,
        they will work thy weal if thou win'st them :
   growl not at guests   nor drive them from the gate
        but show thyself gentle to the poor.

135. Mighty is the bar   to be moved away
        for the entering in of all.
   Shower thy wealth,   or men shall wish thee
        every ill in thy limbs.

136. I counsel thee, Stray-Singer,   accept my counsels,
        they will be thy boon if thou obey'st them,
        they will work thy weal if thou win'st them :
   when ale thou quaffest   call upon earth's might—
        'tis earth drinks in the floods.
   [Earth prevails o'er drink,   but fire o'er sickness,
   the oak o'er binding,   the earcorn o'er witchcraft,
   the rye spur o'er rupture,   the moon o'er rages,
   herb o'er cattle plagues,   runes o'er harm.]

133.—Rennets, *in Iceland the maw rennets of a calf were, and are still hung up to dry, and used for curdling milk.* 136.—*Deals with magic, and belongs to the spell songs rather than here.*

137. (134) Veitk at hekk   vindga meiþi á
          nǽtr allar niu,
        geiri undaþr   ok gefinn Óþni,
          sjalfr sjölfum mér,
        á þeim meiþi,   es manngi veit,
          hvers hann af rótum rinn.

138. (135) Viþ hleifi mik sǽldu   né viþ hornigi;
          nýsta ek niþr:
        namk upp rúnar,   ǽpandi namk;
          fell ek aptr þaþan.

139. (136) Fimbulljóþ niu   namk af enum frǽgja syni
          Bölþorns Bestlu föþur;
        ok drykk of gatk,   ens dýra mjaþar
          ausenn Óþröri.

140. (137) Þá namk frǽvask   ok fróþr vesa
          ok vaxa ok vel hafask:
        orþ mér af orþi   orþs leitaþi,
          verk mér af verki verks.

        *   *   *   *   *

141. (138) Rúnar munt finna   ok ráþna stafi,
          mjök stóra stafi,
          mjök stinna stafi
        es fáþi fimbulþulr   ok görþu ginnregin,
          es reist Hróptr ragna:

142. (139) Óþinn meþ ásum,   en fyr ölfum Daïnn,
          Dvalinn dvergum fyrir,
        Alsviþr jötnum fyr   *en fyr ýta sunum*
          reistk sjalfr sumar.

137.—Vindga, **R**, *H. G. S. Dt. Hl.*; vinga meiþi, *J.*; vinga-meiþi, C.   138.—
Sǽldu, *E. Magnússon, G.*; seldu, **R**. *For comments on these strophes, see B. Stud.,*
E. Magnússon, " Odin's Horse," and Chadwick " Cult of Odin."   142.—Alsviþr, *paper*
MSS., *G. S. R.*; ásviþr, **R**; en fyr ýta sunum, *Mk. S. H. G.*, *missing* **R**.

(Odin's Quest after the Runes.)

137.   I trow I hung   on that windy Tree
        nine whole days and nights,
    stabbed with a spear,   offered to Odin,
        myself to mine own self given,
    high on that Tree   of which none hath heard
        from what roots it rises to heaven.

138.   None refreshed me ever   with food or drink,
        I peered right down in the deep;
    crying aloud   I lifted the Runes,
        then back I fell from thence.

139.   Nine mighty songs   I learned from the great
        son of Bale-thorn, Bestla's sire;
    I drank a measure   of the wondrous Mead,
        with the Soulstirrer's drops I was showered.

140.   Ere long I bare fruit,   and throve full well,
        I grew and waxed in wisdom;
    word following word,   I found me words,
        deed following deed, I wrought deeds.

141.   Hidden Runes shalt thou seek   and interpreted signs,
        many symbols of might and power,
    by the great Singer painted,   by the high Powers fashioned,
        graved by the Utterer of gods.

142.   For gods graved Odin,   for elves graved Daïn,
        Dvalin the Dallier for dwarfs,
    All-wise for Jötuns,   and I, of myself,
        graved some for the sons of men.

137.—A windy Tree, *this must be* Yggdrasil. *The same words are used with regard to it under the name of* Mimir's tree; *see Fj. st. 14.*   138.—Back I fell, *the attainment of the runes had released him from the tree.*   139.—Mimir, *who was a Jötun and Odin's teacher, is presumably the son of the giant* Bale-thorn, *the grandfather of Odin* (Rydberg), *although his name is not given here.*   142.—All-wise, *this giant is unknown, unless identical with* Much-wise; *see Fj.*

* * . * * *

143. (140) Veiztu hvé rísta skal,   veiztu hvé ráþa skal?
veiztu hvé fá skal,   veiztu hvé freista skal?
veiztu hvé biþja skal,   veiztu hvé blóta skal?
veiztu hvé senda skal,   veiztu hvé soa skal?

144. (141) Betra's óbeþit   an sé ofblótit,
   ey sér til gildis gjöf;
betra's ósent   an sé ofsoït
  . . . . . .

Svá Þundr of reist   fyr þjóþa rök,
þar hann upp of reis,   es hann aptr of kvam.

* * * * *

145. (142) Þau ljóþ kannk   es kannat þjóþans kona
   né mannskis mögr:
hjölp heitir eitt,   en þat þér hjalpa mun
   viþ sökum ok sorgum ok sútum görvöllum.

146. (143) Þat kannk annat   es þurfu ýta synir
   þeirs vilja læknar lifa
  . . . .
   . . . .

147. (144) Þat kannk et þriþja,   ef mér verþr þörf mikil
   hapts viþ heiptmögu:
eggjar deyfik   minna andskota,
   bítat þeim vápn né velir.

148. (145) Þat kannk et fjórþa,   ef mér fyrþar bera
   bönd at boglimum:
svá ek gel,   at ek ganga má,
   sprettr af fötum fjöturr,
   en af höndum hapt.

143. Dost know how to write,   dost know how to read,
      dost know how to paint,   dost know how to prove,
      dost know how to ask,   dost know how to offer,
      dost know how to send,   dost know how to spend ?

144. Better ask for too little   than offer too much,
          like the gift should be the boon ;
      better not to send   than to overspend.

                . . . .

      Thus Odin graved   ere the world began ;
      Then he rose from the deep,   and came again.

(The Song of Spells.)

145. Those songs I know,   which nor sons of men
          nor queen in a king's court knows ;
      the first is Help   which will bring thee help
          in all woes and in sorrow and strife.

146. A second I know,   which the son of men
          must sing, who would heal the sick.

147. A third I know :   if sore need should come
          of a spell to stay my foes ;
      when I sing that song,   which shall blunt their swords,
          nor their weapons nor staves can wound.

148. A fourth I know : if men make fast
          in chains the joints of my limbs,
      when I sing that song   which shall set me free,
          spring the fetters from hands and feet.

144.—-Odin, *here called by his name* Thund, *the meaning of which is unknown ; see*
Grm. st. 3.

                                                                P

149. (146) Þat kannk et fimta,   ef sék af fári skotinn
             flein í folki vaþa :
         flýgra svá stint,   at ek stöþvigak,
             ef ek hann sjónum of sék.

150. (147) Þat kannk et sétta,   ef mik sœrir þegn
             á rótum rás viþar :
         ok þann hal,   es mik heipta kveþr,
             eta mein heldr an mik.

151. (148) Þat kannk et sjaunda,   ef sék hávan loga
             sal of sessmögum :
         brinnrat svá breitt,   at ek bjargigak ;
             þann kannk galdr at gala.

152. (149) Þat kannk et átta,   es öllum es
             nytsamlikt at nema :
         hvars hatr vex   meþ hildings sunum,
             þat mák bœta brátt.

153. (150) Þat kannk et niunda,   ef mik nauþr of stendr
             at bjarga fari minu á floti :
         vind ek kyrri   vági á,
             ok svœfik allan sœ.

154. (151) Þat kannk et tiunda,   ef ek sé túnriþur
             leika lopti á :
         ek svá vinnk,   at þær villar fara
             sinna heim hama,
             sinna heim haga.

155. (152) Þat kannk et ellifta,   ef skalk til orrostu
             leiþa langvini :
         und randir gelk,   en þeir meþ ríki fara
             heilir hildar til,
             heilir hildi frá,
             koma þeir heilir hvaþan.

149. A fifth I know :   when I see, by foes shot,
      speeding a shaft through the host,
flies it never so strongly   I still can stay it,
      if I get but a glimpse of its flight.

150. A sixth I know :   when some thane would harm me
      in runes on a moist tree's root,
on his head alone   shall light the ills
      of the curse that he called upon mine.

151. A seventh I know :   if I see a hall
      high o'er the bench-mates blazing,
flame it ne'er so fiercely   I still can save it,—
      I know how to sing that song.

152. An eighth I know :   which all can sing
      for their weal if they learn it well;
where hate shall wax   'mid the warrior sons,
      I can calm it soon with that song.

153. A ninth I know :   when need befalls me
      to save my vessel afloat,
I hush the wind   on the stormy wave,
      and soothe all the sea to rest.

154. A tenth I know :   when at night the witches
      ride and sport in the air,
such spells I weave   that they wander home
      out of skins and wits bewildered.

155. An eleventh I know :   if haply I lead
      my old comrades out to war,
I sing 'neath the shields,   and they fare forth mightily
      safe into battle,
      safe out of battle,
      and safe return from the strife.

154.—*The witches, or "hedge-riders," who could change their shapes or skins (Icel.* hama), *were thus deprived of their magic powers.*

156. (153)   Þat kannk et tolfta   ef sék á tré uppi
      váfa virgilná:
   svá ek ríst   ok í rúnum fák,
     at sá gengr gumi
     ok mælir viþ mik.

157. (154)   Þat kannk et þrettánda,   ef skalk þegn ungan
      verpa vatni á:
   munat hann falla,   þót í folk komi,
     hnígra sá halr fyr hjörum.

158. (155)   Þat kannk et fjogrtánda,   ef skalk fyrþa liþi
      telja tíva fyrir:
   ása ok alfa   ek kann allra skil,
     fár kann ósnotr svá.

159. (156)   Þat kannk et fimtánda,   es gól Þjóþrœrir
      dvergr fyr Dellings durum:
   afl gól hann ásum,   en ölfum frama,
     hyggju Hróptatý.

160. (157)   Þat kannk et sextánda,   ef vilk ens svinna mans
      hafa geþ allt ok gaman:
   hugi ek hverfi   hvítarmri konu
     ok snýk hennar öllum sefa.

161. (158)   Þat kannk et sjautjánda,   *ef* . . . . . .
     . . . .
   svá ek . . . . .   at mik seint mun firrask
     et manunga man.

162. (158)   Ljóþa þessa   mundu, Loddfáfnir!
      lengi vanr vesa,
   þót þér góþ sé,   ef þú getr,
     nýt, ef þú nemr,
     þörf, ef þú þiggr.

156. A twelfth I know: if I see in a tree
         a corpse from a halter hanging,
      such spells I write,   and paint in runes,
         that the being descends and speaks.

157. A thirteenth I know: if the new-born son
         of a warrior I sprinkle with water,
      that youth will not fail   when he fares to war,
         never slain shall he bow before sword.

158. A fourteenth I know: if I needs must number
         the Powers to the people of men,
      I know all the nature   of gods and of elves
         which none can know untaught.

159. A fifteenth I know,   which Folk-stirrer sang,
         the dwarf, at the gates of Dawn;
      he sang strength to the gods,   and skill to the elves,
         and wisdom to Odin who utters.

160. A sixteenth I know: when all sweetness and love
         I would win from some artful wench,
      her heart I turn,   and the whole mind change
         of that fair-armed lady I love.

161. A seventeenth I know: so that e'en the shy maiden
         is slow to shun my love.

162. These songs, Stray-Singer,   which man's son knows not,
         long shalt thou lack in life,   [obey'st them,
      though thy weal if thou win'st them,   thy boon if thou
         thy good if haply thou gain'st them.

156.—*Cf. Bdr. st. 3.*   157.—Sprinkle with water, *an old heathen rite of puri-
fication; see Rp. st. 6.*   159.—Folk-stirrer, *this dwarf is not mentioned elsewhere.*

163. (159) Þat kannk et áttjánda,   es ek ǽva kennik
               mey né manns konu—
          allt es betra   es einn of kann,
               þat fylgir ljóþa lokum—
          nema þeiri einni,   es mik armi verr
               eþa mín systir sé.

164. (160) Nú 'ru Háva mál   kveþin höllu í,
               allþörf ýta sunum,
               óþörf jötna sunum;
          heill sás kvaþ !   heill sás kann !
               njóti sás nam !
               heilir þeirs hlýddu !

163. An eighteenth I know :   which I ne'er shall tell
    to maiden or wife of man,
save alone to my sister,   or haply to her
    who folds me fast in her arms ;
most safe are secrets   known to but one—
    the songs are sung to an end.

164. Now the sayings of the High One   are uttered in the hall
for the weal of men,   for the woe of Jötuns,
Hail, thou who hast spoken !   Hail, thou that knowest !
Hail, ye that have hearkened !   Use, thou who hast learned !

HYMISKVIÞA.

1. Ár valtívar   veiþar námu
   ok sumblsamir,   áþr saþir yrþi,
   hristu teina   ok á hlaut söu:
   fundu at Ægis   örkost hverjan.

2. Sat bergbui   barnteitr fyrir
   mjök glíkr megi   Mistorblinda ;
   leit í augu   Yggs barn í þrá :
   ' Þú skalt ásum   opt sumbl görva.'

*   *   *   *   *

---

*The motive of this illustration is from a pre-Norman monument at Tullie House,
Carlisle.* Hymiskviþa, *in* **R** *No. 7 and* **A**. 1.—Hverjan, *B. G. S. H. Dt. for*
hverja, **R** *L. F. Magnússon, Hold.* 2.—Mistorblinda, *F. Magnússon, R. Gv.* ;
miskorblinda, **R**.

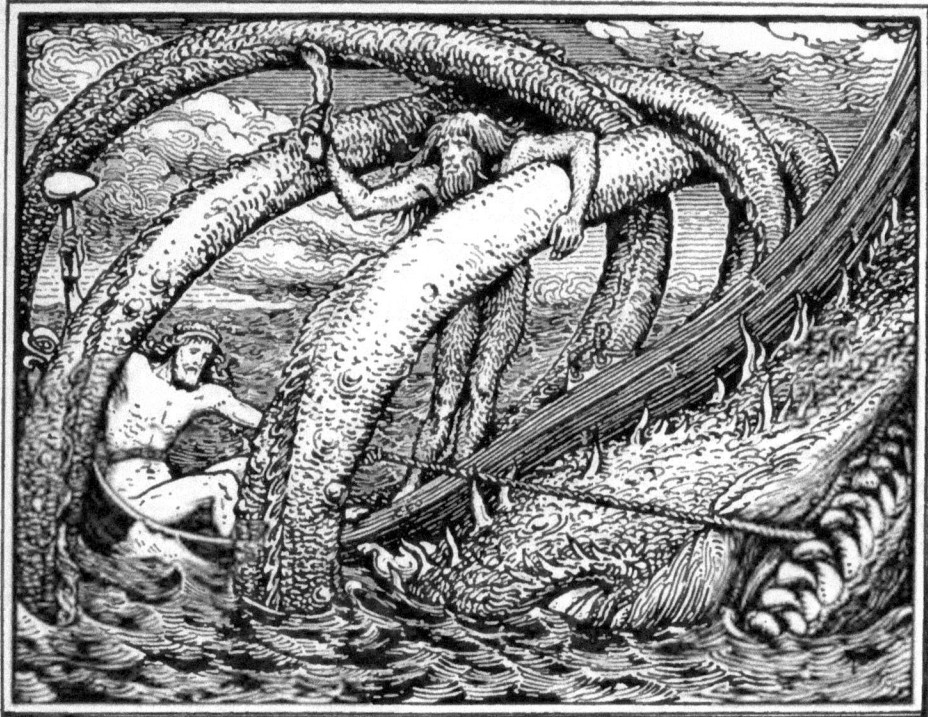

THE LAY OF HYMIR.

1. Of old when the war-gods   their prey had won them,
in mood for feasting,   and still unsated,
they shook divining twigs,   scanned the blood drops,
and found all dainties   in Ægir's halls.

2. As the rock-giant sat   in his wave-brood rejoicing,
and seemed in likeness   the son of Mist-blind,
came Thor and looked   in his eyes with threatening :
'Make now a goodly   feast for the gods!'

1.—Divining twigs, *the oracle; see Vsp. st. 63. Ægir, a sea god, had nine daughters, and "Ægir's children" was a poetical synonym for the waves; see Grm. st. 45; Ls. and Introd.*

℥

3.   Önn fekk jötni   orþbǽginn halr,
        hugþi at hefndum   hann nǽst viþ goþ:
        baþ Sifjar ver   sér fǿra hver,
        'þanns öllum yþr   öl of heitak.'

4.   Né þat máttu   mǽrir tívar
        ok ginnregin   of geta hvergi,
        unz af trygþum   Týr Hlórriþa
        ástráþ mikit   einum sagþi:

5.   'Býr fyr austan   Élivága
        hundvíss Hymir   at himins enda:
        á minn faþir   móþugr ketil,
        rúmbrugþinn hver,   rastar djúpan.'

               þórr kvaþ:

6.   'Veiztu ef þiggjum   þann lögvelli?'

               Týr kvaþ:

      'Ef, vinr! velar   vit görvum til.'

7. (6) Fóru drjúgum   dag þann framan
        Ásgarþi frá,   unz til Egils kvámu;
        hirþi hafra   horngöfgasta;
        hurfu at höllu   es Hymir átti.

8. (7) Mögr fann ömmu   mjök leiþa sér,
        hafþi höfþa   hundruþ niu;
        en önnur gekk   algollin fram
        brúnhvit bera   bjórveig syni:

7.—*Strophe numbering of* **R** *in brackets.*

3. But the harsh-voiced hero   angered the giant,
   who forthwith pondered   revenge on the Powers;
   He bade the Thunderer   bring him a cauldron—
   'Wherein for all of you   ale I may brew;'

4. The glorious gods,   the holy Powers
   such vessel as this   could nowhere find;
   till Tyr the trusty   whispered in secret
   words of friendly   counsel to Thor.

Tyr.

5. 'There dwells to the east   of Stormy Billow
   the all-wise Hymir,   at heaven's end,
   my fierce-souled father,   who owns the kettle,
   the broad-roomed cauldron,   a full mile deep.'

Thor.

6. 'Dost know can we win   that water-seether?'

Tyr.

'If we use wiles   thereto, my friend!'

7. So forth they drove   through the live-long day
   till they came from Asgarth   to Egil's home.
   He stalled the goats   of the splendid horns,
   while they turned to the hall   which Hymir owned.

8. Unsightly seemed   to Tyr his granddam
   for heads she had   nine hundred in all;
   but another came   all golden forth,
   fair-browed, and bearing   to her son the ale-cup.

4.—Tyr, *the god of war, is usually called the son of Odin; see Ls. st. 38.* 5.—Hymir, *a frost giant, who binds the wintry sea.* 7.—Egil *is probably the giant mentioned in st. 39.* The goats, *called* Tooth-gnasher *and* Tooth-cracker, *drew* Thor's *chariot; st. 39.*

9. (8) 'Áttniþr jötna!　　ek viljak ykkr
　　　　hugfulla tvá　　und hvera setja:
　　　　es minn frí　　mörgu sinni
　　　　glöggr viþ gesti,　　görr ills hugar.'

10. (9) En váskapaþr　　varþ síþbuinn
　　　　harþráþr Hymir　　heim af veiþum:
　　　　gekk inn í sal,　　glumþu jöklar,
　　　　vas karls es kvam　　kinnskógr frörinn.

Frilla kvaþ:

11. (10) 'Ves heill, Hymir!　　í hugum góþum:
　　　　nú's sunr kominn　　til sala þinna
　　　　sás vit vǽttum　　af vegi löngum;
　　　　fylgir hánum　　Hróþrs andskoti,
　　　　vinr verliþa,　　Veorr heitir sá.

12. (11) Seþu hvar sitja　　und salar gafli!
　　　　svá forþa sér,　　stendr súl fyrir.'
　　　　Sundr stökk súla　　fyr sjón jötuns,
　　　　en afr í tvau　　áss brotnaþi.

13. (12) Stukku átta,　　en einn af þeim
　　　　hverr harþsleginn　　heill, af þolli;
　　　　fram gengu þeir,　　en forn jötunn
　　　　sjónum leiddi　　sinn andskota.

14. (13) Sagþit hánum　　hugr vel þás sá
　　　　gýgjar grǽti　　á golf kominn:
　　　　þar váru þjórar　　þrir of teknir,
　　　　baþ senn jötunn　　sjóþa ganga.

12.—Afr, *G. S. Gv. Sv. J.*; áþr, **R A.**

Hymir's wife.

9. 'Kinsman of giants!   fain would I hide you
   'neath yon cauldrons,   though bold of heart;
   for my lord and master   ofttimes shows him
   mean to strangers,   moved soon to wrath.'

10. Long tarried that monster,   fierce-mooded Hymir,
    ere he came   from his hunting home.
    He entered the hall,   and icicles clashed—
    all frozen was the bushy   beard on his chin.

Wife.

11. 'Hail to thee, Hymir!   Be gracious in mood:
    for here in thy halls   is come our offspring
    whom long we awaited   from distant ways;
    and with him fares   the foe of giants,
    the friend of man,   whose name is Warder.

12. 'Dost see where they hide,   the hall-gable under,
    sheltering themselves   with a pillar between?'
    But the column was shattered   at the glance of the giant,
    the mighty rafter   was reft asunder:

13. Down from the beam   eight cauldrons crashed,
    one, hard-hammered,   alone was whole.
    Then forth they stepped,   but the ancient Jötun
    ever followed   the foe with his eyes.

14. For evil whispered   his mind when he saw
    the bane of giant-wives   stand on the hearth;
    yet took they soon   of the oxen three,
    and Hymir bade them   cook forthwith.

11.—Warder. *Thor always appears as the defender of mankind against the giants;
see Hrbl. st. 23. In this stanza* Hród, *otherwise unknown, is specified, but his name is
doubtless used in a general sense.*   14.—Bane of giant-wives, *see Hrbl. 23.*

15. (14)   Hverjan létu   höfþi skemra
           auk á seyþi   síþan báru:
           át Sifjar verr,   áþr sofa gengi,
           einn meþ öllu   yxn tvá Hymis.

16. (14)   Þotti hárum   Hrungnis spjalla
           verþr Hlórriþa   vel fullmikill:
           'Munum at apni   öþrum verþa
           viþ veiþimat   vér þrír lifa.'

17.   Veorr kvazk vilja   á vág roa,
           ef ballr jötunn   beitur gǽfi.
           · · · · · · ·   · · · · · ·
           · · · · · · ·   · · · · · ·

               Hymir kvaþ:

18. (15)   'Hverf til hjarþar,   ef hug truir,
           brjótr bergdana!   beitur sǿkja:
           þess vǽntir mik,   at þér myni
           ögn af oxa   auþfeng vesa.'

19. (16)   Sveinn sýsliga   sveif til skógar,
           þars uxi stóþ   alsvartr fyrir:
           braut af þjóri   þurs ráþbani
           hátún ofan   horna tveggja.
           · · · ·   · · · · · · ·

               Hymir kvaþ:

20. (17)   'Verk þykkja þín   verri miklu
           kjóla valdi,   an kyrr sitir.'
           · · · · ·   · · · · · ·

21. (18)   Baþ hlunngota   hafra dróttinn
           áttrunn apa   útar fǿra;
           en sá jötunn   sína talþi
           litla fýsi   lengra at roa.

15. Each one left they	less by a head,
	and laid them soon	on the seething fire;
	then ere he slumbered	the Thunderer ate,
	himself alone,	of the oxen, twain.

16. But Hymir the hoary	friend of Hrungnir
	deemed too ample	the meal of Thor:
	'To-morrow at eve	shall we three have nought
	save our hunting spoil	whereon to sup.'

17. Spake Thor, and said	he would fish in the sea,
	if the fierce-souled giant	would find him bait.

Hymir.

18. 'Go, if thou darest,	slayer of rock-giants,
	seek thy bait	from the herd thyself:
	for such as thou	I ween 'twill seem
	that bait from an ox	were easy to win.'

19. Forthwith sped Thor,	bold youth, to the wood
	and soon, all swart,	stood an ox before him;
	then over its horns	the slayer of Jötuns
	struck, and sundered	the head, high-towering.

Hymir.

20. 'Methinks thou art worse	by far afoot
	than at table sitting,	Steerer of barks!'

21. Then the Lord of goats,	bade the low-born churl
	drive the launched sea-horse	further from shore;
	but little he wished,	that wary giant,
	to row any further	over the ocean.

16.—*Hrungnir, a giant of great renown; Hrbl. st. 15 and Introd.*

22. (19)   Dró mærr Hymir   móþugr hvali
             einn á öngli   upp senn tvá ;
             en aptr í skut   Óþni sifjaþr
             Veorr viþ vélar   vaþ görþi sér.

23. (20)   Egndi á öngul   sás öldum bergr
             orms einbani   oxa höfþi :
             gein viþ agni   sús goþ fía
             umbgjörþ neþan   allra landa.

24. (21)   Dró djarfliga   dáþrakkr Þórr
             orm eitrfán   upp at borþi ;
             hamri kníþi   háfjall skarar
             ofljótt ofan   ulfs hnitbróþur.

25. (22)   Hreingölkn hlumþu,   en hölkn þutu,
             fór en forna   fold öll saman :
             .   .   .   .   . ´ .   .   .   .
             sökþisk síþan   sá fiskr í mar.

26. (22)   .   .   .   .
             óteitr jötunn,   es aptr röru :
             svát at ár Hymir   etki mælti,
             veifþi ræþi   veþrs annars til.

Hymir kvaþ :

27. (23)   'Mundu of vinna   verk halft viþ mik,
             at þu flotbrúsa   festir okkarn,
             eþa heim hvali   haf til bœjar
             ok holtriþa   hver í gögnum.'

27.—*The reversal of lines 2 and 3 and the transposition of line 4, which comes after 28, line 4, in* **R A,** *was made by Gv. H. S.*

22.   Alone the famous   and fierce-souled Hymir
       caught on his hook   two whales at once;
       but aft in the stern   the son of Odin
       fashioned with craft   his fishing line.

23.   Lone Serpent-slayer,   and Shield of Men,
       he baited his hook   with the head of the ox,
       and he whom the gods hate   gaped thereat,
       the Girdle lying   all lands beneath.

24.   Then Thor drew mightily   —swift in his doing—
       the poison-glistening   snake to the side.
       His hammer he lifted   and struck from on high
       the fearful head   of Fenrir's brother.

25.   Moaned the wild monster,   the rocks all rumbled,
       the ancient earth   shrank into itself.
       . . . .

       Then sank the serpent   down in the deep.

26.   So cheerless was the giant   as back they rowed
       that for a while   not a word he spake;
       then anew he turned   the tiller of thought.

Hymir.

27.   'Now half the work   shalt thou share with me:
       or moor thou fast   our floating steed,
       or bear the whales   to the dwellings home,
       all through the hollows   of the wooded hills.

23.—*The* Girdle *is the World-serpent, called also Midgarth's worm. He is one of Loki's children; see Vsp. st. 55, Vsp. en skamma st. 8.*   24.—Fenrir, *the famous Wolf; see Vsp. st. 54, Vsp. en skamma st. 8.*   26.—Hymir *has formed a fresh scheme for defeating Thor (Dt.). G. and others understand simply that he has turned the boat towards land.*

R

28. (24) Gekk Hlórriþi, greip á stafni,
     vatt meþ austri upp lögfáki ;
     einn meþ árum ok austskotu
     bar til bœjar   brimsvín jötuns.

29. (25) Ok enn jötunn of afrendi
     þrágirni vanr viþ Þór senti :
     kvaþat mann ramman, þót roa kynni
     kröpturligan,   nema kalk bryti.

30. (26) En Hlórriþi, es at höndum kvam,
     brátt lét bresta brattstein gleri :
     sló sitjandi   súlur í gögnum,
     báro þó heilan fyr Hymi síþan.

31. (27) Unz þat en fríþa frilla kendi
     ástráþ mikit   eitt es vissi :
     'Drep viþ haus Hymis ! hann's harþari
     kostmóþs jötuns kalki hverjum.'

32. (28) Harþr reis á kné hafra dróttinn,
     fœrþisk allra   í ásmegin :
     heill vas karli   hjalmstofn ofan,
     en vínferill   valr rifnaþi.

Hymir kvaþ :

33. (29) 'Mörg veitk mæti mér gengin frá,
     es kalki sék   ór knëum hrundit ;'
     karl orþ of kvaþ : 'knákak segja
     aptr ævagi :   þú ert, ölþr ! of heitt.

34. (30) Þat's til kostar, ef koma mættiþ
     út ór óru   ölkjól hofi.'
     Týr leitaþi   tysvar hrœra,
     stóþ at hváru hverr kyrr fyrir.

33.—þu ert ölþr of het, **R** ; heitt, **A** (*þ.þt. of* heita, *to brew*), *Sv. G. L. C. J.*
B. suggests þui er áþr of hét, *Gv. B. S.*

28. Then the Thunderer rose,   laid hold on the stem,
    he landed the boat   with the water therein,
    and the ocean-swine,   with the baler and oars
    himself he bore   to the giant's home.

29. But still the Jötun,   stubborn as ever,
    questioned anew   the Thunderer's might.
    'I deem none strong,   row he ne'er so well,
    save he who hath power   to break my cup.'

30. Then the Storm god, swift,   when it came to his hands
    dashed into pieces   a pillar of stone:
    yea, sitting, he hurled   the cup through the columns
    but whole 'twas borne   to Hymir again.

31. At length the fair mistress   with friendly words
    made known the secret   she only knew:
    'Strike at Hymir's skull,   the food-filled giant's,
    'tis harder than ever   a wine cup was.'

32. Then rose to his knees   the strong Lord of goats,
    and girt him with all   the might of the gods;
    still sound above   was the head of Hymir,
    shattered below   was the shapely wine cup.

Hymir.

33. 'Gone already   I trow is my treasure,
    when I see the cup   now cast by thee kneeling.'
    So spake the churl—   "I can say never more,
    'Ale in my cauldron   now art thou brewed.'"

34. 'But 'tis yet to prove   if ye can bear
    the mighty vessel   forth from our court.'—
    Twice in vain   sought Tyr to move it;
    ever unstirred   the cauldron stood.

35. (31) Faþir Móþa   fekk á þremi
ok í gögnum sté   golf niþr í sal ;
hófsk á haufuþ   hver Sifjar verr,
en á hǽlum   hringar skullu.

36. (32) Fórut lengi,   áþr líta nam
aptr Óþins sunr   einu sinni :
sá ór hreysum   meþ Hymi austan
folkdrótt fara   fjölhöfþaþa.

37. (33) Hófsk af herþum   hver standandi,
veifþi Mjöllni   morþgjörnum fram ;
. . . .
ok hraunhvali   hann alla drap.

38. (34) Fórut lengi,   áþr liggja nam
hafr Hlórriþa   halfdauþr fyrir ;
vas skǽr sökuls   skakkr á beini :
þvi enn lǽvísi   Loki of olli.

39. (35) En ér heyrt hafiþ   —hverr kann of þat
goþmálugra   görr at skilja ?—
hver af hraunbua   hann laun of fekk,
es bǽþi galt   börn sín fyrir.

40. (36) Þróttöflugr kvam   á þing goþa
ok hafþi hver   þanns Hymir átti ;
en vear hverjan   vel skulu drekka
ölþr at Ægis   eitt hörmeitiþ.

38.—Skǽr, *Gv. R. S. H. J.;* skirr, **R A**, *Hl.*   40.—Eitt hörmeitiþ, **R A**, *B. Hl. K. D. S. Sv. Gv.*, a doubtful word ; eitr hörmeiti, *J. Thorkelsson, G.*

35. Then the Father of Wrath   laid hold on the rim
    and heaved the cauldron   high on his head,
    against his heels   the handles clinked,
    as across the hearth   he strode down the hall.

36. Far had they fared   ere Odin's son
    had turned him once,   to look behind
    and eastward saw   from the cairns forthcoming
    with Hymir, a war-host   hundred headed.

37. From his shoulders raised he   the resting cauldron,
    swung he Mjöllnir,   death-craving hammer,
    and the monsters all   from the mountains slew.

38. But they fared not far   ere the Thunderer's goat
    had laid him down   half dead in the way;
    for lame in the leg   was the shaft-bound steed,—
    'twas the work of Loki,   crafty in wiles.

39. But ye have heard—   for who knows it better
    of sages learned   in the lore of the gods?—
    what amends   made the dweller in wastes,
    who paid to the Thunderer   both his bairns.

40. Swelling with might   to the meeting of gods
    came Thor with the cauldron   which Hymir had owned,
    and the Holy Ones ever   shall well drink ale
    each harvest of flax   in the Sea-god's hall.

35.—Wrath *or* Módi. *This son is mentioned in Vm. st. 51.* 39.—The dweller in wastes, *or mountain giant (presumably Egil), belongs to another story of Thor's adventures in Jötunheim; see Introd.*

ÞRYMSKVIÞA.

1.   Vreiþr vas Vingþórr   es váknaþi
      ok síns hamars   of saknaþi;
      skegg nam hrista,   skör nam dýja,
      réþ Jarþar burr   umb at þreifask.

2.   Auk þat orþa   alls fyrst of kvaþ:
      'Heyr nú, Loki!   hvat nú mǽlik,
      es engi veit   jarþar hvergi
      né upphimins: áss's stolinn hamri!'

3.   Gengu fagra   Freyju túna,
      ok hann þat orþa   alls fyrst of kvaþ:
      'Muntu mer, Freyja!   fjaþrhams lea,
      ef minn hamar   mǽttak hitta?'

THE LAY OF THRYM.

1.   Wroth was the Thunderer   when he awakened
    aud missed his hammer,   the mighty Mjöllnir.
    His beard was quivering,   his locks were shivering,—
    as he groped around him—   the Son of Earth.

2.   'List now, Loki,   to this I shall tell thee !'—
    these, first of all   his words, he spake—
    'no wight in high heaven   or earth yet weens it :—
    The god of Thunder   is reft of his hammer.'

3.   Then sought they the shining .   halls of Freyja,
    and these, first of all   his words, spake Thor :
    'Wilt thou, Freyja,   lend me thy feather-coat,
    that perchance I may   find my hammer ?'

1.—Mjöllnir, *the* Crusher, *Thor's thunder hammer ; see Vm.* 51, Ls. *st.* 57.
Earth, *or* Jord, *a wife of Odin ; see Ls. st.* 26, Hrbl. *56.*

Freyja kvaþ :

4.   'Munda ek gefa þér   þót væri ór golli,
        ok þó selja   at væri ór silfri.'
        Fló þá Loki,   fjaþrhamr dunþi,
        unz fyr útan kvam   ása garþa
        ok fyr innan kvam   jötna heima.

5. (4) Þrymr sat á haugi,   þursa dróttinn,
        greyjum sínum   gollbönd snöri
        ok mörum sínum   mön jafnaþi.

Þrymr kvaþ :

6. (5) 'Hvat's meþ ásum,   hvat's meþ ölfum ?
        hví'st einn kominn   í jötunheima ? '

Loki kvaþ :

        'Illt's meþ ásum,   illt's meþ ölfum !
        hefr Hlórriþa   hamar of folginn ? '

Þrymer kvaþ :

7. (6) 'Ek hefi Hlórriþa   hamar of folginn
        átta röstum   fyr jörþ neþan ;
        hann engi maþr   aptr of heimtir,
        nema fóeri mér   Freyju at kvæn.'

8. (7) Fló þá Loki,   fjaþrhamr dunþi,
        unz fyr útan kvam   jötna heima
        ok fyr innan kvam   ása garþa ;
        móetti Þóri   miþra garþa,
        ok hann þat orþa   alls fyrst of kvaþ :

9. (8) 'Hefr eyrindi   sem erfiþi ?
        segþu á lopti   löng tíþindi !
        opt sitjanda   sögur of fallask
        ok liggjandi   lygi of bellir.'

4.—*The strophe numbering of* **R** *is marked in brackets.*

Freyja.

4. 'I would give it thee   though 'twere golden,
   still would I grant it   though 'twere silver!'
   Away flew Loki,—   the feather-coat rustled,—
   till he came without   the dwellings of Asgarth,
   came within   the Jötun realms.

5. Thrym sat on a mound,   the lord of giants,
   for his grayhounds twisting   golden circlets,
   smoothing over   the manes of his steeds.

Thrym.

6. 'How do the gods fare?   how do the elves fare?
   Why alone art come   into Jötunheim?'

Loki.

   'Ill do the gods fare,   ill do the elves fare.
   Speak! hast thou hidden   the Thunderer's hammer?'

Thrym.

7. 'Yea, I have hidden   the Thunderer's hammer
   eight miles under,   deep in the earth:
   and never a being   back shall win it
   till he bring me   as bride fair Freyja.'

8. Away flew Loki,   the feather-coat rustled,
   till he came without   the realms of the Jötuns,
   came within   the garths of the gods.
   There 'midst the courts   the Thunderer met he,
   and these, first of all   his words, spake Thor.

9. 'Hast thou had issue   meet for thy labour?
   Tell out aloft   and at length thy tidings.
   For oft when sitting   a tale is broken;
   oft when resting   a lie is spoken.'

5.—Thrym's *name, like that of other Jötuns, signifies* noise; *see Vm. st. 29.*

S

Loki kvaþ :

10. (9) 'Hefk erfiþi   ok eyrindi :
Þrymr hefr hamar,   þursa dróttinn ;
hann engi maþr   aptr of heimtir,
nema hánum féri   Freyju at kvǽn.'

11.   Gengu fagra   Freyju at hitta,
ok hann þat orþa   alls fyrst of kvaþ :
'Bitt þik, Freyja !   brúþar líni,
vit skulum aka tvau   í jötunheima.'

12.   Vreiþ varþ Freyja   ok fnásaþi,
allr ása salr   undir bifþisk,
stökk þat et mikla   men Brísinga :
'Mik veizt verþa   vergjarnasta,
ef ekk meþ þér   í jötunheima.'

13.   Senn váru ǽsir   allir á þingi
ok ásynjur   allar á máli,
ok of þat réþu   ríkir tívar,
hvé Hlórriþa   hamar of sétti.

14.   Þá kvaþ Heimdallr,   hvítastr ása—
vissi vel fram   sem vanir aþrir—:
Bindum Þór þa   brúþar líni,
hafi et mikla   men Brísinga !

15.   Látum und hánum   hrynja lukla
ok kvennváþir   of kné falla,
en á brjósti   breiþa steina,
ok hagliga   of höfuþ typpum !'

16.   Þá kvaþ þat Þorr,   þrúþugr áss :
'Mik munu ǽsir   argan kalla,
ef bindask létk   brúþar líni.'

Loki.

10. 'I have had toil   and issue also.
  Thrym has thy hammer,   lord of giants:
  never a being   back shall win it
  till he bring him   as bride fair Freyja.'

11. Forthwith went they   to find fair Freyja,
  and these, first of all   his words, spake Thor:
  'Bind thee, Freyja,   in bridal linen,
  we twain must drive   into Jötunheim.'

12. Wroth then was Freyja;   fiercely she panted;
  the halls of Asgarth   all trembled under,
  burst that mighty   necklet of Brisings.
  'Know me to be   most wanton of women
  if I drive with thee   into Jötunheim.'

13. Straight were gathered   all gods at the doomstead;
  goddesses all were   in speech together;
  and the mighty Powers   upon this took counsel,
  how the Thunderer's hammer   they should win again.

14. Spake then Heimdal,   of gods the fairest;—
  even as the Wanes   could he see far forward—
  'Come bind we Thor   in bridal linen,
  let him wear the mighty   Brisinga-men.

15. Let us cause the keys   to jingle under him,
  weeds of a woman   to dangle round him,
  and over his breast   lay ample jewels,
  and daintily let us   hood his head.'

16. Spake the Thunderer   of gods the sturdiest:
  'Womanish then   the Powers will call me
  if I let me be bound   in bridal linen.'

12.—Necklet of Brisings. *This famous mythological treasure, called* **Brisinga-men,** *like many others, was won from the dwarfs; see Introd.*

17.   Þá kvaþ þat Loki,   Laufeyjar sunr :
             ' Þegi þú, Þórr !   þeira orþa :
             þegar munu jötnar   Ásgarþ bua,
             nema þinn hamar   þér of heimtir.'

18.   Bundu Þór þá   bruþar líni
             auk enu miklu   meni Brísinga.

19. (18)   Létu und hánum   hrynja lukla
             ok kvennváþir   of kné falla,
             en á brjósti   breiþa steina,
             ok hagliga   of höfuþ typþu.

20. (19)   Þá kvaþ þat Loki,   Laufeyjar sunr :
             ' Munk auk meþ þér   ambátt vesa,
             vit skulum aka tvær   í jötunheima.'

21. (20)   Senn váru hafrar   heim of vreknir,
             skyndir at sköklum,   skyldu vel rinna :
             björg brotnuþu,   brann jörþ loga,
             ók Óþins sunr   í jötunheima.

22. (21)   Þa kvaþ þat Þrymr,   þursa dróttinn :
             ' Standiþ upp, jötnar !   ok straiþ bekki :
             nú fœriþ mér   Freyju at kvæn,
             Njarþar dóttur   ór Noatúnum.

23. (22)   Ganga hér at garþi   gollhyrndar kýr,
             öxn alsvartir,   jotni at gamni :
             fjölþ ák meiþma,   fjölþ ák menja,
             einnar Freyju   ávant þykkjumk.'

24. (23)   Vas þar at kveldi   of komit snimma
             auk fyr jötna   öl fram borit ;
             einn át oxa,   átta laxa,
             krásir allar   þærs konur skyldu,
             drakk Sifjar verr   sáld þriu mjaþar.

22.—Fœriþ, **R** ; fœra, *B. G. H. S. J.*

17. Spake then Loki,   the son of Laufey:
   'Silence, Thor!   with words so witless!
   Soon shall the Jötuns   dwell in Asgarth
   unless thou get thee   again thy hammer.'

18. Then bound they Thor   in bridal linen,
   eke with the mighty   Brisinga-men.

19. They caused the keys   to jingle under him,
   weeds of a woman   to dangle round him,
   and over his breast   laid ample jewels
   and daintily   they hooded his head.

20. Spake then Loki,   the son of Laufey:
   'I will fare with thee   as thy serving-maiden:
   we twain will drive into Jötunheim.'

21. Forthwith the goats   were homeward driven,
   sped to the traces,—   well must they run!
   Rent were the mountains,   earth was aflame;
   fared Odin's son   into Jötunheim.

22. Spake then Thrym,   the lord of giants:
   'Stand up, Jötuns!   and strew the benches!
   Now shall ye bring me   as bride fair Freyja,
   daughter of Njörd,   from Noatun.

23. 'Golden-horned kine   are found in my dwellings
   and oxen all swarthy,   the joy of the giant.
   I own many treasures   I rule many riches,
   and Freyja alone   to me seems lacking.'

24. Swiftly drew   the day to evening,
   borne was the ale cup   forth to the Jötuns,
   Thor ate an ox   and eight whole salmon,
   with dainties all   as should a damsel,
   three full cups   of mead he quaffed.

17.—Loki, *see Ls. and Introd.* Laufey, *or Leaf-isle, Loki's mother; also called Nâl, or Pine-needle, by Snorri.*

25. (24) Þá kvaþ þat Þrymr, þursa dróttinn:
'Hvar sátt brúþir bíta hvassara?
sákak brúþir bíta breiþara,
né enn meira mjöþ mey of drekka.

26. (35) Sat en alsnotra ambátt fyrir,
es orþ of fann viþ jötuns máli:
'Át vætr Freyja átta náttum,
svá vas óþfús í jötunheima.'

27. (26) Laut und línu, lysti at kyssa,
en útan stökk endlangan sal:
'Hví 'ru öndótt augu Freyju?
þykkjumk ór augum *eldr* of brinna.'

28. (27) Sat en alsnotra ambátt fyrir,
es orþ of fann viþ jötuns máli:
'Svaf vætr Freyja átta náttum,
svá vas óþfús í jötunheima.'

29. (28) Inn kvam en arma jötna systir,
hins brúþfear biþja þorþi:
'Lát þér af höndum hringa rauþa,
ef öþlask vill ástir mínar
ástir mínar alla hylli.'

30. (29) Þa kvaþ þat Þrymr, þursa dróttinn:
'Beriþ inn hamar brúþi at vígja,
leggiþ Mjöllni í meyjar kné,
vígiþ okkr saman Várar hendi!'

31. (30) Hló Hlórriþa hugr í brjósti,
es harþhugaþr hamar of þekþi;
Þrym drap fyrstan, þursa dróttin,
ok ætt jötuns alla lamþi.

27.—Eldr, *a word missing in* R *supplied by paper MSS.*

25. Spake then Thrym,   the lord of giants,
'Didst ever see damsel   eat so bravely?
Ne'er have I seen one   bite so boldly,
nor a maiden quaff   more cups of mead!'

26. All crafty sat by   the serving-maiden,
who answer found   to the giant's asking:
'Nought has Freyja   these eight nights eaten,
so sore her yearning   for Jötunheim.'

27. Stooped then Thrym   'neath the veil, to kiss her,
back he leapt   the hall's whole length:
'Why are fair Freyja's   eyes so fearful?
Meseems from those eyes   a fire is flaming.'

28. All crafty sat by   the serving-maiden,
who answer found   to the giant's asking:
'Not a whit has Freyja   these eight nights slumbered,
so sore her yearning   for Jötunheim.'

29. In came the wretched   sister of Jötuns
and dared to beg   for a bridal token:
'Take the red rings   from off thy fingers
if thou wilt win thee   mine affection,
mine affection,   all my favour!'

30. Spake then Thrym,   the lord of giants:
'Bring in the hammer,   the bride to hallow.
Mjöllnir lay   on the knee of the maiden!
Hallow us twain   with the hand of the Troth-goddess!'

31. Laughed in his breast   the heart of the Thunderer;
strong was his soul   when he spied his hammer.
He first smote Thrym,   the lord of giants,
and all the Jötun's   kindred crushed.

27.—Eyes so fearful. *When Thor was angry he let his bushy brows drop over his eyes "so that you could scarce get a glimpse of them" (Snorri).* 30.—Thor *was called on by the old Norse peasants to bless their marriage feasts with his hammer.* Troth-goddess, *or Var, was the guardian of oaths and plightings.*

32. (31) Drap ena öldnu   jötna systur
          hinas brúþfear   of beþit hafþi:
          hón skell of hlaut fyr skillinga,
          en högg hamars   fyr hringa fjölþ.

    (32) Sva kvam Óþins sunr   endr at hamri.

32. Smote he the ancient   sister of Jötuns,—
her who had begged   for a bridal token.
She got but a stroke   in the place of shillings;
Mjöllnir's mark   and never a ring.

And thus Thor won him   again his hammer.

SKIRNISMÁL.

Freyr sonr Njarþar hafþi einn dag sez í Hliþskjálf ok sá um heima alla; hann sá í jötunheima ok sá þar mey fagra, þá er hon gekk frá skála föþur síns til skemmu. Þar af fekk hann hugsóttir miklar. Skirnir hét skósveinn Freys; Njörþr baþ hann kveþa Frey máls. Þá mælti Skaþi:

1. 'Rís nú, Skirnir!   ok gakk at beiþa
       okkarn mála mög,
   ok þess at fregna,   hveim enn fróþi sé
       ofreiþi afi.'

Skirnismál.—In **R**, No. 5; st. 1-27 in **A**.

THE STORY OF SKIRNIR.

Once Frey, son of Njörd, had seated himself on Window-shelf, and was gazing out over all worlds. When he looked into Jötunheim he beheld a fair maiden going from her father's hall to the bower, and at the sight of her he was seized with great sickness of heart.

Now Frey's servant was called Skirnir, and Njörd bade him ask speech of his master; and Skadi, wife of Njörd, said:—

1.   Rise, bright Skirnir!   run thou swiftly,
     and beseech our son to speak:
   ask the wise youth   to answer thee this,
    'gainst whom his wrath is aroused.

Frey, *see Introd. and Ls., st. 42.*   Njörd, *see Ls., st. 34.*   Window-shelf, *Odin's high seat.*   Skirnir's *name means the* Light-bringer.

Skirnir kvaþ:

2. 'Illra orþa　　　erumk ón at ykrum syni,
　　　ef gengk at mæla viþ mög,
　　ok þess at fregna,　　hveim enn fróþi sé
　　　ofreiþi afi.'

Skirnir kvaþ:

3. 'Segþu þat, Freyr,　　folkvaldi goþa!
　　　auk ek vilja vita:
　　hví einn sitr　　endlanga sali,
　　　minn dróttinn! of daga?'

Freyr kvaþ:

4. 'Hvi of segjak þér,　　seggr enn ungi!
　　　mikinn móþtrega?
　　þvít alfröþull　　lýsir of alla daga,
　　　ok þeygi at mínum munum.'

Skirnir kvaþ:

5. 'Muni þína　　hykkak svá mikla vesa,
　　　at mér, seggr! né segir;
　　þvít ungir saman　　várum í árdaga,
　　　vel mættim tveir truask.'

Freyr kvaþ:

6. 'Í Gymis görþum　　ek sá ganga
　　　mér tíþa mey;
　　armar lýstu,　　en af þaþan
　　　allt lopt ok lögr.

7. Mær's mér tíþari　　an manni hveim
　　　ungum í árdaga;
　　ása ok alfa　　þat vil engi maþr,
　　　at vit samt sém.

Skirnir.

2. If I seek for speech   with him, your son,
     ill words I shall haply win,
if I ask the wise youth   to answer me this,
     'gainst whom his wrath is aroused.

(Skirnir (to Frey).

3. Tell me truly, Frey,   thou ruler of gods,
     what I fain would learn from thy lips:
why sitt'st thou lone   in the hall, my lord,
     lingering the live-long day?

Frey.

4. How shall I ever   own to thee, youth,
     the great heart's burden I bear?
the Elf-light shines   each day the same,
     but works not yet my will.

Skirnir.

5. Scarce are the longings   of thy love so great
     but I trow thou canst tell them to me;
we were young together   in days of yore,
     we twain may well trust each other.

Frey.

6. In the courts of Gymir,   the frost-giant, saw I
     that maiden most dear to me;
light shone out   from her arms and thence
     all the air and sea were ashine.

7. She is dearer to me   than ever was maiden
     to youth in days of yore:
but none among all   the gods and elves
     hath willed that we twain should wed.

4.—Elf-light, *a name for the sun from its power over dwarfs or elves; see Alv.,* st. 16.

Skírnir kvaþ:

8. 'Mar gef mér þá,　　þanns mik of myrkvan beri
　　　vísan vafrloga,
　　ok þat sverþ,　　es sjalft vegisk
　　† viþ jötna ǽtt.'

Freyr kvaþ:

9. 'Mar þér þann gefk,　　es þik of myrkvan berri
　　　vísan vafrloga,
　　ok þat sverþ,　　es sjalft mun vegask,
　　ef sá's horskr es hefr.'

Skírnir mælti viþ hestinn:

10. 'Myrkt es úti,　　mál kveþk okkr fara
　　　úrig fjöll yfir,
　　þursa þjóþ yfir;
　　báþir vit komumk,　　eþa okkr báþa tekr
　　enn ámátki jötunn.'

Skírnir reiþ í jötunheima til Gymis garþa.　Þar váru hundar ólmir ok bundnir fyr skíþsgarþs hliþi þess er um sal Gerþar var.　Hann reiþ at þar er féhirþir sat á haugi ok kvaddi hann:

11. 'Seg þat, hirþir!　　es þu á haugi sitr
　　　ok varþar alla vega:
　　hve at andspilli　　komumk ens unga mans
　　fyr greyjum Gymis?'

Hirþir kvaþ:

12. 'Hvárt est feigr　　eþa estu framgenginn,
　　. . . . . . . ?
　　andspillis vanr　　þú skalt ǽ vesa
　　góþrar meyjar Gymis.'

Skirnir.

8. Give me steed to bear me   safe through the dim
    enchanted flickering flame,
and the sword which wages   war of itself
    'gainst the fearful Jötun folk.

Frey.

9. Here is steed to bear thee   safe through the dim
    enchanted flickering flame,
and the sword which wages   war of itself,
    if he who bears it be bold.

Skirnir (speaking to the horse).

10. Dark 'tis without!   'tis time, I ween,
    to fare o'er the dewy fells:
'mid the throng of giants   we shall both win through,
    or the awful Jötun have both.

Then Skirnir rode into Jötunheim to the dwellings of Gymir, where fierce dogs were chained up before the gate of the enclosure which surrounded Gerd's hall. He rode up to a herdsman who was sitting on a mound, and said :—

11. Speak, thou herdsman,   who sitt'st on a mound
    and watchest every way!
How, for Gymir's hounds,   shall I e'er hold speech
    with that Jötun's youthful maid?

Herdsman.

12. Either doomed art thou,   or one of the dead
    going forth to the halls of Hel!
never a word   shalt thou win, I ween,
    with Gymir's goodly maid.

8, 9.—The sword, *see Ls., st. 42; Vsp., st. 53.*   12.—Going forth to the halls
of Hel, *see Introd. to Bdr.*

Skirnir kvaþ :

13. 'Kostir'u betri   heldr an at klökkva sé
        hveims fúss es fara ;
      einu dœgri   vörumk aldr of skapaþr
      ok allt líf of lagit.'

Gerþr kvaþ :

14. 'Hvat's þat hlymja   es ek hlymja heyri til
        ossum rönnum í ?
      jörþ bifask,   en allir fyrir
      skjalfa garþar Gymis.'

Ambótt kvaþ :

15. 'Maþr's hér úti,   stiginn af mars baki,
      jó lætr til jarþar taka.'

Gerþr kvaþ :

16. 'Inn biþ hann ganga   í okkarn sal
        ok drekka enn mæra mjöþ ;
      þo ek hitt oumk,   at hér úti sé
      minn bróþurbani.'

Gerþr kvaþ :

17. 'Hvat's þat alfa   né ása suna
        né víssa vana ?
      hvi einn of kvamt   eikinn fúr yfir
      ór salkynni at sea ?'

Skirnir kvaþ :

18. 'Emkak alfa   né ása suna
        né víssa vana :
      þó einn of kvamk   eikinn fúr yfir
      yþur salkynni at sea.

Skirnir.

13. A wiser choice   than to whine makes he
     who is ready to run his race :
my time was set   to a certain day
     and my length of life decreed.

Gerd (within the hall).

14. What is the clanking   and clashing of sounds
     which echoing I hear in our halls ?
Trembles the earth   and before it all
     the courts of Gymir are shook.

A Serving-maid.

15. See ! A man without !   He is sprung from his steed,
     which he now lets graze on the grass.

Gerd.

16. Bid him come in ;   let him enter our halls,
     let him quaff the glorious mead !
Yet I fear me much   lest that man without
     the slayer of my brother should be.

Gerd to Skirnir (who has entered).

17. Who comes, nor of elves'   nor of gods' race seeming,
     nor yet of the all-wise Wanes ?
why hast fared alone   through the raging fire
     to visit the folk in our halls ?

Skirnir.

18. I come, nor of elves'   nor of gods' race am I,
     nor yet of the all-wise Wanes ;
yet have I fared   through the raging fire
     to visit the folk in your halls.

16.—Slayer of my brother. *Frey slew the giant Beli, who was perhaps Gerd's brother ; but, according to Snorri, this was after the loss of his sword, for he used a stag's horn ; see Vsp., st. 53.*

U

19. Eleven apples all golden have I:
these will I give thee, Gerth,
to win thy heart that from henceforth Frey
be deemed thy dearest in life.

Gerth.

20. Not the eleven will I take these eleven apples
at the will of any wight,
nor will we twain live, Frey and I,
together while life shall last.

Skirnir.

21. Then a ring I offer thee, once 'twas burned
with Othin's youthful son:
it lets fall ever eight golden rings
of a like weight each ninth night.

Gerth.

22. No ring do I want, though once 'twas burned
with Othin's youthful son.
Gold is not lacking in Gymir's courts,
nor my father's riches to rule.

Skirnir.

23. Seest thou this sword, maiden, slender, rune-graven,
which here I hold in my hand?
Thy head will I hew from off thy neck,
if thou speak not soon thy consent.

Gerth.

24. It shall ne'er befall me to suffer force
to the will of any wight.
I ween if thou meet'st with Gymir in war
that fiercely ye twain will fight.

19—Apples all golden. These were the products of Idun; see Lokasol, 7 n. 21. A ring, Draupnir, the dropper, which was forged for Othin by the dwarfs, was burned with Baldr; see Lokasol, 22 n. and v. 30.

Skirnir kvaþ:

25. 'Sér þú þenna mæki, mær!   mjóvan, málfán,
    es hefk í hendi hér?
    fyr þessum eggjum   hnígr sa enn aldni jötunn,
    verþr þinn feigr faþir.

26. Tamsvendi þik drepk,   en ek þik temja mun,
    mær! at mínum munum;
    þar skalt ganga,   es þik gumna synir
    síþan æva sea.

27. Ara þúfu á   skaltu ár sitja,
    horfa [heimi ór, snugga] heljar til;
    matr sé þer leiþari   an manna hveim
    enn fráni ormr meþ firum.

28. At undrsjónum verþir,   es þú út kömr,
    á þik Hrimnir hari,
    á þik hotvetna stari;
    viþkunnari verþir   an vörþr meþ goþum;
    gapi þú grindum frá.

29. (30) Tramar gneypa   þik skulu görstan dag
    jötna görþum í;
    til hrímþursa hallar   þú skalt hverjan dag
    kranga kostalaus,
    kranga kostavön.
    grát at gamni   skaltu í gögn hafa,
    ok leiþa meþ tárum trega.

30. (31) Meþ þursi þríhöfþuþum   þú skalt æ nara
    eþa verlauss vesa;
    þitt geþ grípi,   þik morn morni!
    ves sem þistill   sás þrunginn vas
    í önn ofanverþa.

29.—*The strophe arrangement of* **R A** *is marked in brackets.*   30.—þitt, **R**, *Dt.*
Hl.; þik, *B. G. H. S.*

Skirnir.

25. See'st thou this sword, maiden,   slender, rune-graven,
      which here I hold in my hand?
  Before its keen edge   shall fall that old Giant,—
      thy father is doomed to death.

26. With a taming wand   I will touch thee, maid!
      and win thee soon to my will.
  I will send thee far off   where thou shalt be seen
      never more by the sons of men.

27. On an eagle's mound   shalt thou sit from morn,
      gazing out of the world toward Hel:
  thy food shall seem loathlier   than bright-hued serpent
      seemed ever to man among men.

                                        [on thee,
28. Sight of wonder when thou walkest,   all beings shall stare
      and the Frost Giant fix thee with his eye!
  Known wider than Heimdal   the Watchman of gods,
      thou shalt gape through the gates of Hel.

29. Trolls shall torment thee   from morn till eve
      in the realms of the Jötun race,
  each day to the dwellings   of Frost giants must thou
      creep helpless, creep hopeless of love;
  thou shalt weeping have   in the stead of joy,
      and sore burden bear with tears.

30. With a three-headed giant   must thou abide
      or lack ever husband in life.
  Care shall lay hold   on thy heart and mind,
      thou shalt waste with mourning away,
  as a thistle shalt be   which hath thrust itself up
      in the latter season full late.

27.—An eagle, Corpse-swallower, *who sits at the end of heaven; Vm., st. 37.*
30.—The latter season, *so Dt. Hl. Others,* a loft, under the roof.

31. (35) Hrímgrimnir heitir þurs   es þik hafa skal
           fyr nágrindr neþan:
           þar þér vílmegir   á viþar rótum
           geita hland gefi:
  (36) œþri drykkju   fá þú aldrigi,
           mær! af þínum munum,
           mær! at mínum munum!

32. (29) Tópi ok ópi,   tjösull ok óþoli
           vaxi þér tár meþ trega;
           sezktu niþr,   mun ek segja þér
           sváran súsbreka
           ok tvinnan trega.

33. Vreiþr's þér Óþinn   vreiþr's þér ása bragr,
           þik skal Freyr fiask,
           en firinilla mær!   es þú fengit hefr
           gambanvreiþi goþa.

34. Heyri hrímþursar,   heyri jötnar,
           Suttunga synir,
           sjalfir ásliþar:
           hvé fyrbýþk,   hvé fyrbannak
           manna glaum mani,
           manna nyt mani.

35. (32) Til holts èk gekk   ok til hrás viþar,
           gambantein at geta:
      . . . .
           gambantein ek gat.

31. The Frost-hooded giant   shall hold thee fast
     beneath the doors of the dead;
at the tree's roots there   shall wretched thralls
     give thee foul water of goats;
and other draught   shalt thou never drink,
     at thy wish, maiden, with my will, maid.

32. Sit thee down! I will further   woes two-fold bespeak thee,
     a whelming wave of care.
May madness and shrieking,   bondage and yearning,
     burden thee, with trouble and tears.

33. Wroth is Odin!   Wroth is the Thunderer!
     Frey too shall hate thee, I trow:
thou evil maiden,   well hast thou earned
     the awful anger of the gods!

34. Hear now, Jötuns,   Frost-giants hear me,
     Suttung's sons 'neath the earth,
ye god-folk, too!   how I ban and forbid
     man's love to the maiden, man's joy to the maid.

35. I went to the forest   to find and fetch
     a magic wand of might;
to a green-wood tree,   and I got me there
     this mighty magic wand.

31.—At the tree's roots. *Presumably Yggdrasil's root stretching over Jötunheim;* (*Nd. D.Alt. xxx.*). 33.—Thunderer. *Thor is here called* prince of gods. *These three—Odin, Thor, and Frey—are usually ranked together, and appear as the chief gods in temple worship.* 34.—Sutting, *a giant of the underworld; see Háv., st. 102.* 35.—A green-wood tree, *see Háv., st. 150.*

36. (36) Þurs rístk þér   ok þria stafi:
        ergi ok œþi ok óþola;
    svá ek þat af ríst,   sem ek þat á reist,
        ef görvask þarfar þess.'

Gerþr kvaþ:

37.   'Heill ves heldr, sveinn!   ok tak viþ hrímkalki
        fullum forns mjaþar:
    þó hafþak ætlat,   at myndak aldrigi
        unna vaningja vel.'

Skirnir kvaþ:

38.   'Eyrindi mín   viljak öll vita,
        áþr ríþak heim heþan:
    nær þu at þingi   munt enum þroska
        nenna Njarþar syni.'

Gerþr kvaþ:

39.   'Barri heitir,   es vit bæþi vitum,
        lundr lognfara:
    en ept nætr niu   þar mun Njarþar syni
        Gerþr unna gamans.'

Þá reiþ Skirnir heim. Freyr stóþ úti ok kvaddi hann ok spurþi
tíþinda:

40.   'Seg mer þat, Skirnir!   áþr verpir söþli af mar
        ok stígir feti framarr:
    hvat þu árnaþir   í jötunheima
        þíns eþa míns munar?'

36. I have cut thee a giant,   and carved thee three staves,
    lust and raving and rage.
  Even as I cut them on   so can I cut them off,
    if haply I have the will.

(Gerd offers him a foaming cup.)

37. Be gracious rather, youth!   Take now this rimy cup
    filled with famous old mead.
  Little I thought   that ever in life
    I should love a Waneling well.

Skirnir.

38. All my errand   will I know to the end
    before I ride homeward hence.
  When wilt thou, maiden,   meet at the trysting
    the stalwart son of Njörd?

Gerd.

39. Pine-needle is the wood   of peaceful faring,
    we twain know well the way:
  there shall Gerd bestow   on the son of Njörd
    her heart's love nine nights hence.

Then Skirnir rode home. Frey was standing without, and he greeted him and asked for tidings.

Frey.

40. Speak, Skirnir! Cast not   saddle from the steed,
    and stir not one step hence:
  what hast thou won   of thy will and mine
    in the realms of the Jötun race?

36.—Giant: *Icelandic* þurs. *The name of some object was given to each runic letter, and here the symbol* þ *would represent* þurs. 37.—Waneling. *Frey's father Njörd was a Wane; see Ls., st. 35; Vm., st. 39.*

X

SKIRNISMÁL.

Skirnir kvaþ:

41. 'Barri heitir,   es vit báþir vitum,
        lundr lognfara:
    en ept nǽtr niu   þar mun Njarþar syni
    Gerþr unna gamans.'

Freyr kvaþ:

42. 'Löng es nótt,   langar'u tvǽr,
        hvé of þreyjak þriar?
    opt mér mánuþr   minni þótti

Skirnir.

41. Pine-needle is the wood   of peaceful faring,
    we twain know well the way :
there shall Gerd bestow   on the son of Njörd
    her heart's love nine nights hence.

Frey.

42. Long is one night,—   long are two nights—
    how shall I live through three !
Shorter a month   has seemed to me oft
    than waiting this half night here.

GRÓUGALDR.

Svipdagr kvaþ:

1. 'Vaki þú, Groa!   vaki þú, góþ kona!
    vekk þik dauþra dura:
    ef þat mant,   at þinn mög bǽþir
    til kumbldysjar koma.'

Gróa kvaþ:

2. 'Hvat's nú ant   mínum einga syni,
    hverju 'st bölvi borinn:
    es þú móþur kallar   es til moldar es komin
    ok ór ljóþheimum liþin?'

Grógaldr.—*In paper* **MSS.** *of the seventeenth century.*

DAY-SPRING AND MENGLOD.

PART I.—The Spell-songs of Groa.

Son.

1. Wake thou, Groa,   wake, sweet woman,
    at the doors of the dead, awake!
   Thy child, thou bad'st me,   —dost thou not mind thee?—
    come to the cairn of thy grave.

Groa.

2. What sorrow grieves thee,   mine only son,
    with what burden art overborne,
   that thou callest thy mother   who is turned to dust
    and gone from the folk-world forth?

Svipdagr kvaþ :

3. 'Ljótu leikborþi   skaut fyr mik en lǽvísa kona
     sús 'faþmaþi minn föþur :
   þar baþ mik koma,   es kvǽmtki veit,
     móti Menglöþu.'

Gróa kvaþ :

4. 'Löng es för,   langir'u farvegar,
     langir'u manna munir ;
   ef þat verþr,   at þu þinn vilja bíþr,
     ok skeikar þó Skuldar at sköpum.'

Svipdagr kvaþ :

5. 'Galdra mer gal   þás góþir'u,
     · bjarg þú, móþir ! megi :
   á vegum allr   hykk at ek verþa muna,
     þykkjumk til ungr afi.'

Gróa kvaþ :

6. 'Þann gelk þér fyrstan,   þann kveþa fjölnýtan,
     þann gól Rindr Rani :
   at of öxl skjótir   þvís þér atalt þykkir ;
     sjalfr leiþ sjalfan þik !

7. Þann gelk þér annan,   ef þú árna skalt
     viljalauss á vegum :
   Urþar lokur   haldi þér öllum megum,
     es þu á smán sér !

8. Þann gelk þer enn þriþja,   ef þér þjóþaar
     falla at fjörlotum :
   til heljar heþan   snuisk Horn ok Ruþr,
     en þverri ǽ fyr þér.

3.—Kvǽmtki, B. G. S. Gv. J.; kveþki, **MSS.**   4.—Menglöþu, *a proper name* G. B. Gv. S. C.; menglöþu(m), **MSS.**, K. R. M. Hl. J.   7.—Á smán, **MSS.**, Dt. *and* Hl.; á sinnum, Gv. G. S.   8.—Fjörlotum, **MSS.**, Hl. J., *life-spring—from* fjör, *life, and* lota, *energy ;* Fjör-lokum, B. Gv. S. G.

Son.

3. A fearful task   hath that false woman set me,
    who fondly my father hath clasped :
  she hath sent me where none   may go, to seek
    the gay-necklaced maiden Menglod.

Groa.

4. Long is the faring,   long are the pathways,
    long are the loves of men :
  well it may be   that thou gain thy will,
    but the end must follow fate.

Son.

5. Sing me spell-songs,   sweet and strong ones !
    Mother, shield me thy child !
  Dead on the way   I ween I shall be,
    for I feel me too young in years.

Groa.

6. I sing thee the first   —well it serves, they say—
    which Rindr sang to Ran :
  be thy burden too heavy,   may it fall from thy back
    and may self lead self at will.

7. I sing thee the second :   if haply thou strayest
    joyless on journeys far,
  may the web of Weird   be around thy way
    and save thee from shameful plight.

8. I sing thee the third :   if mighty streams
    with their waters o'erwhelm thy life,
  may those floods of Hel   flow back, and dry
    be the paths before thy feet.

6.—Rindr, *another name for Odin as husband of the giantess Rind (Bdr., st. 11),* *who is here called Ran. Odin long wooed her in vain, and won her at last by enchant-* *ments (Saxo Grammaticus) ; cf. the same use of the masculine and feminine forms in* Fjorgynn *and* Fjorgyn ; *see Ls., st. 26.*   7.—Weird *or* Urd, *the goddess of fate ; see* *Vsp., 20.*   8.—Floods of Hel, *here called* Horn *and* Rud, *not mentioned in the list of* *the rivers which flow from* Roaring-kettle ; *see Grm., st. 28, 29.*

9.   Þann gelk þer enn fjórþa,   ef þik fiandr standa
       görvir á galgvegi :
       hugr þeim hverfi   til handa þér
       ok snuisk til sátta sefi.

10.   Þann gelk þer enn fimta,   ef þér fjöturr verþr
       borinn at boglimum :
       leysigaldr   lætk þer fyr legg of kveþinn,
       ok stökkr þá láss af limum,
       en af fótum fjöturr.

11.   Þann gelk þer enn sétta,   ef á sjó kömr
       meira an menn viti :
       lopt ok lögr   gangi þer í lúþr saman
       ok lé þer æ friþdrjúgrar farar.

12.   Þann gelk þer enn sjaunda,   ef þik sœkja kömr
       frost á fjalli há :
       hrævakulþi   megit þínu holdi fara,
       ok haldi þér lík at liþum.

13.   Þann gelk þer enn átta,   ef þik úti nemr
       nótt á niflvegi :
       at því firr megi   þér til meins görva
       kristin dauþ kona.

14.   Þann gelk þer enn niunda,   ef viþ enn naddgöfga
       orþum skiptir jötun :
       máls ok mannvits   sé þer á *munn ok* hjarta
       gnóga of gefit.

15.   Far þú nu æva   þas foraþ þikkir
       ok standit þer mein fyr munum !

     *   *   *   *   *

       á jarþföstum steini   stóþk innan dura,
       meþan þér galdra gólk.

10.—Leysigaldr, *B. Gv. S. G. J.;* leifnis elda, **MSS.**   11.—Lopt, *Gv. S. G.;*
logn, **MSS.**   14.—Munn ok, *B. Gv. S. G. C.;* minnis, **MSS.**

9.   I sing thee the fourth: if foes should lurk
          in ambush, armed for thy death,
    be their hearts forthwith   toward thee turned
          and their minds be moved to peace.

10.   I sing thee the fifth: if men make fast
          a charm on the joints of thy limbs,
    that loosening spell   which I sing o'er thy legs
          shall break fetters from hands and feet.

11.   I sing thee the sixth: if thou fare o'er seas
          mightier than men do know,
    may wind and wave for thee   work thy boat,
          and make peaceful thy path o'er the deep.

12.   I sing thee the seventh: if thou art assailed
          by frost on the rimy fell,
    may thy flesh not die   in the deadly cold;
          be thou sound in life and limb.

13.   I sing thee the eighth: if night o'ertake thee,
          wandering on the misty way,
    none the more may ghosts   of Christian women
          have power to work thy woe.

14.   I sing thee the ninth: when thou needs must stand
          in speech with that spear-famed giant,
    may words and wisdom   to lips and heart
          in abundance be bestowed.

15.   May thou ne'er be led,   where danger lurks,
          may harm not hinder thy will!

    *   *   *   *   *

    At the doors I stood,   on an earth-bound stone,
          while I sang these songs to thee.

13.—Ghosts of Christian women. *This line must have been written in heathen days, when Christianity was regarded as a mysterious power of evil.* 14.—That spear-famed giant *must be* Much-wise, *the warder of Menglod's halls.*

Y

16.   Móþur orþ   berþu, mögr! heþan
       ok lát þer í brjósti bua!
       iþgnóga heill   skalt of aldr hafa,
       meþan mín orþ of mant.'

FJÖLSVINNSMÁL

1.   Útan garþa   hann sá upp of koma
     þursa þjóþar sjöt.

Svipdagr kvaþ :

(2) 'Hvat's þat flagþa,   es stendr fyr forgörþum
    ok hvarflar umb háettan loga?'

Fjölsviþr kvaþ :

2. (1) 'Hvers þú leitar   eþa hvers á leitum est,
       eþa hvat vilt, vinlauss! vita?
       úrgar brautir   árnaþu aptr heþan!
       áttat hér, verndarvanr! veru.'

Svipdagr kvaþ :

3.   'Hvat's þat flagþa,   es stendr fyr forgarþi
     ok býþrat liþöndum löþ?
     Sæmþarorþa lauss   hefr þú, seggr! of lifat,
     ok haltu heim heþan!'

Fjölsviþr kvaþ :

4.   'Fjölsviþr ek heiti,   en ek á fróþan sefa,
     þeygi emk míns mildr matar:
     innan garþa   þú kömr aldrigi,
     ok dríf þu nú vargr at vegi!'

1.—*This transposition from* **MSS.** *made by B. Mb. Gv. C. G.*

16. Child, bear with thee   a mother's words,
     let them abide in thy breast!
Wealth enough   in life thou shalt win
     if thou keepst my counsel in mind.

PART II.—The Sayings of Much-wise.

1. Stood Day-spring without   the walls, and saw
     loom high the Jötuns' home.

Day-spring.

What monster is that   who guards the threshold,
     and prowls round the perilous flames?

Much-wise.

2. Whom dost thou seek?   Of whom art in search?
     What, friendless wight, wouldst thou learn?
Back wander hence   on thy dewy way;
     not here is thy haven, lone one!

Day-spring.

3. What monster is that   who guards the threshold
     and bids not welcome to wanderers?
Lacking all seemly   speech wert thou born;
     hence, speaker, hie thee home!

Much-wise.

4. Much-wise I am called,   for I am wise in mind,
     though none too free with my food.
Here in the courts   shalt thou never come;
     get thee hence like a wolf on thy way!

Svipdagr kvaþ :

5. 'Augna gamans　　　fýsir aptr at fá,
　　　hvars getr svást at sea :
　　garþar gloa　　　þykkjumk of gollna sali,
　　　hér mundak öþli una.'

Fjölsviþr kvaþ :

6. 'Seg mér, hverjum　　　estu, sveinn ! of borinn
　　　eþa hverra'st manna mögr ? '

Svipdagr kvaþ :

'Vindkaldr heitik,　　　Várkaldr hét minn faþir,
　þess vas Fjölkaldr faþir.

7. Seg mér þat, Fjölsviþr !　　　es ek þik fregna mun
　　　auk ek vilja vita :
　　hverr hér ráeþr　　　—ok ríki hefr—
　　　eign ok auþsölum ? '

Fjölsviþr kvaþ :

8. 'Menglöþ of heitir,　　　en hana móþir of gat
　　　viþ Svafnþorins syni :
　　hón hér ráeþr　　　—ok ríki hefr—
　　　eign ok auþsölum.'

Svipdagr kvaþ :

9 'Seg mér þat, Fjölsviþr !　　　es ek þik fregna mun
　　　auk ek vilja vita :
　　hvat sú grind heitir,　　　es meþ goþum söut
　　　menn at meira foraþ ? '

5.—Aptr at fá, *Hl. and F. adopt this conjecture on the margin of the* **MSS.** Aptr
fán, **MSS.,** *B. S. L. Gv.*　8.—Svafnþorins, *S.* Svafrþorins, *Dt. and Hl.*

Day-spring.

5. Longs the lover again for the light of his eyes,
  with his sweet-heart back in sight:
glowing are the walls of that golden hall;
  I would fain make here my home.

Much-wise.

6. Tell me, bold youth, from whom thou art sprung,
  son of what being wert born?

Day-spring.

They call me Wind-cold, the son of Spring-cold,
  whose father was Fierce-cold named.

7. Now answer me, Much-wise, this that I ask
  and fain would learn from thy lips:
who here doth rule and hold in power
  the wealth and wondrous halls?

Much-wise.

8. There is one called Menglod, who of her mother
  was born to Sleep-thorn's son:
'tis she doth rule and hold in power
  the wealth and wondrous halls.

Day-spring.

9. Now answer me, Much-wise, this that I ask
  and fain would learn from thy lips:
what is that gate called? Ne'er among gods
  was more fearful barrier found.

5.—*This strophe, like 49, suggests that Svipdagr and Menglod have met before.*

Fjölsviþr kvaþ :

10. 'Þrymgjöll hón heitir,　　en hana þrír görþu
　　　Sólblinda synir ;
　　fjöturr fastr　　verþr viþ faranda hverjan,
　　es hana hefr frá hliþi.'

Svipdagr kvaþ :

11. 'Seg mér þat, Fjölsviþr !　　es ek þik fregna mun
　　　auk ek vilja vita :
　　hvat sá garþr heitir,　　es meþ goþum söut
　　menn et meira foraþ ?'

Fjölsviþr kvaþ :

12. 'Gaststropnir heitir,　　en ek hann görvan hefk
　　　ór Leirbrimis limum ;
　　svá hefk studdan,　　at hann standa mun
　　æ meþan öld lifir.'

Svipdagr kvaþ :

13. (19) 'Seg mér þat, Fjölsviþr !　　es ek þik fregna mun
　　　auk ek vilja vita :
　　hvat þat barr heitir,　　es breiþask of
　　lönd öll limar ?'

Fjölsviþr kvaþ :

14. (20) 'Mimameiþr hann heitir,　　en þat mangi veit,
　　　hvers hann af rótum rinnr ;
　　viþ þat hann fellr,　　es fæstan varir :
　　flærat hann eldr né jarn.'

12.—Gast-stropnir, *Dt. and Hl.*; Gat-stropnir, *B. Gv. F.*; Gastropnir, most
MSS.　13-18.—*The transposition of these strophes, suggested by Möller, adopted by
S. G., gives more sequence to S.'s questions.*

Much-wise.

10. Sounding-clanger   the gate is called,
      wrought by three sons of Solblind.
   Fast is the chain   to each wanderer who seeks
      to lift that door from the latch.

Day-spring.

11. Now answer me, Much-wise,   this that I ask
      and fain would learn from thy lips:
   what is that wall named?   Ne'er among gods
      was more fearful barrier found.

Much-wise.

12. Guest-crusher 'tis called;   from the Clay-giant's limbs
      I built that barrier myself:
   so fast have I set it   that firm 'twill stand,
      for ever while life shall last.

Day-spring.

13. Now answer me, Much-wise,   this that I ask
      and fain would learn from thy lips:
   what is that tree,   which far and wide,
      spreads limbs over every land?

Much-wise.

14. 'Tis the tree of Mimir,   but no man knows
      by what roots it rises to heaven:
   'twill fall at last   by what least one weens,
      for nor fire nor weapons will wound it.

10.—Solblind *or* Sun-blinded *must be a dwarf name for one who, like All-wise (st. 35), fears the light, and whose children are forgers like Brokk and Sindri; see Vsp. 37, Grm. st. 43, and Introd.* 12.—The Clay-giant *or* Leirbrimir. *From the giant Ymir or Brimir (Vm., st. 21) was made the whole framework of earth, and the expression is only a poetical term for the solid ground.* 14.—The tree of Mimir, Yggdrasil; *see Vsp. 19, 29; Vm. 45. Mimir's well, like that of Weird, was situated beneath it, and here, in Giant-home, the tree would be called his.*

Svipdagr kvaþ :

15. (21) 'Seg mér þat, Fjölsviþr!   es ek þik fregna mun
          auk ek vilja vita :
          hvat af moþi verþr   þess ens mǽra viþar,
          es hann flǽrat eldr né jarn ?'

Fjölsviþr kvaþ :

16. (22) 'Út af hans aldni   skal á eld bera
          fyr killisjúkar konur :
          útar hverfa þess   þeirs innar skyldu,
          sás hann meþ mönnum mjötuþr.'

Svipdagr kvaþ :

17. (23) 'Seg mér þat, Fjölsviþr!   es ek þik fregna mun
          auk ek vilja vita :
          hvat sá hani heitir,   es sitr í enum háva viþi,
          allr viþ goll gloïr ?'

Fjölsviþr kvaþ :

18. (24) 'Viþofnir heitir,   en hann stendr veþrglasi
          á meiþs kvistum Mima :
          einum ekka   þryngr hann örófsaman
          Surt ok Sinmöru.'

Svipdagr kvaþ :

19. (13) 'Seg mér þat, Fjölsviþr!   es ek þik fregna mun
          auk ek vilja vita :
          hvat þeir garmar heita,   es gífrir rata
          görþum fyr . . . . . .

16.—*G.*, þess þeirs innar skyli, *S.;* þaz þǽr innar skyli, *Dt. and Hl.*
Mjötuþr, *Dt. and Hl. suggest* mjötviþr; *see Vsp.,* 2.   18.—Surt ok, *G. S. Gv.;*
surtar, *B.;* surtar, **MSS.** Sinmöru, *G. B. Gv. S. J.;* sinmantu, **MSS.**   19, lines
3 and 4.—*These lines are corrupt, and the exact wording has not been determined.*

Day-spring.

15. Now answer me, Much-wise,   this that I ask
        and fain would learn from thy lips:
    what befalls the fruit   of that famous tree
        which nor fire nor weapons will wound?

Much-wise.

16. The fruit thereof   must be laid on the fire
        for the weal of travailing women;
    they shall then come out   who had been within.
        To mankind 'tis the giver of life.

Day-spring.

17. Now answer me, Much-wise,   this that I ask
        and fain would learn from thy lips:
    what cock sits perched   in yon lofty tree,
        who is glistening all with gold?

Much-wise.

18. Wood-snake he is called,   who storm-bright sits
        in the boughs of Mimir's Tree:
    with one long dread   he galls beyond measure
        giant and giant-wife.

Day-spring.

19. Now answer me, Much-wise,   this that I ask
        and fain would learn from thy lips:
    what fierce hounds watch   in front of the courts
        ravening and roaming around?

16.—*Giver of life, or, according to another reading, the* Fate-tree, *as in Vsp., st. 2.*
17.—Wood-snake, *a poetical name for bird. This cock may be* Golden Comb, *who wakes the gods at the coming of the giants (Vsp., st. 43), and is hence the dread of giant and giant-wife, or, more probably, Fjalar (Vsp., st. 42), who sits "in the roosting tree," and sounds the first note of doom. The names of* Surt *and* Sinmara, *found in the text, are used in a general sense.*

Z

Fjölsviþr kvaþ :

20. (14) 'Gífr heitir annarr,   en Geri annarr,
         ef þú vill þat vita :
   verþir'u öflgir,   er þeir varþa,
         unz rjúfask regin.'

Svipdagr kvaþ :

21. (15) 'Seg mér þat, Fjölsviþr !   es ek þik fregna mun
         auk ek vilja vita :
   hvárt sé manna nekkvat   þats megi inn koma,
   meþan sókndjarfir sofa ? '

Fjölsviþr kvaþ :

22. (16) 'Missvefni mikit   vas þeim mjök of lagit,
         síþans þeim vas varzla vituþ :
   annarr of nǽtr sefr,   en annarr of daga,
   ok kömsk þá vǽtr, ef kvam.'

Svipdagr kvaþ :

23. (17) 'Seg mér þat, Fjölsviþr !   es ek þik fregna mun
         auk ek vilja vita :
   hvárt sé matar nekkvat   þats menn hafi,
   ok hlaupi inn, meþan eta ? '

Fjölsviþr kvaþ :

24. (18) 'Vǽngbráþir tvǽr   liggja í Viþofnis liþum,
         ef þú vill þat vita :
   þat eitt's svá matar,   at þeim menn of gefi,
   ok hlaupi inn, meþan eta.'

Svipdagr kvaþ :

25. 'Seg mér þat, Fjölsviþr !   es ek þik fregna mun
         auk ek vilja vita :
   hváɪt sé vápna nekkvat,   þats knegi Viþofnir fyrir
   hníga á Heljar sjöt ? '

20.—*S. G.*, varþir ellifu, **MSS.**, *Dt. and Hl. J. B.*

Much-wise.

20. One is called Greed,   the other Glutton,
        if haply thou wouldst hear:
    mighty warders   they are who watch
        for aye till the Powers perish.

Day-spring.

21. Now answer me, Much-wise,   this that I ask
        and fain would learn from thy lips:
    is there never a being   may pass within
        while the fierce hounds are held in sleep?

Much-wise.

22. Division of sleep   was ever their lot
        since 'twas given them to guard:
    sleeps one by night,   and the other by day,
        and none who comes may win through.

Day-spring.

23. Now answer me, Much-wise,   this that I ask
        and fain would learn from thy lips:
    is there no food   which man can find them
        and dart through the doors while they feast?

Much-wise.

24. There lie two wings   in the Wood-snake's sides,
        if haply thou wouldst hear:
    this alone is that food   which if man can find,
        he shall dart through the doors while they feast.

Day-spring.

25. Now answer me, Much-wise,   this that I ask
        and fain would learn from thy lips:
    is there no weapon   to strike the Wood-snake
        down to the halls of Hel?

20.—Mighty warders, *or, if another reading is taken,* eleven warders there are who watch, *named perhaps in st. 34.*

Fjölsviþr kvaþ :

26. 'Lævateinn heitir,   es görþi Loptr rúinn
     fyr nágrindr neþan ;
     í Sægjarns keri   liggr hjá Sinmöru,   .
     ok halda njarþlásar niu.'

Svipdagr kvaþ :

27. 'Seg mér þat, Fjölsviþr !   es ek þik fregna mun
     auk ek vilja vita :
     hvárt aptr kömr   sás eptir ferr
     ok vill þann tein taka ? '

Fjölsviþr kvaþ :

28. 'Aptr mun koma   sás eptir ferr
     ok vill þann tein taka,
     ef þat fœrir,   sem faïr eigu,
     eiri aurglasis.'

Svipdagr kvaþ :

29. 'Seg mér þat, Fjölsviþr !   es ek þik fregna mun
     auk ek vilja vita :
     hvárt sé mæta nekkvat,   þats menn hafi,
     ok verþr því en fölva gýgr fegin ? '

Fjölsviþr kvaþ :

30. 'Ljósan lea   skaltu í lúþr bera
     þanns liggr í Viþofnis völum,
     Sinmöru at selja,   áþr hón söm telisk
     vápn til vígs at lea.'

26.—Sægjarns, *R. M.;* sægjarns *or* segiarns, **MSS.**; seig-jarn, B.

Much-wise.

26. 'Tis the Wounding Wand   which Loki plucked
         beneath the doors of the dead :
    Sinmara keeps it   with nine fast locks,
         shut in Sea-lover's chest.

Day-spring.

27. Now answer me, Much-wise,   this that I ask
         and fain would learn from thy lips :
    comes he ever again,   who goes to seek,
         and craves to win that wand ?

Much-wise.

28. He shall come again   who goes to seek
         and craves to win that wand ;
    if he brings the treasure   which none doth own,
         the gold-bright goddess to please.

Day-spring.

29. Now answer me, Much-wise,   this that I ask
         and fain would learn from thy lips :
    is there no treasure   which man can take
         to rejoice that pale-hued giantess ?

Much-wise.

30. In its quill must thou bear   the bright sickled plume,
         which was taken from Wood-snake's tail,
    and give to Sinmara   ere she will grant thee
         that weapon of war to use.

26.—The Wounding Wand *must be the mistletoe with which Baldr was slain. Snorri tells us that it grew to the west of Vallhöll; see Bdr., st. 9.* Sinmara : *This giantess is only mentioned in st. 18, where she is coupled with Surt, as though his wife.* 28.—Gold-bright goddess. *A poetical term for woman.* 30.—Quill, *a suggestion for* lutr, *which means case or box; but whose significance is here doubtful.*

Svipdagr kvaþ ;

31. 'Seg mér þat, Fjölsviþr!   es ek þik fregna mun
auk ek vilja vita :
hvat sá salr heitir   es slunginn es
vísum vafrloga ? '

Fjölsviþr kvaþ :

32. 'Hyrr hann heitir,   en hann lengi mun
á brodds oddi bifask ;
auþranns þess   munu of aldr hafa
frétt eina firar.'

Svipdagr kvaþ :

33. 'Seg mér þat, Fjölsviþr!   es ek þik fregna mun
auk ek vilja vita :
hverr þat görþi,   es fyr garþ sák
innan ásmaga ? '

Fjölsviþr kvaþ :

34. 'Uni ok Iri,   Bari ok Ori,
Varr ok Vegdrasill,
Dori ok Uri, Dellingr, Atvarþr,
Líþskjalfr, Loki.'

Svipdagr kvaþ :

35. 'Seg mér þat, Fjölsviþr!   es ek þik fregna mun
auk ek vilja vita :
hvat þat bjarg heitir,   es ek sé brúþi á
þjóþmæra þruma ? '

Fjölsviþr kvaþ :

36. 'Lyfjaberg heitir,   en þat hefr lengi verit
sjúkum ok sárum gaman :
heil verþr hver,   þót hafi + árs sótt,
ef þat klífr, kona.'

32.—Hyrr, **MSS.**, K. M. Dt. and Hl. B ; Lýr, Gv. S. G.   34.—Atvarþr. at
varþar, ok varþar, **MSS.** Líþskjalfr, Hl. M. B. C.

Day-spring.

31. Now answer me, Much-wise,   this that I ask
    and fain would learn from thy lips:
what hall is yonder,   all girt around
    by enchanted flickering flames?

Much-wise.

32. Ember 'tis called   and long must it quiver
    as though on the spear's point set;
far tidings only,   throughout all time,
    man hears of this wondrous hall.

Day-spring.

33. Now answer me, Much-wise,   this that I ask
    and fain would learn from thy lips:
what beings, born   of the gods have built
    what I saw inside the court?

Much-wise.

34. Uni and Iri,   Bari and Ori,
    Var and Vegdrasil,
Dori and Uri,   Delling, Atvard,
    Lidskjalf and Loki were these.

Day-spring.

35. Now answer me, Much-wise,   this that I ask
    and fain would learn from thy lips:
what hill is that   on whose height I see
    yon wondrous Woman resting?

Much-wise.

36. 'Tis the Hill of Healing;   long hath it held,
    for the sick and sorrowful, joy:
each woman is healed   who climbs its height,
    even of year-long ills.

35.—Dori, Ori, *and* Delling *are dwarfs (see Vsp., st. 15; Vm., st. 25); Loki, the god. The others are unknown; their names do not seem to indicate their powers like those of st. 38.*

Svipdagr kvaþ :

37. 'Seg mér þat, Fjölsviþr!   es ek þik fregna mun
    auk ek vilja vita :
    hvat þér meyjar heita,   es fyr Menglaþar knëum
    sitja sáttar saman ? '

Fjölsviþr kvaþ :

38. 'Hlíf heitir ein,   önnur Hlífþrasa,
    þriþja þjóþvara,
    Björt ok Blíþ,   Blíþr ok Fríþ,
    Eir ok Aurboþa.'

Svipdagr kvaþ :

39. 'Seg mér þat, Fjölsviþr!   es ek þik fregna mun
    auk ek vilja vita :
    hvárt þér bjarga   þeims blóta þér,
    ef görvask þarfar þess ? '

Fjölsviþr kvaþ :

40. '*Bjarga svinnar*   hvars menn blóta þér
    á stallhelgum staþ :
    ey svá hátt foraþ   kömr at hölþa sunum,
    hverjan ór nauþum nema.'

Svipdagr kvaþ :

41. 'Seg mér þat, Fjölsviþr!   es ek þik fregna mun
    auk ek vilja vita :
    hvárt sé manna nekkvat,   þats knegi á Menglaþar
    svásum armi sofa ? '

Fjölsviþr kvaþ :

42. 'Vætr's þat manna,   es knegi á Menglaþar
    svásum armi sofa,
    nema Svipdagr einn,   hánum vas en sólbjarta
    brúþr at kván of gefin.'

40.—Bjarga svinnar, *B. Gv. G. F. J.;* sumur hvar, **MSS.**

Day-spring.

37. Now answer me, Much-wise,   this that I ask
      and fain would learn from thy lips:
who are the maidens,   at Menglod's knees
      all gathered in peace together?

Much-wise.

38. They are spirits, Sheltering,   Shielding giants,
      Guarding warriors in war,
Bright and Tender,   Blithe and Peaceful,
      Gentle, Generous maids.

Day-spring.

39. Now answer me, Much-wise,   this that I ask
      and fain would learn from thy lips:
will they shelter all   who make offering to them,
      if need thereof arise?

Much-wise.

40. Those Wise Ones shelter   where men make offering
      in the sacred altar-stead:
no peril so mighty   can man befall
      but they save him soon from need.

Day-spring.

41. Now answer me, Much-wise,   this that I ask
      and fain would learn from thy lips:
is there never being   in the world may lie
      in Menglod's soft arms sleeping?

Much-wise.

42. There is never being   in the world may lie
      in Menglod's soft arms sleeping
save Day-spring, to whom   of yore was given
      that sun-bright maiden as bride.

Svipdagr kvaþ :

43. 'Hritt á hurþir,   láttu hliþ rúm !
    hér mátt Svipdag sea ;
    þó vita far,   ef vilja muni
    Menglöþ mitt gaman.'

Fjölsviþr kvaþ :

44. 'Heyrþu, Menglöþ !   hér es maþr kominn,
    gakk á gest sea !
    hundar fagna,   hús hefr upp lokizk :
    hykk at Svipdagr seï.'

Menglöþ kvaþ :

45. 'Horskir hrafnar   skulu þer á hám galga
    slíta sjónir ór,
    ef þat lýgr,   at hér sé langt kominn
    mögr til minna sala.

46. Hvaþan þú fórt,   hvaþan þú för görþir,
    hvé þik hétu hiu ?
    at ætt ok nafni   skalk jartegn vita,
    ef ek vas þer at kván of kveþin.'

Svipdagr kvaþ :

47. 'Svipdagr heitik,   Sólbjartr hét faþir,
    þaþan vrákumk vindar kalda vegu ;
    Urþar orþi   kveþr engi maþr,
    þót sé viþ löst lagit.'

Menglöþ kvaþ :

48. 'Vel þú nú kominn !   hefk minn vilja beþit,
    fylgja skal kveþju koss ;
    forkunnar sýn   mun flestan glaþa,
    hverrs hefr viþ annan ást.

Day-spring.

43. Fling open the door,   make wide the gate,
    Day-spring is here, behold!
  Yet hie thee first,   and find if in truth
    Menglod longs for my love.

Much-wise to Menglod.

44. Hearken, Menglod,   a guest is here!
    Come thou this stranger behold!
  The hounds are joyous,   the hall hath opened.
    'Tis Day-spring, well I ween!

Menglod.

45. Now may fierce ravens   rend thine eyes out,
    high on the gallows hanging,
  if falsely thou sayest   that from far away
    comes Day-spring here to my halls!

To Day-spring.

46. Whence hast thou come,   whence made thy way,
    how do thy home-folk call thee?
  Show race and name   ere I know that to thee
    in truth I have been betrothed.

Day-spring.

47. Day-spring am I,   the child of Sun-bright,
    by winds on my chill way wafted;
  the doom of Weird   may no wight withstand
    e'en though meted amiss.

Menglod.

48. Now welcome art thou!   My will is won;
    with greeting comes the kiss.
  Never sweeter is sight   of heart's desire
    than when one brings love to another.

47.—The doom of Weird, see *Spell-songs*, st. 4.

49. Lengi satk   Lyfjabergi á,
       beiþk þín dœgr ok daga :
     nú þat varþ   es ek vætt hefi,
       at aptr kvamt, mögr! til minna sala.

50. Þrár hafþar   es ek hef til þíns gamans,
       en þú til míns munar ;
     nú's þat satt,   es vit slíta skulum
       ævi ok aldr saman.'

49.—Lyfjabergi, *B. Gv. C. G. S.;* liúfu bergi, **MSS**.   At aptr kvamt : at þu ert aptr kominn, **MSS**.

49. Long have I sat   on the Hill of Healing,
    awaiting thee day by day;
till that I looked for   at length is come,—
    thou art back, youth, here in my halls.

50. Yearnings had I   oft for thy heart,
    and thou didst long for my love:
now all is made sure,   we twain shall share
    together the days of time.

HÁRBARÐSLJÓÞ.

Þórr fór ór austrvegi ok kom at sundi einu; öþrum megum sundsins var ferjukarlinn meþ skipit. Þórr kallaþi :

1. 'Hverr es sá sveinn sveina,   es stendr fyr sundit handan ?'

Ferjukarlinn kvaþ:

2. 'Hverr es sá karl karla,   es kallar of váginn ?'

GREYBEARD AND THOR.

As Thor was journeying from the Eastern Land of the Jötuns he came to a sound. On the other side was a ferryman with his boat.

Thor.

1. What swain of swains   art thou who thus
   on yonder side of   the sound art standing?

Greybeard.

2. Tell me rather   what carle of carles
   thus calls across the wave.

Prose.—*Presumably Odin in disguise ; see Introd.*

Þórr kvaþ :

3. 'Ferþu mik of sundit !   fǿþik þik á morgin :
meis hefk á baki   verþra matr enn betri.
Át ek í hvílþ,   áþr ek heiman fór,
sildr ok hafra :   saþr emk enn þess.'

Ferjukarlinn kvaþ :

4. 'Árligum verkum hrósar þú verþinum;   veiztattu fyrir görla :
döpr eru þín heimkynni,   dauþ hykk at þín móþir sé.'

Þórr kvaþ :

5. 'Þat segir þú nú,   es hverjum þykkir
mest at vita,   at mín móþir dauþ sé.'

Ferjukarlinn kvaþ :

6. 'Þeygi es sem þú   þrjú bú góþ eigir :
berbeinn þú stendr   ok hefr brautinga görvi ;
þatki at þú hafir brǿkr þínar !'

Þórr kvaþ :

7. 'Stýrþu hingat eikjunni !   ek mun þér stöþna kenna ;
eþa hverr á skipit   es þú heldr viþ landit ?'

Ferjukarlinn kvaþ :

8. 'Hildolfr sá heitir,   es mik halda baþ,
rekkr enn ráþsvinni,   es býr í Ráþseyjarsundi ;
baþat hann hlennimenn flytja   eþa hrossa þjófa,
góþa eina   ok þás ek görva kunna.
Segþu til nafns þíns,   ef þú vill of sundit fara.

Thor.

3. Row me over! A meal   this morn I'll pay thee,
choicer fare . thou shalt never find thee.
Here on my back   there hangs a basket ;
in peace I ate,   myself, ere I started,
herrings and goat's flesh,   and still am I sated.

Greybeard.

4. As a morning's work   thou dost boast thy meal ;
but thou art not all forseeing :
filled with care   at home are thy kindred,
dead I trow is thy mother.

Thor.

5. Worst of all tidings   art thou telling,
when thou sayest me now   that dead is my mother.

Greybeard.

6. At least thou lookst not   like one who owns
a lot of three fair lands ;
bare-legged thou standest,   clad like a beggar,
and not even breeks hast thou on.

Thor.

7. Steer the bark hither !   I will show thee a haven.
Who owns yon boat   which by the brink thou holdest ?

Greybeard.

8. Battle-wolf bade me—   wise-counselled hero,
who dwells in Counsel-Isle Sound—
to keep it and ferry   nor rogues nor robbers
but the worthy and those I know well.
Now shalt thou tell me   thy name if thou fain
wouldst hither fare o'er the flood.

3.—*Herrings and goat's flesh. For Thor as a fisherman, see Hym., st. 17-25. He usually ate his goats for supper, and restored them to life in the morning; see Introd. Hym. This rendering of* hafra *seems more probable than the more common alternative* oats; *for Thor's meal of goat's flesh was famous, and a burlesque like the present poem would be incomplete without some allusion to it.* 8.—*Battle-wolf, meaning himself, the patron of war.*

Þórr kvaþ :

9. 'Segja munk til nafns míns, þót ek sekr seak,
ok til alls öþlis : ek em Óþins sunr,
Meila bróþir, en Magna faþir,
þrúþvaldr goþa ; viþ Þór knáttu hér dœma.
Hins viljak nú spyrja, hvat þú heitir.'

Ferjukarlinn kvaþ :

10. 'Hárbarþr ek heiti. hylk of nafn sjaldan.'

Þórr kvaþ :

11. 'Hvat skaltu of nafn hylja, nema þú sakar eigir ?'

Hárbarþr kvaþ :

12. 'En þót ek sakar eiga, fyr slíkum sem þú est
munk forþa þó fjörvi mínu,
nema ek feigr sé.'

Þórr kvaþ :

13. 'Harm ljótan mér þikkir í þuí at vaþa,
of váginn til þín ok væta ögur minn ;
skyldak launa kögursveini þínum kanginyrþi,
ef ek komumk of sundit.'

Hárbarþr kvaþ :

14. 'Hér munk standa ok þín heþan bíþa ;
fanntattu mann enn harþara at Hrungni dauþan.'

Þórr kvaþ :

15. 'Hins vildu nú geta, es vit Hrungnir deildum,
sá enn stórúþgi jötunn, es ór steini vas höfuþit á ;
þó létk hann falla ok fyrir hníga.—
Hvat vanntu þá meþan, Hárbarþr ?'

12, lines 1 and 2.—*Transposed G. from* þá mun ek forþa fjörvi minu **fyr**, *&c.*, **R.**

Thor.

9. Were I outlawed, yet   my name would I tell thee,
eke my race.   I am son of Odin,
the brother of Meili,   and father of Magni,
gods' Strength-wielder;   thou speak'st with Thor.
Fain would I know now   thy name and kinship.

Greybeard.

10. They call me Grey-beard;   'tis seldom I care
to hide my own name from any.

Thor.

11. Wherefore shouldst thou   not show thy name,
except thou have cause   of strife with thy foemen?

Greybeard.

12. Have I cause, 'gainst such   as thee will I hold
my life unless I be doomed.

Thor.

13. Sore shame 'twould be   to wet my burden
in wading thus   thro' the water toward thee.
Those mocking words   would I pay thee, mannikin,
could I but reach   yon side of the sound now.

Greybeard.

14. Here I stand and await thee!   Ne'er metst thou with sturdier
hero since Hrungnir was slain,

Thor.

15. Dost tell how we once fought,   I and Hrungnir,
that hard-hearted giant   whose head was rock-hewn?
Yet did he fall   and bow before me.
What, the while, wast thou   working, Greybeard?

9.—Meili. *Nothing is known concerning this son of Odin.* Magni *or* Might, *see* Vm., *st. 51.* 10.—Greybeard. *Odin's wonted disguise was that of a grey-bearded old man.* 11.—*Cause of strife, see* G. gloss. 14.—Hrungnir. *The slaying of this giant was one of Thor's famous deeds; see* Hym., *st. 16.*

Hárbarþr kvaþ :

16. 'Vask meþ Fjölvari   fimm vetr alla
    í eyju þeiri   es Algrœn heitir;
    vega vér þar knáttum   ok val fella,
    margs at freista,   mans at kosta.'

Þórr kvaþ :

17. 'Hversu snúnuþu yþr konur yþrar?'

Hárbarþr kvaþ :

18. 'Sparkar áttum vér konur,   ef oss at spökum yrþi;
    horskar áttum vér konur,   ef oss hollar véri:
    þér ór sandi   síma undu
    ok ór dali djúpum   grund of grófu
    Varþk þeim einn öllum   öfri at ráþum,
    hvíldak hjá þeim systrum sjau
    ok hafþak geþ þeira allt ok gaman.
    Hvat vanntu þá meþan, Þórr?'

Þórr kvaþ :

19. 'Ek drap Þjaza,   enn þrúþmóþga jötun,
    upp ek varp augum   Alvalda sunar
    á þann enn heiþa himin ;
    þau eru merki mest   minna verka,
    þaus allir menn síþan of sé.
    Hvat vanntu meþan, Hárbarþr?'

Hárbarþr kvaþ :

20. 'Miklar manvélar   ek hafþa viþ myrkriþur,
    þás ek vélta þér frá verum;
    harþan jötun   hugþak Hlébarþ vesa:
    gaf hann mér gambantein,
    en ek vélta hann ór viti.'

Greybeard.

16. I dwelt with Wary-wise   five whole winters
in the island called All-green.
Battles we fought there   and felled the doomed,
much daring, and wiling women.

Thor.

17. Got ye weal or woe   from those wives of your winning?

Greybeard.

18. Merry wives had we owned   had they borne them wisely;
shrewd wives, had they shown them true:
all out of sand   they spun them ropes
and dug from the deep dales earth.
Yet slyest was I,   who with seven sisters slept,
and won all their liking and love.
What, the while, wast thou   working, Thunderer?'

Thor.

19. Slew I Thiazi,   son of All-wielder,
strong-souled Jötun,   and flung his eyes up
where men shall behold   in the shining heavens
the tokens great   of my deeds hereafter.
What, the while, wast thou   working, Greybeard?

Greybeard.

20. I had dealings in love   with the dark witch-riders,
from their husbands I wiled them away:
stout giant seemed Hlebard   till his wand he gave me
and I wiled him out of his wits.

16.—Wary-wise, *unknown.*   19.—Thiazi. *See I.s., st. 50, and Introd.; Vsp. en skamma, st. 3.*

Þórr kvaþ:

21. 'Illum huga launaþir þú þá góþar gjafar.'

Hárbarþr kvaþ:

22. 'Þat hefr eik   es af annarri skefr:
of sik es hverr í slíku.
Hvat vanntu meþan, Þórr?'

Þórr kvaþ:

23. 'Ek vas austr   ok jötna barþak
brúþir bölvísar   es til bjargs gengu:
mikil mundi ætt jötna,   ef allir lifþi,
vætr mundi manna   und miþgarþi.
Hvat vanntu meþan, Hárbarþr?'

Hárbarþr kvaþ:

24. 'Vask á Vallandi   ok vígum fylgþak,
attak jöfrum,   en aldri sættak.
Óþinn á jarla   þás í val falla,
en Þórr á þræla kyn.'

Þórr kvaþ:

25. 'Ójafnt skipta   es þú mundir meþ ásum liþi,
ef þú ættir vilgi mikils vald.'

Hárbarþr kvaþ:

26. 'Þórr á afl œrit,   en etki hjarta:
af hræzlu ok hugbleyþi   vas þér í hanzka troþit
[ok þóttiska þú þá Þórr vesa;]
hvárki þú þá þorþir   fyr hræzlu þinni
hnjósa ne físa,   svát Fjalarr heyrþi.'

Thor.

21, Then spite for those goodly   gifts thou gavest ?

Greybeard.

22. Let one oak take   what it scrapes off another,
and let each man seek his own.
What, the while, wast thou   working, Thunderer ?

Thor.

23. Slew I the evil   wives of Jötuns,
far in the east,   as they fled to the mountains :
were they all left   in the land of the living,
huge would have been now   the host of giants,
and never a man   would there be in Midgarth.
What, the while, wast thou   working, Greybeard ?

Greybeard.

24. In the Land of the Slain   I warred and stirred up
princes to strife without peace.
Odin has earls   who fall on the battlefield,
Thor has the race of thralls.

Thor.

25. Unfairly wouldst thou   divide the slain
among gods if power   too great were given thee !

Greybeard.

26. Strength enough has the Thunderer,   nought of daring ;
from fear and faintness of heart
thou wert thrust, I ween,   in a glove-thumb once,
and scarce couldst deem thyself Thor :
lest Fjalar should hear thee,   for fright thou durst not
sneeze nor stir a hair.

26.—Fjalar, *a giant, otherwise known as Utgard-loki ; see Introd.*

Þórr kvaþ :

27. 'Hárbarþr enn ragi!   ek munda þik í hel drepa,
ef ek mǽtta seilask of sund.'

Hárbarþr kvaþ :

28. 'Hvat skyldir þú of sund seilask,   es sakar'u alls öngvar ?
Hvat vanntu þá, Þórr ?'

Þórr kvaþ :

29. 'Ek vas austr   ok ána varþak,
þás mik sóttu   þeir Svárangs synir ;
grjóti þeir mik börþu,   gagni urþu þeir þó lítt fegnir,
urþu þeir mik fyrri   friþar at biþja.
Hvat vanntu þá meþan, Hárbarþr ?'

Hárbarþr kvaþ :

30. 'Ek vas austr   ok viþ einhverja dœmþak,
lék ek viþ ena línhvítu   ok launþing háþak,
gladdak ena gollbjörtu,   gamni mǽr unþi.'

Þórr kvaþ :

31. 'Góþ áttuþ ér mankynni þar þá.'

Hárbarþr kvaþ :

32. 'Liþs þíns vǽrak þá þurfi, Þórr!   et ek helda þeiri enni
línhvítu mey.'

Þórr kvaþ :

33. 'Ek munda þér þá þat veita,   ef ek viþr of kvǽmumk.'

Thor.

27. Greybeard, thou craven!   Could I but stretch
o'er the sound I would smite thee   soon into Hel-home.

Greybeard.

28. Why shouldst thou stretch   o'er the sound and smite me?
No reason have we for wrath.
What, the while, wast thou   working, Thunderer?

Thor.

29. Eastward held I   the flood of Ifing
against the sons   of Svarang the Whelmer;
with stones they beset me   but small gain got they
and first were found   to ask peace of foemen.
What, the while, wast thou   working, Greybeard?

Greybeard.

30. In the East I dallied   with one, my chosen;
I played with that linen-fair lass,
kept secret trysting,   and gladdened the gold-bright
maiden, merry in the game.

Thor.

31. Glad meetings of love   had ye there with maidens?

Greybeard.

32. Need had I then   of help from Thor,
to have kept that linen-fair lass.

Thor.

33. Fain would I give it thee   could I but get there.

29.—**Ifing.** *The name is not mentioned in the text, but it may be assumed that the river is that which flowed between the realms of gods and giants ; see Vm. 16.*

2 C

Hárbarþr kvaþ :

34. 'Ek munda þér þá trua,   nema þú mik í trygþ véltir.'

Þórr kvaþ :

35. 'Emkat ek sá hǽlbítr   sem húþskór forn á vár.'

Hárbarþr kvaþ :

36. 'Hvat vanntu meþan, Þórr ? '

Þórr kvaþ ;

37. 'Brúþir berserkja   barþak í Hléseyju,
      þǽr höfþu verst unnit   vilta þjóþ alla.'

Hárbarþr kvaþ :

38. 'Klǽki vanntu þá, Þórr !   es þú á konum barþir.'

Þórr kvaþ :

39. 'Vargynjur váru þǽr,   en varla konur ;
      skeldu skip mitt   es ek skorþat hafþak ;
      œgþu mér ïarnlurki,   en eltu þjalfa.
      Hvat vanntu meþan, Hárbarþr ? '

Hárbarþr kvaþ :

40. 'Ek vask í hernum   es hingat görþisk
      gnǽfa gunnfana,   geir at rjóþa.'

Þórr kvaþ :

41. 'Þess vildu nú geta, es þú fórt oss óljúfan at bjóþa.'

Hárbarþr kvaþ :

42. 'Bǿta skal þér þat þá   munda baugi,
      sem jafnendr unnu   þeirs okkr vilja sǽtta.'

Greybeard.

34. Fain would I now   put trust in thy faith,
    wert thou not wont to betray me.

Thor.

35. No heelbiter I,   like an old shoe in spring-time!

Greybeard.

36. What, the while, wast thou   working, Thunderer?

Thor.

37. Slew I berserk-wives   in the Isle of Ægir;
    vile things wrought they,   all men-folk wiling.

Greybeard.

38. A base deed then   wast thou doing, Thunderer—
    waging war with women!

Thor.

39. She-wolves were they,   and scarcely women.
    My ships laid up   on the shore they shattered,
    with clubs they threatened me,   Thialfi chased they.
    What, the while, wast thou   working, Greybeard?

Greybeard.

40. To raise the war flag   and redden the spear,
    hither I came in the host.

Thor.

41. Wouldst tell how with hate   thou cam'st to harm us?

Greybeard.

42. Let a ring make atonement   as the daysmen meted,
    who sought to set us at peace.

34.—Wont to betray me. *This rendering seems justified by the ensuing st.; see*
Introd. 37.—*Ægir, here called by his other name* Hlér.

Þórr kvaþ :

43. 'Hvar namtu   þessi en hnœfiligu orþ,
    es ek heyrþa aldri   in hnœfiligri ?'

Hárbarþr kvaþ :

44. 'Nam ek at mönnum   þeim enum aldrœnum
    es bua í heimis haugum.'

Þórr kvaþ :

45. 'Þá gefr þú   gott nafn dysjum,
    es þú kallar þǽr heimis hauga.'

Hárbarþr kvaþ :

46. 'Svá dœmi ek of slíkt far.'

Þórr kvaþ :

47. 'Orþkringi þín   mun þér illa koma,
    ef ek rǽþ á vág at vaþa ;
    ulfi hǽra   hykk þik œpa munu,
    ef þú hlýtr af hamri högg.'

Hárbarþr kvaþ :

48. 'Sif á hór heima,   hans mundu fund vilja,
    þann mundu þrek drýgja,   þat es þér skyldara.'

Þórr kvaþ :

49. 'Mǽlir þú at munns ráþi,   svát mér skyldi verst þykkja,
    halr enn hugblauþi !   hykk at þú ljúgir.'

44.—Haugum ; 45, bauga, *B. Gv. G. S. C. J.* Skógum, skógu, **R.**

Thor.

43. Where didst thou learn those scornful speeches?
Never were words more wounding said me.

Greybeard.

44. I learnt them once from ancient beings
who dwell in the hills of home.

Thor.

45. Fair name for cairns to call them home-hills!

Greybeard.

46. 'Tis even as I think concerning such things.

Thor.

47. Sorely thy skill in words should serve thee,
could I but wade to thee through the water.
Louder, I ween, than a wolf wilt thou howl
if haply thou get'st a stroke from my hammer.

Greybeard.

48. Sif has a lover, thy wife at home,
art thou not eager to meet him?
That a deed of daring now must thou do,
a work which well befits thee.

Thor.

49. Faint-heart! Speak'st thou as worst meseems,
by the counsel of thy lips; for I trow thou liest!

44.—Hills of home, *the ancestral graves.* 48.—Sif's *lover* is Loki; *see Ls.,*
st. 54.

Hárbarþr kvaþ :

50. 'Satt hykk mik segja ;   seinn estu at för þinni ;
langt mundir þú nú kominn, Þórr !   ef þú litum fœrir.'

Þórr kvaþ :

51. 'Hárbarþr enn ragi !   heldr hefr þú nú mik dvalþan.'

Hárbarþr kvaþ :

52. 'Ásaþórs   hugþak aldri mundu
glepja farhirþi farar.'

Þórr kvaþ :

53. 'Ráþ munk þér nú ráþa :   ró þú hingat bátinum ;
hǽttum hœtingi,   hittu föþur Magna !'

Hárbarþr kvaþ :

54. 'Farþu firr sundi !   þér skal fars synja.'

Þórr kvaþ :

55. 'Vísa þú mér nú leiþina,   alls þú vill mik eigi of váginn
ferja !'

Hárbarþr kvaþ :

56. 'Lítit es at synja,   langt es at fara :
stund es til stokksins,   önnur til steinsins,
haltu svá til vinstra vegsins,   unz þú hittir Verland.
Þar mun Fjörgyn   hitta Þór sun sinn
ok mun hón kenna hánum áttunga brautir   til Óþins
landa.'

Þórr kvaþ :

57. 'Mun ek taka þangat í dag ?'

Greybeard.

50. Truly I ween that   my words are spoken:
too slow art thou in thy travelling.
Far on thy way   hadst thou fared now, Thor,
if thou hadst but gone in disguise.

Thor.

51. Greybeard, thou craven!   Too long thou delay'st me.

Greybeard.

52. I had ne'er weened boatman   would hinder the way
of Thor, the Thunderer of gods.

Thor.

53. Now will I counsel thee;   come in thy boat hither;
fetch Magni's father,   and cease we from mocking.

Greybeard.

54. Hie thee hence   away from the sound!
The ferry to thee is refused.

Thor.

55. Show me a path then,   since thou wilt not
ferry me over   the flood betwixt us.

Greybeard.

56. 'Tis little to withhold,   'tis far to fare
a while to the stock and the stone:
thus shalt thou hold   to the left-hand path,
till thou light on the Land of Men;
there will Earth meet her son   and show him the way
of his race to the realms of Odin.

Thor.

57. Shall I to-day reach   the dwellings of Odin?

56.—Earth, *or* Jord, *who is here called* Fjörgyn, *is one of* Odin's *wives; see* Ls.,
st. 26.

Hárbarþr kvaþ :

58. 'Taka viþ víl ok erfiþi
　　at uppvesandi sólu, es ek get þána.'

Þórr kvaþ :

59. 'Skamt mun nú mál okkat,　　alls þú mér skœtingu einni svarar;
　　launa munk þér farsynjun,　　ef vit finnumsk í sinn annat.'

Hárbarþr kvaþ :

60. 'Farþu nú þars þik hafi allan gramir !'

58.—þána, **R**, *B. Gv. J. C.;* þá-na, *G.*

Greybeard.

58. With weariness and toil   when the dew is wet
at sunrise, I ween, thou wilt win them.

Thor.

59. Short be our speech now,   with but jeering thou answerest.
When we meet next I'll pay thee   for denying me passage.

Greybeard.

60. Hie thee hence   away where the fiends
may seize thee, body and soul!

58.—When the dew is wet, *B's interpretation*; about that time, *G.*

2 D

RÍGSÞULA.

Svá segja menn í fornum sögum, at einhverr af ásum, sá er Heimdallr hét, fór ferþar sinnar ok fram meþ sjóvarströndu nökkurri, kom at einum húsaboe ok nefndiz Rígr. Eptir þeiri sögu er kvæþi þetta :

1. Ár kvöþu ganga groenar brautir
öflgan ok aldinn ás kunnigan,
ramman ok röskvan Ríg stíganda,
. . . .

2. Gekk meirr at þat miþrar brautar ;
kvam hann at húsi, hurþ vas á gætti ;
inn nam ganga, eldr vas á golfi,
hjón sátu þar hár at arni.
Ai ok Edda aldinfalda.

Rígsþula.—*In* **W**. 2.—At arni, *R. S. H. G. Gv.* ; af árni, **W**, *Hl. J.*

THE SONG OF RIG.

It is told in the sagas of old time that a certain god called Heimdal was passing on his way along the sea shore when he came to a farm. He entered, calling himself Rig according to the story which thus relates:

I.—THE BIRTH OF THRALL.

1.   Once walked, 'tis said,   the green ways along,
       mighty and ancient,   a god most glorious;
       strong and vigorous,   striding, Rig.
      . . . .

2.   Ever on he went   in the middle of the way,
       till he came to a house   with door unclosed.
       He entered straight;   there was fire on the floor
       and a hoary couple   sitting by the hearth,
       Great-grandfather and mother   in ancient guise.

Heimdal.—*See Vsp. en skamma, st. 14; Grm. 13 and Vsp., st. 1, where men are called his children.* Rig or King.—*A Celtic word.*

3. Rígr kunni þeim   ráþ at segja,
    meirr settisk hann   miþra fletja,
    en á hliþ hvára   hjón salkynna.

4. Þá tók Edda   ökkvinn hleif,
    þungan ok þykkvan,   þrunginn sáþum ;
    bar meirr at þat   miþra skutla,
    soþ vas í bolla,   setti á bjóþ.

5. (4) Reis upp þaþan,   rézk at sofna ;
  (5) Rígr kunni þeim   ráþ at segja,
    meirr lagþisk hann   miþrar rekkju,
    en á hliþ hvára   hjón salkynna.
    Þar vas at þat   þriar nætr saman,
    gekk meirr at þat   miþrar brautar,
    liþu meirr at þat   mánuþr niu.

6. Jóþ ól Edda,   jósu vatni,
    hörvi svartan   hétu Þræl.
    Hann nam at vaxa   ok vel dafna,
    vas þar á höndum   hrokkit skinn,
    kropnir knuar, ...
    fingr digrir,   fúlligt andlit,
    lútr hryggr,   langir hælar.
  (7) Nam meirr at þat   megins of kosta,
    bast at binda,   byrþar görva,
    bar heim at þat   hrís görstan dag.

7. Þar kvam at garþi   gengilbeina,
    örr vas á iljum,   armr sólbrunninn,
    niþrbjúgt es nef,   nefndisk Þír.

8. Meirr settisk hón   miþra fletja,
    sat hjá henni   sunr húss,
    rœddu ok rýndu,   rekkju görþu
    Þræll ok Þír   þrungin dœgr.

4, line 4.—*Followed by a line in* **W**, *transposed to st. 15.*   **5.**—*Strophe numbering of* **W** *is marked in brackets.*

3. Well knew Rig   how to give them counsel,
     he sat him down   in the middle of the floor,
     with the home-folk twain   upon either side.

4. Great-grandmother fetched   a coarse-baked loaf,
     all heavy and thick   and crammed with husk:
     she bore it forth   in the middle of the dish,
     with broth in a bowl,   and laid the board.

5. Thence Rig uprose,   prepared to rest;—
     well he knew   how to give them counsel—
     he laid him down   in the middle of the bed
     and the home-folk twain   upon either side.
     Thus he tarried   three nights together,
     then on he strode   in the middle of the road
     while thrice three moons   were gliding by.

6. Great-grandmother bore   a swarthy boy;
     with water they sprinkled him,   called him Thrall.
     Forthwith he grew   and well he throve,
     but rough were his hands   with wrinkled skin,
     with knuckles knotty   and fingers thick;
     his face was ugly,   his back was humpy,
     his heels were long.   . . . . .
     Straightway 'gan he   to prove his strength,
     with bast a-binding   loads a-making,
     he bore home faggots   the livelong day.

7. There came to the dwellings   a wandering maid,
     with wayworn feet,   and sunburned arms,
     with down-bent nose,—   the Bond-maid named.

8. She sat her down   in the middle of the floor;
     beside her sat   the son of the house:
     they chatted and whispered,   their bed preparing—
     Thrall and Bond-maid—   the long day through.

6.—Sprinkled him with water, *see Háv., st. 157.* Thrall, *the lowest class, who were little better than slaves.* 7.—Wandering. *The other brides (st. 18 and 30) came, not on foot, but driving to their husbands.*

9. (8)   Börn álu þau,   bjuggu ok unþu;
       hykk at héti   Hreimr ok Fjósnir,
       Klúrr ok Kleggi,   Kefsir, Fúlnir,
       Drumbr, Digraldi,   Dröttr ok Hösvir,
       Lútr, Leggjaldi: lögþu garþa,
       akra töddu,   unnu at svínum,
       geita gǽttu,   grófu torf.

10. (9)   Dǿtr váru þǽr   Drumba ok Kumba,
       Ökkvinkalfa   ok Arinnefja,
       Ysja ok Ambátt,   Eikintjasna,
       Tötrughypja   ok Trönubeina:
       þaþan eru komnar   þrǽla ǽttir.

11. (10)   Gekk Rígr at þat   réttar brautir;
       kvam hann at höllu,   hurþ vas á skíþi;
       inn nam ganga,   eldr vas á golfi:
       Afi ok Amma   áttu hús.

12. (10)   Hjón sátu þar,   heldu á sýslu:
       maþr telgþi þar   meiþ til rifjar;
       vas skegg skapat,   skör vas fýr enni,
       skyrtu þröngva,   skokkr vas á golfi.

13. (11)   Sat þar kona,   sveigþi rokk,
       breiddi faþm,   bjó til váþar;
  (12)   sveigr vas á höfþi,   smokkr vas á bringu,
       dúkr vas á halsi,   dvergar á öxlum.

14.   Rígr kunni þeim   ráþ at segja,
       meirr settisk hann   miþra fletja,
       en á hliþ hvára   hjón salkynna.

11, line 4.—*Transposed from st. 13 by S. B. G.*   14, lines 2 and 3.—*Not found in* **W** ; *supplied from other parts of the poem, B. S. G.*

9. Joyous lived they   and reared their children.
    Thus they called them: Brawler, Cowherd,
    Boor and Horsefly,   Lewd and Lustful,
    Stout and Stumpy,   Sluggard, Swarthy,
    Lout and Leggy.   They fashioned fences,
    they dunged the meadows,   swine they herded,
    goats they tended   and turf they dug.

10. Daughters were there,—   Loggy and Cloggy,
    Lumpy-leggy,   and Eagle-nose,
    Whiner, Bondwoman,   Oaken-peggy,
    Tatter-coat   and the Crane-shanked maid.
    Thence are come   the generations of thralls.

II.—THE BIRTH OF CHURL.

11. Ever on went Rig   the straight roads along
    till he came to a dwelling   with door unclosed;
    he entered straight;   there was fire on the floor;
    Grandfather and Grandmother   owned the house.

12. The home-folk sat there   hard aworking;
    by them stood   on the floor a box;
    hewed the husband   wood for a warp-beam;
    trim his beard   and the locks o'er his brow,
    but mean and scanty   the shirt he wore.

13. The wife sat by him   plying her distaff,
    swaying her arms   to weave the cloth,
    with snood on her head   and smock on her breast,
    studs on her shoulders,   and scarf on her neck.

14. Well knew Rig   how to give them counsel;
    he sat him down   in the middle of the floor,
    and the home-folk twain   upon either side.

15.   Þá tók Amma   . . . . . .
        . . . .
        fram setti hón   fulla skutla,
        vas kalfr soþinn   krása baztr.
        Reis frá borþi,   rézk at sofna,
        Rígr kunni þeim   ráþ at segja,
        meirr lagþisk hann   miþrar rekkju,
        en á hliþ hvára   hjón salkynna.

16.   Þar vas at þat   þriar nætr saman,
        gekk meirr at þat   miþrar brautar,
        liþu meirr at þat   mánuþr niu.

17. (15)   Jóþ ól Amma,   jósu vatni,
        kölluþu Karl;   kona sveip ripti
        rauþan ok rjóþan,   riþuþu augu.
        Hann nam at vaxa   ok vel dafna,
        öxn nam temja,   arþr at görva,
        hús at timbra   ok hlöþur smíþa,
        karta at görva   ok keyra plóg.

18. (16)   Heim óku þá   hanginluklu,
        geitakyrtlu,   giptu Karli;
        Snör heitir sú,   settisk und ripti,
        bjuggu hjón,   bauga deildu,
        breiddu blæjur   ok bú görþu.

19. (16)   Börn ólu þau,   bjuggu ok unþu;
        hét Halr ok Drengr,   Hölþr, þegn ok Smiþr,
        Breiþr, Bóndi,   Bundinskeggi,
        Bui ok Boddi,   Brattskeggr ok Seggr.

20. (16)   Enn hétu svá   öþrum nöfnum:
        Snót, Brúþr, Svanni,   Svarri, Sprakki,
        Fljóþ, Sprund ok Víf,   Feima, Ristill:
        þaþan eru komnar   karla ættir.

15, lines 3 and 4.—*Transposed from st. 4, B. S. G. J.*   16, line 2.—*Not found in*
W; *supplied B. S. G.*

15. Grandmother set forth   plenteous dishes ;
cooked was the calf,   of dainties best.
Thence Rig uprose   prepared to rest.—
Well he knew   how to give them counsel—
he laid him down   in the middle of the bed
and the home-folk twain   upon either side.

16. Thus he tarried   three nights together,
then on he strode   in the middle of the road
while thrice three moons   were gliding by.

17. A child had Grandmother,   Churl they called him,
and sprinkled with water   and swathed in linen,
rosy and ruddy,   with sparkling eyes.
He grew and throve,   and forthwith 'gan he
to break in oxen,   to shape the harrow,
to build him houses   and barns to raise him,
to fashion carts   and follow the plough.

18. Then home they drove   with a key-hung maiden
in goat-skin kirtle,   named Daughter-in-Law.
They wed her to Churl   in her bridal linen :
the twain made ready,   their wealth a-sharing,
kept house together,   and joyous lived.

19. Children reared they   thus they called them :
Youth and Hero,   Thane, Smith, Yeoman,
Broad-limb, Peasant,   Sheaf-beard, Neighbour,
Farmer, Speaker   and Stubbly-beard.

20. By other names   were the daughters called :
Dame, Bride, Lady,   Gay, and Gaudy,
Maid, Wife, Woman,   Bashful, Slender.
Thence are come   the kindreds of churls.

17.—Churl *or* karl, *the free-born peasant proprietor.*

21. (17)   Gekk Rígr þaþan   réttar brautir,
             kvam hann at sal,   suþr horfþu dyrr ;
             vas hurþ hnigin,   hringr vas í gǽtti,
             gekk inn at þat :   golf vas straït.
             Sátu hjón,   söusk í augu,
             Faþir ok Móþir,   fingrum at leika.
             Sat húsgumi   ok snöri streng,
             alm of bendi,   örvar skepti ;
             en húskona   hugþi at örmum,
             strauk of ripti,   sterti ermar,
             keistr vas faldr,   kinga á bringu,
             síþar slǿþur   serk bláfaan,
             brún bjartari,   brjóst ljósara,
             hals hvítari   hreinni mjöllu.

22. (18)   Rígr kunni þeim   ráþ at segja,
             meirr settisk hann   miþra fletja,
             en á hliþ hvára   hjón salkynna.

23. (19)   Þa tók Móþir   merkþan dúk,
             hvítan af hörvi,   hulþi bjóþ ;
             hón tók at þat   hleifa þunna,
             hvíta af hveiti,   ok hulþi dúk.
             Fram setti hón   fulla skutla
             silfri varþa,   *setti* á bjóþ,
             faïn fleski,   fogla steikþa ;
             vín vas í könnu,   varþir kalkar,
             drukku ok dǿmþu,   dagr vas á sinnum.

24. (21)   Rígr kunni þeim   ráþ at segja,
             reis hann at þat,   rekkju görþi ;
             meirr lagþisk hann   miþrar rekkju,
             en á hliþ hvára   hjón salkynna.

21.—Keistr vas faldr, *C. G. S. ;* keisti falld, **W.**   24, lines 3 and 4.—*Not found in* **W** ; *supplied B. G. S.*

III.—THE BIRTH OF EARL.

21. Still on went Rig   the straight roads along
    till he came to a hall   whose gates looked south.
    Pushed was the door to,   a ring in the post set:
    he forthwith entered   the rush-strewn room.
    Each other eyeing,   the home-folk sat there—
    Father and Mother,—   twirling their fingers.
    There was the husband,   string a-twining,
    shafting arrows   and shaping bows:
    and there was the wife   o'er her fair arms wondering,
    smoothing her linen,   stretching her sleeves.
    A high-peaked coif   and a breast-brooch wore she,
    trailing robes   and a blue-tinged sark.
    Her brow was brighter,   her breast was fairer,
    her throat was whiter   than driven snow.

22. Well knew Rig   how to give them counsel;
    he sat him down   in the middle of the floor,
    and the home-folk twain   upon either side.

23. Then took Mother   a figured cloth,
    white, of linen,   and covered the board;
    thereafter took she   a fine-baked loaf,
    white, of wheat   and covered the cloth:
    next she brought forth   plenteous dishes,
    set with silver,   and spread the board
    with brown-fried bacon   and roasted birds.
    There was wine in a vessel   and rich-wrought goblets;
    they drank and revelled   while day went by.

24. Well knew Rig   how to give them counsel;
    he rose ere long   and prepared his couch:
    he laid him down   in the middle of the bed,
    and the home-folk twain   upon either side.

21.—Pushed to: *Icelandic* hnigin, *is usually rendered* open *in this passage, but* Vigfússon's, the door was down *or* shut, *suggests a contrast to the humbler dwellings;* st. 2, 11. *The ring was for the visitor to "tirl" at, as in old ballads.*

25. (22)   Þar vas at þat   þriar nǽtr saman,
              gekk meirr at þat   miþrar brautar,
              liþu meirr at þat   mánuþr niu.

26. (23)   Svein ól Móþir,   silki vafþi,
              jósu vatni,   Jarl létu heita ;
              bleikt vas hár,   bjartir vangar,
              ötul váru augu   sem yrmlingi.

27. (24)   Upp óx þar   Jarl á fletjum,
              lind nam skelfa   leggja strengi,
              alm at beygja,   örvar skepta,
              fleini fleygja,   frökkur dýja,
              hestum ríþa,   hundum verpa,
              sverþum bregþa,   sund at fremja.

28. (25-27)   Kvam þar ór runni   Rígr gangandi,
              Rígr gangandi,   rúnar kendi ;
              sitt gaf heiti,   sun kvezk eiga,
              þann baþ eignask   óþalvöllu,
              óþalvöllu,   aldnar bygþir.

29. (28)   Reiþ meirr þaþan   myrkvan viþ,
              hélug fjöll,   unz at höllu kvam.
              Skapt nam dýja   skelfþi lind,
              hesti hleypþi   ok hjörvi brá ;
              víg nam vekja,   völl nam rjóþa,
              val nam fella,   vá til landa.
    (29)   Réþ einn at þat   átján buum,
    (30)   auþ nam skipta,   öllum veita :
              meiþmar ok mösma,   mara svangrifja ;
              hringum hreytti,   hjó sundr baug.

30. (31)   Óku ǽrir   úrgar brautir,
              kvámu at höllu   þars Hersir bjó ;
              mey átti hann   mjófingraþa,
              hvíta ok horska :   hétu Ernu.

30.—Mey átti hann, *B. Gv. G. S. J. C.;* mǽtti hann, **W.**

25. Thus he tarried   three nights together;
    then on he strode   in the middle of the road
    while thrice three moons   were gliding by.

26. Then a boy had Mother;   she swathed him in silk,
    and with water sprinkled him;   called him Earl.
    Light were his locks,   and fair his cheeks,
    flashing his eyes   like a serpent's shone.

27. Grew Earl forthwith   in the halls and 'gan
    to swing the shield,   to fit the string,
    to bend the bow,   to shaft the arrow,
    to hurl the dart,   to shake the spear,
    to ride the horse,   to loose the hounds,
    to draw the sword,   and to swim the stream.

28. Forth from the thicket   came Rig a-striding,
    Rig a-striding,   and taught him runes,
    his own name gave him,—   as son he claimed him,
    and bade him hold   the ancestral fields,—
    the ancestral fields—   and the ancient home.

29. Then on rode Earl   through the murky wood,
    through the rimy fells   till he reached a hall.
    His shaft he shook,   his shield he brandished,
    his steed he galloped,   his sword he drew;
    war he wakened,   the field he reddened,
    the doomed he slew,   and won him lands—
    till alone he ruled   over eighteen halls.
    Gold he scattered   and gave to all men
    treasures and trinkets   and slender-ribbed horses;
    wealth he strewed   and sundered rings.

30. Along dewy roads   his messengers drove
    till the hall they reached   where Ruler dwelt.
    A daughter owned he,   dainty fingered,
    fair and skilful,   Erna called.

30.—Erna. *No satisfactory meaning has been suggested for this name.*

31. (32)   Báþu hennar   ok heim óku,
           giptu Jarli,   gekk und líni ;
           saman bjuggu þau   ok sér unþu,
           ættir jóku   ok aldrs nutu.

32. (33)   Burr vas enn elzti,   en Barn annat,
           Jóþ ok Aþal,   Arfi, Mögr,
           Niþr ok Niþjungr   (námu leika)
           Sunr ok Sveinn   (sund ok tafl) ;
           Kundr hét einn,   Konr vas enn yngsti.

33. (34)   Upp óxu þar   Jarli bornir,
           hesta tömþu   hlífar bendu,
           skeyti skófu,   skelfþu aska.
           En Konr ungr   kunni rúnar,
           æfinrúnar   ok aldrrúnar ;
           meirr kunni hann   mönnum bjarga,
           eggjar deyfa,   ægi lægja.
           Klök nam fogla,   kyrra elda,
           sefa of svefja,   sorgir lægja ;
           afl ok eljun   átta manna.

34. (34)   Hann viþ Ríg Jarl   rúnar deildi,
           brögþum beitti   ok betr kunni ;
           þá öþlaþisk   ok eiga gat
           Rígr at heita,   rúnar kunna.

35.   Reiþ Konr ungr   kjörr ok skóga,
           kolfi fleygþi,   kyrþi fogla ;
           þá kvaþ þat kráka,   sat á kvisti ein :
           'hvat skalt, Konr ungr !   kyrra fogla ?
           Heldr mættiþ ér   hestum ríþa

           . . . .

           . . . .

           [hjörum of bregþa]   ok her fella.

35.—*S. H. think five half lines are missing.* Hjörum of bregþa *supplied by*
B. Gv. S. J.

31. They wooed her and brought her   home a-driving;
    to Earl they wed her   in veil fine-woven:
    husband and wife   lived happy together,
    their children waxed   and life enjoyed.

IV.—THE BIRTH OF KING.

32. Heir was the eldest,   Bairn the second,
    Babe, Successor,   Inheritor, Boy,
    Descendent, Offspring,   Son, Youth, Kinsman;
    Kon the kingly   was youngest born.

33. Forthwith grew up   the sons of Earl;
    games they learned,   and sports and swimming,
    taming horses,   round shields bending,
    war shafts smoothing.   ash spears shaking;
    but King the youngest   alone knew runes,
    runes eternal   and runes of life.
    Yet more he knew,—   how to shelter men,
    to blunt the sword-edge   and calm the sea:
    he learnt bird language,   to quench the fire flame,
    heal all sorrows   and soothe the heart;
    strength and might   of eight he owned.

34. Then he strove in runes   with Rig, the Earl,
    crafty wiles   he used and won,
    so gained his heritage,   held the right thus
    Rig to be called   and runes to know.

35. Young King rode once   through thicket and wood,
    shooting arrows   and slaying birds,
    till spake a crow,   perched lone on a bough:
    'Why wilt thou thus   kill birds, young King?
    'Twould fit thee rather   to ride on horses,
    to draw the sword   and to slay the foe.

32.—*Kon* is *the masculine of* kona, *a woman. It is a word only found in poetry, applied to men of gentle or royal birth. The poet plays upon its resemblance to* konungr, *a king, and suggests a false derivation from* kon *and* ungr, *the young in order to show that Kon rose to the highest rank and became* Rig, *the* king; *st. 34.* 33, line 2.— *Transposed from 32. For the power of* runes, *see Háv. st. 145-163 and Introd.*

36. Á Danr ok Danpr   dýrar hallir,
  œþra óþal   an ér hafiþ;
  þeir kunnu vel   kjól at ríþa,
  egg at kenna,   undir rjúfa.'   . . .

36. 'Dan and Damp have   dwellings goodlier,
    homesteads fairer   than ye do hold ;
    and well they know   the keel to ride,
    the sword to prove   and wounds to strike.' . . .

36.—Dan and Damp *appear as Danish kings in the historical sagas. The end of this poem is missing, which tells of* Kon's *descendants, and probably of his invasion and conquest of Denmark.*

VÖLUSPÁ EN SKAMMA.

1. (28) Váru ellifu   æsir talþir,
          Baldr es hné   viþ banaþúfu;
          þess lézk Váli   verþr at hefna,
          es síns bróþur   sló handbana.

2. (29) Vas Baldrs faþir   Burs arfþegi

         . . . .
         . . . .
         . . . .

3. (29) Freyr átti Gerþi,   vas Gymis dóttir,
          jötna ǽttar   ok Aurboþu:
          þá vas Þjazi   þeira frǽndi,
          skautgjarn jötunn,   vas Skaþi dóttir.

This poem, found after st. 29 in **F**, *is generally regarded as an independent work;*
B. Mh. G. S. H. J. 1.—*The strophe numbering of Hdl. in* **F** *is marked in brackets.*
Line 4 is followed by alt's þat ǽtt þín Óttar heimski; **F**.

THE VALA'S SHORTER SOOTHSAYING.

1.   Eleven only   the war gods numbered
when Baldr sank   on the bale fire down;
but Váli showed him   strong to avenge it
and slew ere long   his brother's slayer.

2.   Father of Baldr   was Odin, Bur's son.

      *   *   *   *   *

3.   Frey wedded Gerd;   she was Gymir's daughter,
and Aurboda's   of Jötun race;
Thiazi also   came of their kindred,
the shape-shifting giant,   Skadi's sire.

Vala *or* Witch, *see Bdr, st. 4.*   1.—Vali, *see Bdr., st. 11 ; Vm., st. 51.*   2.—
Bur *means* son, *e.g. of Buri, the first-born of the god's race, and according to Snorri, the grandfather of Odin ; see Vsp. st. 4 and Introd. to Vm.*   3.—Gerd, *see Skm.* Aurboda, *or* Moisture-bringer?   Thiazi *took the form o an eagle; see Ls. st. 50, Introd., and Hrbl. st. 19.*

4. (30) Mart segjum þér   ok munum fleira;
         vörumk at viti svá,   vilt enn lengra?

5. (31) Heiþr ok Hrossþjófr   Hrimnis kindar.

6. (31) Eru völur allar   frá Víþolfi,
         vitkar allir   frá Vilmeiþi,
         en seiþberendr   frá Svarthöfþa,
         jötnar allir   frá Ymi komnir.

7. (32) Mart segjum þér   ok munum fleira;
         vörumk at viti svá,   vilt enn lengra?

8. (38) Ól ulf Loki   viþ Angrboþu,
         en Sleipni gat   viþ Svaþilfera;
         eitt þótti skars   allra feiknast,
         þat vas bróþur frá   Býleists komit.

9. (39) Loki *át* hjarta—   lindi brendu
         fann halfsviþinn   hugstein konu—;
         varþ Loptr kviþugr   af konu illri:
         þaþan's á foldu   flagþ hvert komit.

10. (34) Mart segjum þér   ok munum fleira;
          vörumk at viti svá,   vilt enn lengra?

11. (35) Varþ einn borinn   í árdaga
          rammaukinn mjök   ragna kindar;
          niu báru þann,   naddgöfgan mann,
          jötna meyjar   viþ jarþar þröm.

12. (35) Hann Gjölp of bar,   hann Greip of bar,
          bar hann Eistla   ok Eyrgjafa,
          hann bar Ulfrún   ok Angeyja,
          Imþr ok Atla   ok Iarnsaxa.

5.—*For the transposed lines, see Hdl.* 28.   6.—*Also found in* **Wr.**

4.   Much have I told thee,   yet more I remember;
     needs must one know it thus,—   wilt thou yet further?

5.   Witch and Horse-thief   are sprung from Rime-bringer,

6.   All the Valas   sprung from Forest-wolf,
     all the wizards   sprung from Wish-giver,
     all the sorcerers   sprung from Swart-head;
     and all the Jötuns   come from Ymir.

7.   Much have I told thee,   yet more I remember;
     needs must one know it thus,—   wilt thou yet further?

8.   Woe-bringer bore   the wolf to Loki,
     with Swadilfari   begat he Sleiphir.
     But one was deemed   the deadliest of all—
     the monster brood   from Loki born.

9.   When the heart of a woman—   home of love—
     he ate half-burned   with linden wood,
     and bore ere long   a loathly being
     whence witches all   in the world are sprung.

10.   Much have I told thee,   yet more I remember,
     needs must one know it thus,—   wilt thou yet further?

11.   One was there born   in days of old,
     girt with great power,   of the kindred of gods.
     Nine giant maidens   bore that being
     armed with glory   on the rim of earth.

12.   Yelper bore him,   Griper bore him,
     Foamer bore him,   Sand-strewer bore him,
     She-wolf bore him,   Sorrow-whelmer,
     Dusk and Fury   and Ironsword.

6.—Ymir, *see Vm. st. 21.*   8.—Woe-bringer, *or Angrboþa, a giantess, who was the mother of Fenrir, the World Serpent and Hel (Sn. E.).* Sleiphir, *see Bdr., st. 2.* 9.—*This strophe is perhaps explained by Vsp. st. 21, when the gods burn Golden-draught, the witch who is ever born anew.*   11-14.—*No name is mentioned in the text, but these strophes clearly refer to Heimdal or Rig; see Introd., Vsp. st. 1, and Rþ.*

13. (36) Sá vas aukinn jarþar megni,
    svalköldum sǽ ok sonardreyra.

14. (41) Varþ einn borinn öllum meiri,
    sá vas aukinn jarþar megni;
    þann kveþa stilli stórúþgastan,
    sif sifjaþan, sjötum görvöllum.

15. (37) Mart segjum þér ok munum fleira;
    vörumk at viti svá, vilt enn lengra?

16. (40) Haf gengr hríþum viþ himin sjalfan,
    líþr lönd yfir, en lopt bilar;
    þaþan koma snjóvar ok snarir vindar,
    þá's í ráþi, at regin of þrjóti.

17. (44) Þa kömr annarr enn mátkari,
    þó þorik eigi þann at nefna;
    faïr sea nú fram of lengra,
    an Óþinn mun ulfi mǿta.

14.—*After 16 in* **F**; *placed after 13 by Gv. S. G., who connect it with 11.*

13. He was girt with all   the power of Earth,
    of the ice-cold sea,   and of sacred swine-blood.

14. He was the One born   greater than any;
    girt with all   the power of Earth.
    Men call him ever   the richest ruler,
    Rig, the kinsman   of every race.

15. Much have I told thee,   yet more I remember,
    needs must one know it thus,—   wilt thou yet further?

16. The sea shall rise   in storms to heaven
    it shall sweep o'er the land   and the skies shall yield
    in showers of snow   and biting blasts
    at the Doom of the Powers,   the gods of war.

17. There shall come hereafter   another mightier
    whose name I dare not   now make known:
    few there are   who may see beyond
    when Odin fares   to fight with the Wolf.

17.—Another mightier *probably anticipates the coming of Christianity.*

HYNDLULJÓÞ.

Freyja kvaþ :

1. 'Vaki, mær meyja !   vaki, mín vina !
   Hyndla systir,   es í helli býr !
   nú's rökkr rökkra :   ríþa vit skulum
   til Valhallar,   til vés heilags.

2. Biþjum Herföþr   í hugum sitja ;
   hann geldr ok gefr   goll verþungu :
   gaf Hermóþi   hjalm ok brynju,
   en Sigmundi   sverþ at þiggja.

Hyndluljóþ.—*In F. and W. Freyja kvaþ, etc., is supplied. The speeches are not assigned in the MSS.*

THE LAY OF HYNDLA.

Freyja.

1.   Wake, maid of maidens,   friend, awaken,
    sister Hyndla,   in a rock-hole biding!
    Comes the gloom of gloaming,   we twain together
    must ride to Valhöll,   the holy dwelling.

2.   The War-father bid we   be mild in his mood,
    who grants and gives   to his followers gold;
    he gave to Hermod   a helm and byrnie
    and to Sigmund gave   a sword to take.

2.—*Hermod belongs to some lost tradition. He appears now as a god and now as a hero. In the Prose Edda he is the son of Odin (see Introd. Bdr.); in the old English poem of Beowolf he is a Danish King, mighty and beneficent in his youth, but a blood-*

2 G

3. Gefr sigr sonum,   en sumum aura,
    mælsku mörgum   ok mannvit firum;
    byri gefr brögnum   en brag sköldum,
    gefr mannsemi   mörgum rekki.

4. Þór mun blóta,   þess munk biþja,
    at æ viþ þik   einart láti;

. . . .
    þó's hánum ótítt   viþ jötuns brúþir.

5. Nú tak ulf þinn   einn af stalli,
    lát hann rinna   meþ runa mínum.

Hyndla kvaþ:

seinn es göltr þinn   goþveg troþa,
vilkak mar minn   mætan hlœþa.'

6. 'Flá est, Freyja!   es freistar mín,
    vísar augum   á oss þanig,
    es hefr ver þinn   í valsinni,
    Óttar unga,   Innsteins bur.'

Freyja kvaþ:

7. 'Dulin est, Hyndla!   draums ætlak þér,
    es kveþr ver minn   í valsinni,
    þars göltr gloar   gollinbursti,
    Hildisvíni,   as mer hagir görþu
    dvergar tveir   Daïnn ok Nabbi.

8. Sennum vit ór söþlum: sitja skulum
    auk of jöfra   ættir dœma;
    gumna þeira   es frá goþum kvámu

. . . .

4.—Mun, *Sv. S. J.;* mun hón, **F.**   5, lines 1 and 2.—*These lines are assigned to Freyja by B. Gv. H. Hl.; to Hyndla, G. Simrock.*   Lines 3 and 4.—*Spoken by Hyndla, B. Gv. Dt. Hl.; by Freyja, G. S. J., who have* minn *for* þinn.

3. To some grants he wealth,   to his children war-fame,
word-skill to many   and wisdom to men:
fair winds to sea-farers,   song-craft to skalds,
and might of manhood   to many a warrior.

4. To Thor will I offer   and this will I ask him,
to bear him truly   ever toward thee,
e'en though foe   of the wives of Jötuns.

5. Now of thy wolves   take one from the stall
and swift let him run   by the side of my boar.

Hyndla.

Nay! loth is thy swine,   to tread the gods' way,
nor will I burden   my noble beast.

6. False art thou, Freyja!   thou fain wouldst tempt me;
thine eyes betray thee;   thou turnest ever
to where on the Dead's way   thy lover is with thee,—
Ottar the youthful,   Instein's son.

Freyja.

7. Dull art thou, Hyndla!   I trow thou art dreaming,
when thou deemst my lover   is here on the Dead's road,
where Golden-bristle,   the boar, is glowing,
the swine of battle   which once they made me,
Daïn and Nabbi,   the crafty dwarfs.

8. Let us now strive   in our saddles sitting,
and hold converse o'er   the long long lines of kings,
heroes all   who are come from the gods.

---

thirsty tyrant when old, who is deserted by his subjects. Sigmund, *father of* Sigurd (*st. 25*). *At a wedding feast Odin entered and thrust his sword into a tree from which only Sigmund, the gods' favourite, could draw it.* 3.—Song-craft to skalds, *see Háv., st. 105, 139.* 6.—The Dead's way: *A road by which the dead warriors went to Valhöll.* Ottar: *The story of Freyja's human lover Ottar or Odd is told by Snorri.* 7.—The boar: Frey *owned the boar called* Golden-bristle, *which was forged by the dwarfs; see* Introd. Grm. Freyja, *according to Snorri, rode on a cat.* Daïn, the Dead one, *is mentioned in Vsp.*

9. (8) Þeir hafa veþjat   Vála malmi,
        Óttarr ungi   ok Angantýr :
        skylt's at veita,   svát skati enn ungi
        föþurleifþ hafi   ept frændr sína.

10.   Hörg mér görþi   *of* hlaþinn steinum—
        nú es grjót þat   at gleri orþit—,
   (10) rauþ í nýju   nauta blóþi ;
        æ trúþi Óttarr   á ásynjur.

11.   Nú lát forna   niþja talþa
        ok upp bornar   ættir manna :
        hvat's Skjöldunga,   hvat's Skilfinga,
        hvat's Öplinga,   hvat's Ynglinga,
        hvat's hölþborit,   hvat's hersborit,
        mest manna val   und miþgarþi ? '

                Hyndla kvaþ :

12.   ' Þú est, Óttarr !   borinn Innsteini,
        en Innsteinn vas   Alfi gamla,
        Alfr vas Ulfi,   Ulfr Sæfara,
        en Sæfari   Svan enum rauþa.

13.   Móþur áttir   menjum göfga,
        hykk at héti   Hlédís gyþja ;
        Fróþi vas faþir,   en † Friaut móþir :
        öll þótti ætt sú   meþ yfirmönnum.

14. (17) Vas Hildigunn   hennar móþir,
        Svávu barn   ok Sækonungs ;
        allt's þat ætt þín,   Óttarr heimski !
        varþar at viti svá,   vilt enn lengra ?

11.—Hvat's Öplinga, *B. Gv. H. G. S. C., missing in* F ; ynglinga *for* ylfinga, F ;
see st. 20.   13.—Móþur áttir, *Sv. S. G.;* átti faþir þinn, F, *Hl. J.*   14, etc.—
*The rearrangement of strophes has been made for the sake of clearness in the translation
to show the probable connection of names in Óttar's line. The numbers in brackets,* F.

9. Ottar the youthful,   and Angantyr—
on this have wagered   their wealth of gold;
needs must I help   the youthful hero
to hold the heritage   after his fathers.

10. He built me an altar   with stone o'erlaid;
like glass all riven   is that rock with fire,
for he reddened it oft   with the fresh blood of oxen;
aye to the goddesses   Ottar was true.

11. Come now let ancient   kinsman be numbered,
and let be told   the long lines of men:
who is of Skjöldungs,   who of Skilfings,
who is of Athlings,   who of Ynglings,
who is freeborn,   who is gentleborn,
choicest of all   the men under Midgarth?

Hyndla.
(Óttar's race.)

12. Thou art Ottar,   born of Instein;
Instein came   from Alf the Old,
Alf was from Wolf,   Wolf from Seafarer,
and Seafarer sprang   from Swan the Red.

13. Thou hadst a mother   shining in jewels,
Hledis, I ween,   she was named, the priestess;
her father was Frodi,   and Friaut her mother.
All of this race   among lords are reckoned.

14. Hildigunn was   the mother of Friaut;
child was she   of Svafa and Sea-king.
All this race is thine   Ottar the Simple!
Needs must one know it thus,   wilt thou yet further?

9.—Gold *is here called foreign metal. Icelandic* Valsk; *English* Welsh *originally meant* foreign. 11.—Skjöldings, *etc., see Introd. for these traditional race names.*

15. (19)   Ketill vas vinr þeirar,   Klypps arfþegi,
          vas móþurfaþir   móþur þinnar ;
          þar vas Fróþi   fyrr an Kári,
          enn eldri vas   Álfr of getinn.

16.   Nanna vas næst þar   Nökkva dóttir,
          vas mögr hennar   mágr þíns föþur ;
          fyrnd es sú mægþ,   fram telk lengra :
          allt's þat ætt þín,   Óttarr heimski !

17.   Ísolfr ok Ásolfr   Ölmóþs synir
          ok Skúrhildar   Skekkils dóttur,
          skalt til telja   skatna margra :
          allt's þat ætt þín,   Óttarr heimski !

18. (14)   Áli vas áþr   öflgastr manna,
          Halfdanr fyrri   hæstr Skjöldunga ;
          fræg vöru folkvíg   þaus framir görþu,
          hvarfla þóttu hans verk   meþ himins skautum.

19. (15)   Efldisk viþ Eymund,   œztan manna,
          en Sigtrygg *slô*   meþ svölum eggjum ;
          átti Almveigu,   œzta kvenna,
          ólu ok áttu   átján sunu.

20. (16)   Þaþan Skjöldungar,   þaþan Skilfingar,
          þaþan Öþlingar,   þaþan Ynglingar,
          þaþan hölþborit,   þaþan hersborit,
          mest manna val   und miþgarþi ;
          allt's þat ætt þín,   Óttarr heimski !

21. (18)   Dagr átti Þóru   drengja móþur,
          ólusk í ætt þar   œztir kappar :
          Fraþmarr ok Gyrþr   ok Frekar báþir,
          Ámr ok Josurmarr,   Álfr enn gamli :
          varþar at viti svá,   vilt enn lengra ?

15.—Þeirar, *S. G.;* þeirra, **F.**   16, line 3.—*Followed by a repetition of 24, line 3,* **F.**

15. Klyp's son Ketil   was spouse of Hildigun;
he was the father   of thy mother's mother.
Older than Kari   yet was Frodi,
but Alf was of all   the eldest born.

16. Next came Nanna,   the daughter of Nökkvir;
her son was thy father's   brother by wedlock.
Old is that kindship,   still on will I tell thee,
for all this race is thine,   Ottar the Simple.

17. Isolf and Osolf   were sons of Ölmod,
and born of Skurhild,   daughter of Skekkil.
Thou shalt reckon back   to many a chieftain.
All this race is thine   Ottar the Simple!

(Halfdan's Race.)

18. Far back was Ali,   mightiest of men:
Halfdan before him   highest of Skjöldungs,
whirled were his deeds   round the skirts of heaven,
great wars of nations   the chieftains waged.

19. He joined him to Eymund,   highest of heroes;
Sigtrygg slew   with the icy sword-edge,
wedded Almveig,   loftiest of ladies;
so he begat him   sons eighteen.

20. Thence are the Skjöldungs,   thence the Skilfings,
thence are the Athlings,   thence the Ynglings,
thence are freeborn,   thence are gentleborn,
all the choicest   of men under Midgarth.
All this race is thine,   Ottar the Simple;

21. Dag's wife was Thora,   mother of warriors;
reared in that race   were the mightiest heroes,
Fradmar and Gyrd,   and both the Wolf-cubs,
Josurmar, Am,   and Alf the Old.
Needs must one know it thus,   wilt thou yet further?

18.—Halfdan, *a mythical King of Denmark.*   19.—Eymund, *King of Novgorod and father of* Almveig *(Skaldskm).*   21.—Dag, *son of* Halfdan, *father of* Arngrim *(st. 22).*

22. (23) Þeir í Bolm austr   bornir váru
Arngríms synir   ok Eyfuru;
brökun berserkja,   böls margskonar,
of lönd ok of lög   sem logi fóeri:

23. (25) Hervarþr, Hjörvarþr,   Hrani, Angantýr,
Bui ok Brámi,   Barri ok Reifnir,
Tindr ok Tyrfingr,   tveir Haddingjar:
allt's þat ǽtt þín,   Óttarr heimski!

24. (22) Gunnarr balkr,   Grímr harþskafi,
jarnskjöldr Þórir,   Ulfr gínandi;
kunnak báþa   Brodd ok Hörvi,
váru þeir í hirþ   Hrolfs ens gamla.

25. (27) Þeir váru gumnar   goþum signaþir,
allir bornir   Jörmunreki,
(24) Sigurþar mági,   —hlýþ sögu minni!—
folkum grims   es Fáfni vá.

26. (25) Sá vas vísir   frá Völsungi
ok Hjördís   frá Hrauþungi,
en Eylimi   frá Öþlingum:
allt's þat ǽtt þín,   Óttarr heimski!

27. (26) Gunnarr ok Högni   Gjúka arfar
ok et sama Guþrún,   systir þeira:
eigi vas Gotþormr   Gjúka ǽttar,
þó vas bróþir   beggja þeira:
allt's þat ǽtt þín,   Óttarr heimski!

22, line 1.—*B. G. S. J.'s emendation to agree with* Örvar Odd's S., ani ómi váru bornir, **F.**   Line 4.—*Followed by* allt's, *etc.*, **F**, *om.* G S. J.   23, line 1.—*Supplied from* Örvar Odds S., *C. 14, and* Hervarar S., B. Gv. H. C. G. S. J.   24.—*B. suggests this transposition, because* Grim *and* Thorir *are mentioned at* Hrólf's Court *in* Forn. S., III., 57, G. H. S. J.   25, lines 1 and 2.—*Transposed by B. G. H. S. J.*

(The Berserks.)

22. Born in Bolm   in the eastern land
     were Arngrim's sons   and Eyfora's;
     woes unnumbered   the berserks worked,
     like the faring of fire   o'er land and sea.

23. Hervard, Hjörvard,   Hrani, Angantyr,
     Bui and Brami,   Barri and Reifnir,
     Tind and Tyrfing,   and Haddungs twain.
     All this race is thine,   Ottar the Simple!

24. Gunnar Battle-wall,   Grim Strongminded,
     Thorir Iron-shield,   Wolf the Gaper;
     Brod and Hörvi,   once I knew them,
     both in the train   of Hrolf the Old.

(The Völsung race.)

25. Given to the gods   were the warrior sons,
     all the children   of Jörmunrek,
     the kinsman of Sigurd—   list to my saga!—
     Fear of Nations,   who Fafnir slew.

26. That ruler was born   of the race of Völsungs,
     and Hjördis came,   his mother, of Hraudungs,
     and Eylimi,   her sire, of Athlings.
     All this race is thine,   Ottar the Simple!

27. Gunnar and Högni   were sons of Gjuki;
     Gudrun their sister,   was eke his offspring;
     but not of their kin   was Guthorm Battle-snake,
     though of the twain   he was held the brother.
     All this race is thine,   Ottar the Simple!

22-23.—*The story of* Angantyr *and the famous berserks is told in Hervarar S. and* Örvar Odds S.   24.—Hrolf, *probably* Hálf, *a famous King of Gauta-land, and hero of Hálf's S.*   25.—Jörmunrek, *the heroicised* Ermanric, *King of the Goths in the fourth century.* Sigurd, *the hero of the Völsunga S., and later Niebelungen lied.*   27.—Gjuki, *of Niflung race, a King of the Burgundians.* Guthorm, *his stepson, slew* Sigurd *at the desire of* Brynhild.

2 H

28. (31)　Haki vas Hveþnu　　hóti baztr sona,
　　　　　en Hveþnu vas　　Hjörvarþr faþir
　　　. . . . . . . 　　. . . . . .
　　　. . . . . . . 　　. . . . . .

29. (27)　Haraldr hilditönn　　borinn Hrœreki
　　　　　slöngvanbauga,　　sunr vas hann Auþar,
　　　　　Auþr djúpúþga　　Ívars dóttir,
　　　　　en Ráþbarþr vas　　Randvés faþir :
　　　　　allt's þat ætt þín,　　Óttarr heimski !'

Freyja kvaþ :

30.　　'Ber minnisöl　　mínum gelti,
　　　svát öll muni　　orþ at tína,
　　　þessa rœþu,　　á þriþja morni,
　　　þás þeir Angantýr　　ættir rekja.'

Hyndla kvaþ :

31.　　'Snuþu braut heþan !　　sofa lystir mik,
　　　fœr fátt af mér　　fríþra kosta :
　　　hleypr, eþlvina !　　úti á náttum,
　　　sem meþ höfrum　　Heiþrún fari.

32.　　Rannat at Óþi　　ey þreyjandi :
　　　skutusk þér fleiri　　und fyrirskyrtu ;
　　　hleypr, eþlvina !　　úti á náttum,
　　　sem meþ höfrum　　Heiþrún fari.'

Freyja kvaþ :

33.　　'Ek slæ eldi　　of íviþju,
　　　svát eigi kömsk　　óbrend heþan.

28.—*Transposed by B. G. S. J.*

28.   Best was Haki   of Hvedna's children;
     the father of Hvedna   was Hjörvard.

(Race of Harald War-tooth.)

29.   Born from Aud   was Harald War-tooth,
     son of Hrœrik,   Slinger of Rings.
     Aud Deep-thoughted   was Ivar's daughter,
     and Randver the son   of Radbard born.
     All this race is thine,   Ottar the Simple!

*   *   *   *   *

Freyja.

30.   To my boar now bear   the ale of memory,
     so shall he tell forth   all this tale
     when the third morn comes,   and with Angantyr
     he shall trace back the mighty   men of their race.

Hyndla.

31.   Hie away hence!   for I fain would sleep,
     and few fair words   shalt thou win from me.
     Thou gaddest forth,   good friend, at nights
     like a she-goat straying   bold among bucks.

32.   Yearning ever   thou hast followed Odd;
     many a sweetheart   has slept in thine arms.
     Thou gaddest forth,   good friend, at nights
     like a she-goat straying   bold among bucks.

Freyja.

33.   I will strike fire   about thee, giantess,
     so that unburnt   thou hie not hence.

29.—Harald War-tooth, *a King of Denmark.* Hrœrik, *a King of Sweden, husband of* Aud. *The saga of these mythical personages is told in Sögubrot and by Saxo Grammaticus.* 31.—A she-goat: *The name of the mythical goat* Heidrun *(Grm., st. 25) is here used in a general sense.*

Hyndla kvaþ :

'Hleypr, eþlvina !   úti á náttum,
sem meþ höfrum   Heiþrun fari.'

34. 'Hyr sék brinna   en hauþr loga,
verþa flestir   fjörlausn þola :
ber Óttari   bjór at hendi
eitrblandinn mjök,   illu heilli !
Hleypr, eþlvina !   úti á náttum
sem meþ höfrum   Heiþrun fari.'

Freyja kvaþ :

35. 'Orþheill þín skal   öngu ráþa,
þót, brúþr jötuns !   bölvi heitir ;
hann skal drekka   dýrar veigar,
biþk Óttari   öll goþ duga.'

Hyndla.

Thou gaddest forth,   good friend, at nights
like a she-goat straying   bold among bucks.

34. Lo ! all around us   the earth is flaming !
Many must render   their lives as ransom.
Bear now the ale-cup   to Ottar's hand,
all mingled with poison   and omens of ill.
Thou gaddest forth,   good friend, at nights
like a she-goat straying   bold among bucks.

Freyja.

35. The word of thine omen   shall work no evil,
albeit thou cursest,   vile wife of Jötuns;
sweet shall the draught be   that Ottar drinks,
for I pray all the Powers   to shield him well.

BALDRS DRAUMAR.

1.   Senn váru ǽsir   allir á þingi
ok ásynjur   allar á máli,
ok of þat réþu   ríkir tívar,
hví vǽri Baldri   ballir draumar.

2.   Upp reis Óþinn,   aldinn gautr,
auk á Sleipni   söþul of lagþi;
reiþ niþr þaþan   Niflheljar til,
mǿtti hvelpi   es ór helju kvam.

3. (2) Sá vas blóþugr   of brjóst framan
ok galdrs föþur   gó of lengi;
    (3) fram reiþ Óþinn   foldvegr dunþi,
hann kvam at hávu   Heljar ranni.

Baldrs Draumar.—*In* **A.**   3.—*Strophe numbering in* **A** *marked in brackets.*

BALDR'S DREAMS.

1. Straight were gathered   all gods at the doomstead,
   goddesses all were   in speech together;
   and the mighty Powers   over this took counsel,—
   why to Baldr   came dreams forboding.

2. Up rose Odin   the ancient creator;
   he laid the saddle   on gliding Sleipnir,
   and downward rode   into Misty Hel.
   Met him a hound   from a cavern coming;

3. all its breast   was blood-besprinkled,
   long it bayed   at the Father of Spells.
   Onward he rode,   the Earth's way rumbled,
   to the lofty hall   of Hel came Odin.

2.—Sleipnir: *Odin's eight-footed steed; see Vsp. en skamma, st. 8.* Misty Hel: *The dwelling place of the goddess Hel, daughter of Loki and Angrboþa; see Vsp. en skamma, st. 8, Ls. Introd.* A hound: *Garm; see Vsp. 44.* 3.—*The father of spells or magic, as in Háv. Odin sang some such song as that mentioned in Háv., st. 156.*

4.   þá reiþ Óþinn   fyr austan dyrr,
          þars hann vissi   völvü leiþi,
   (4)   nam vittugri   valgaldr kveþa,
          unz nauþug reis   nás orþ of kvaþ :

5. (4)   'Hvat's manna þat   mér ókunnra
          es höfumk aukit   erfitt sinni ?
   (5)   vask snivin snjóvi   ok slegin regni
          ok drifin döggu,   dauþ vask lengi.'

                    Óþinn kvaþ :

6.   'Vegtamr heitik,   sunr emk Valtams ;
          seg mer ór helju,   ek mun ór heimi :
          hveim eru bekkir   baugum sánir.
          flet fagrliga   flóiþ gulli ? '

                    Völva kvaþ :

7. (6)   'Hér stendr Baldri   of brugginn mjöþr,
          skírar veigar,   liggr skjöldr yfir ;
          en ásmegir   í ofvǽni.
          Nauþug sagþak,   nú munk þegja.'

                    Óþinn kvaþ :

8. (6)   'Þegjat, völva !   þik vilk fregna,
          unz alkunna,   vilk enn vita :
          hverr mun Baldri   at bana verþa
          ok Óþins sun   aldri rǽna ? '

                    Völva kvaþ :

9. (7)   'Höþr berr hávan   hróþrbaþm þinig,
          hann mun Baldri   at bana verþa
          ok Óþins sun   aldri rǽna.
          Nauþug sagþak,   nú munk þegja.'

6.—Flóiþ, *B. G. S.;* flóþ, **A.**

4. Round he rode   to a door on the eastward
where he knew   was a witch's grave.
He sang there spells   of the dead to the Vala;
needs she must rise—   a corpse—and answer:

5. 'What man is this   to me unknown,
who torment adds   to my toilsome way?
I was snowed on with snow,   and dashed with rain,
I was drenched with dew,   I have long been dead.'

Odin.

6. 'They call me Waywont   I am son of Warwont;
tell me tidings of Hel,   I will tell of the world.
For whom are the benches   strewn with rings,
for whom is the fair daïs   flooded with gold?'

Vala.

7. 'Here stands for Baldr   brewed the mead,
the shining cup,   the shield lies over,
but the gods' race all   are in despair.
Needs have I spoken,   now will I cease.'

Odin.

8. 'Cease not, Vala!   still will I ask thee,
I must see yet onward   till all I know:—
who will be   the slayer of Baldr,
who Odin's son   will of life bereave?'

Vala.

9. 'Höd shall bear thither   the high-grown Fame-bough,
he will be   the slayer of Baldr,
yea, Odin's son   will of life bereave.
Needs have I spoken,   now will I cease.'

6.—Waywont: *Odin as wanderer; Cf. Gangleri, Grm., st. 49.* 9.—The Fame-bough *or mistletoe which, according to Snorri, Loki puts into the hands of blind Höd; see Vsp. 32, Ls. st. 28, Fj. st. 26.*

Óþinn kvaþ :

10. (7) 'Þegjat, völva !   þik vilk fregna,
unz alkunna,   vilk enn vita :
hverr mun heiptar [Heþi]   hefnt of vinna
eþa Baldrs bana   á bál vega ?'

Völva kvaþ :

11. (8) 'Rindr berr Vála   í vestrsölum,
sa mun Óþins sunr   einnǽttr vega ;
hönd of þvǽrat   né höfuþ kembir,
áþr á bál of berr   Baldrs andskota.
Nauþug sagþak,   nú munk þegja.'

Óþinn kvaþ :

12. (8) 'Þegjat, völva !   þik vilk fregna,
unz alkunna,   vilk enn vita :
(9) hverjar'u meyjar   es at muni gráta
ok á himin verpa   halsa skautum ?'

Völva kvaþ :

13. (10) 'Estat Vegtamr,   sem ek hugþa,
heldr est Óþinn,   aldinn gautr !'

Óþinn kvaþ :   .

'Estat völva   né vís kona,
heldr est þriggja   þursa móþir !'

Völva kvaþ :

14. (11) 'Heim ríþ, Óþinn !   ok ves hróþugr :
svá komir manna   meirr aptr á vit,
es lauss Loki   líþr ór böndum
ok í ragna rök   rjúfendr koma.'

14.—Ok í ragna rök, *B. G. S.*, **A** ; ok ragna rök, *Dt. and Hl.*

Odin.

10. 'Cease not, Vala, still will I ask thee,
 I must see yet onward till all I know :—
 who shall work revenge for the woe on Höd,
 and lay on the bale fire Baldr's foe ?'

Vala.

11. 'Rind shall bear Vali in the western halls;
 he, Odin's son, shall fight one night old.
 Nor hand will he wash, nor head will he comb
 till he lay on the bale fire Baldr's foe.
 Needs have I spoken, now will I cease.'

Odin.

12. 'Cease not, Vala, still will I ask thee,
 I must see yet onward till all I know :—
 who are the maidens who weep at will,
 and up toward heaven their neck veils fling ?'

Vala.

13. 'Not Waywont art thou as I had weened,
 but thou art Odin, the ancient creator !'

Odin.

'No Vala art thou nor woman wise,
but of three giants thou art mother !'

Vala.

14. 'Ride homeward, Odin, glorying in thy gain !
 for thus shall no being ever meet me more,
 ere Loki roves from his fetters free,
 and the Destroyers come at the Powers' great Doom.'

11.—Rind, *the giant wife of Odin; see Gg., st. 6.* Vali, *see Vm. 51; Vsp. en skamma, st. 1.* 12.—Their neck veils : *Icelandic,* halsa skautum, *is of uncertain meaning.* Skaut *is used for* sheet, corner, quarter of the heavens, sail, part of a woman's dress. *Dt. inclines to the above ; G.,* sail corners. *If the expression is nautical, Wimmer suggests that the maidens are wave daughters of Ægir ; see Hym., st. 2.*

LOKASENNA.

FRÁ ÆGI OK GOÞUM.

Ægir, er öþru nafni hét Gymir, hann hafþi búit ásum öl, þá er hann hafþi fengit ketil inn mikla, sem nú er sagt. Til þeirar veizlu kom Óþinn ok Frigg kona hans. Þórr kom eigi, þuiat hann var í austrvegi. Síf var þar, kona Þórs; Bragi ok Iþunn kona hans. Týr var þar, hann var einhendr: Fenrisúlfr sleit hönd af hánum, þá er hann var bundinn. Þar var Njörþr ok kona hans Skaþi, Freyr ok Freyja, Víþarr sonr Óþins. Loki var þar, ok þjónustumenn Freys Byggvir ok Beyla. Mart var þar ása ok álfa. Ægir atti twá þjonustu-

LOKI'S MOCKING

AT THE BANQUET OF ÆGIR.

Ægir, who is also called Gymir (the Binder), bade the gods to an ale feast after he had got possession of the great cauldron—as already told. To this banquet came Odin and Frigg, his wife. Thor came not because he was journeying in the East-country, but his wife Sif was there, and Bragi, with his wife Idun; Tyr also, who was one-handed, because the wolf Fenrir had torn off the other hand while the gods were binding him. There were Njörd and his wife Skadi, Frey and his servants Barley and Beyla, Freyja, Vidar, the son of Odin, with many other gods and elves; there, moreover, was Loki. Ægir had two servants—Nimble-snatcher and Fire-stirrer. Shining gold was

---

As already told.—*See Hm.*   East-country, *or Jötunheim.*

menn : Fimafengr ok Eldir. Þar var lýsigull haft fyrir elds ljós;
sjálft barsk þar öl; þar var griþstaþr mikill. Menn löfuþu mjök hversu
góþir þjonustumenn Ægis váru. Loki mátti eigi heyra þat, ok draþ
hann Fimafeng. Þa skóku œsir skjöldu sina ok œpþu at Loka ok eltu
hann braut til skógar, en þeir faru at drekka. Loki hvarf aptr ok hitti
úti Eldi; Loki kvaddi hann:

Loki kvaþ :

1. 'Seg þat, Eldir! svát þú einugi
   feti gangir framarr :
   hvat hér inni hafa at ölmálum
   sigtíva synir ? '

Eldir kvaþ:

2. 'Of vápn sín dœma ok of vígrisni sína
   sigtíva synir :
   ása ok alfa es hér inni 'rú
   mangi's þér í orþi vinr.'

Loki kvaþ :

3. 'Inn skal ganga Ægis hallir í
   á þat sumbl at sea ;
   joll ok áfu fœrik ása sunum
   ok blentk þeim meini mjöþ.'

Eldir kvaþ :

4. 'Veiztu, ef inn gengr Ægis hallir í
   á þat sumbl at sea,
   hróþi ok rógi ef þú eyss á holl regin,
   á þér munu þerra þat.'

Loki kvaþ :

5. 'Veizt þat, Eldir! ef vit einir skulum
   sáryrþum sakask,
   auþugr verþa munk í andsvörum,
   ef þú mælir til mart.'

used in the hall for the light of fire, the ale bore itself, and the place was held as a holy peace-stead. Men praised Ægir's servants, and said oft how good they were; but Loki could not brook this, and he slew Nimble-snatcher. The gods all shook their shields and cried out against Loki, and chased him away to the woods, and then betook themselves again to drink. But Loki turned back, and finding Fire-stirrer standing without, he hailed him :—

Loki.

1. Tell me, Fire-stirrer—   but whence thou standest
        move not a single step—
   what are the sons   of the war-gods saying
        o'er the ale-cup here within ?

Fire-stirrer.

2. Of their weapons are speaking   the sons of the war-gods,
        they boast of their battle-fame ;
   but 'mid gods and elves   who within are gathered,
        not one is thy friend in his words.

Loki.

3. I shall now enter   the halls of Ægir
        this banquet to behold :
   mockery and strife   will I bring to the god's sons,
        and mingle sorrow with their mead.

Fire-stirrer.

4. Know, if thou enter   the halls of Ægir
        this banquet to behold,
   if reproach and slander   on the blest Powers thou pour
        they shall wipe out thy words upon thee.

Loki.

5. Know thou, Fire-stirrer,   if we twain must fight
        together with wounding words,—
   if thou talk too freely   thou soon shalt find me
        in answering ready and rich.

Síþan gekk Loki inn í höllina, en er þeir sá, er fyrir váru, hverr inn var kominn, þögnuþu þeir allir.

Loki kvaþ:

6.　'Þyrstr ek köm　　þessar hallar til,
　　　Loptr, of langan veg,
　　ásu at biþja,　　at mér einn gefi
　　　mæran drykk mjaþar.

7. (6)　Hví þegiþ ér svá,　　þrungin goþ!
　　　at ér mæla né meguþ?
　　sessa ok staþi　　veliþ mér sumbli at,
　　　eþa heitiþ mik heþan.'

Bragi kvaþ:

8. (7)　'Sessa ok staþi　　velja þér sumbli at
　　　æsir aldrigi;
　　þvít æsir vitu,　　hveim þeir alda skulu
　　　gambansumbl of geta.'

Loki kvaþ:

9. (8)　'Mant þat, Óþinn!　　es vit í árdaga
　　　blendum blóþi saman?
　　ölvi bergja　　lézt eigi mundu,
　　　nema okkr væri báþum borit.'

Óþinn kvaþ:

10. (9)　'Rís þá, Víþarr!　　ok lát ulfs föþur
　　　sitja sumbli at,
　　síþr oss Loki kveþi　　lastastöfum
　　　Ægis höllu í.'

7.—*Strophe numbering of* **R** *in brackets.*

Then Loki entered the hall, and when those assembled saw who was come in they all became silent.

Loki.

6. Thirsty come I,   the Rover of Air,
    to this feasting hall from afar;
I would ask the gods   to give me but one
    sweet draught of the mead to drink.

7. Why all silent   ye sullen gods?
    Can ye speak no single word?
Make me room on the bench,   give me place at the banquet,
    or bid me hie homeward hence.

Bragi.

8. Nor place at the banquet   nor room on the bench
    the gods shall give to thee;
well they know   for what manner of wight
    they should spread so fair a feast.

Loki.

9. Mindest thou, Odin,   how we twain of old
    like brothers mingled our blood?
Then saidst thou that never   was ale-cup sweet
    unless 'twere borne to us both.

Odin.

10. Rise up, Vidar,   and give the Wolf's father
    bench-room at the banquet,
lest Loki shame us   with scornful speeches
    here in Ægir's halls.

8.—Bragi, *the god of poetry.*   9.—*The mingling of blood sealed a brotherhood in arms.* Loki, Odin, *and* Hœnir *were companions in many strange adventures.*   10.— Vidar, *see* Grm. *17;* Vsp., *st. 54.* Loki *was the father of* Fenrir, *see st. 39;* Vsp. en skamma, *st. 8.*

þá stóþ Víþarr upp ok skenkþi Loka; en áþr hann drykki, kvaddi hann ásuna:

11. (10) 'Heilir æsir,   heilar ásynjur
              ok öll ginnheilug goþ!
           nema einn áss   es innar sitr,
              Bragi, bekkjum á.'

                    Bragi kvaþ:

12. (11) 'Mar ok mæki   gefk þer míns fear
              ok bœtir svá baugi Bragi,
           síþr þú ásum   öfund of gjaldir;
              gremjat goþ at þér!'

                    Loki kvaþ:

13. (12) 'Jós ok armbauga   mundu æ vesa
              beggja vanr, Bragi!
           ása ok alfa   es hér inni 'rú
              þú'st viþ víg varastr
              ok skjarrastr viþ skot.'

                    Bragi kvaþ:

14. (13) 'Veitk, ef fyr útan værak,   sem fyr innan emk
              Ægis höll of kominn,
           haufuþ þitt   bærak í hendi mér:
              létak þér þat fyr lygi.'

                    Loki kvaþ:

15. (14) 'Snjallr est í sessi,   skalta svá göra,
              Bragi, bekkskrautuþr!
           vega þú gakk,   ef þú vreiþr seïr!
              hyggsk vætr hvatr fyrir.'

                    Íþunn kvaþ:

16. (15) 'Biþk þik, Bragi!   barna sifjar duga
              ok allra óskmaga,
           at þú Loka kveþjat   lastastöfum
              Ægis höllu í.'

Then Vidar arose and poured out ale for Loki, who thus greeted the gods before he drank :—

11.   Hail, ye gods,   and goddesses, hail !
          hail all ye holy Powers !—
      save only one   who sits within,
          thou, Bragi, upon the bench !

Bragi.

12.   Steed and sword   from my store will I give thee
          and reward thee well with rings
      lest thou pour thy hate   on the gracious Powers.
          Rouse not their wrath against thee !

Loki.

13.   Nor steeds nor rings   wilt thou ever own
          as long as thou livest, Bragi :
      thou art wariest in war,   and shyest at shot
          of all gods and elves herein.

Bragi.

14.   Were I without now   even in such mood
          as within the halls of Ægir,
      that head of thine   would I hold in my hand :—
          'twere little reward for thy lie !

Loki.

15.   Bold seemst thou sitting,   but slack art thou doing,
          Bragi, thou pride of the bench !
      Come forth and fight   if in truth thou art wroth ;
          a bold warrior bides not to think.

Idun.

16.   Nay Bragi, I beg   for the sake of blood-kindred,
          and of all the war-sons of Odin,
      upbraid not Loki   with bitter speeches
          here in Ægir's halls.

16.—Idun, *Bragi's wife. The myth of st. 17 is unknown.*

LOKASENNA.

Loki kvaþ :

17. (16) 'Þegi þú, Íþunn !   þik kveþk allra kvenna
vergjarnasta vesa,
síztu arma þína   lagþir ítrþvegna
umb þinn bróþurbana.'

Íþunn kvaþ :

18. (17) 'Loka ek kveþka   lastastöfum
Ægis höllu i ;
Braga ek kyrri   bjórreifan :
vilkak at vreiþir vegisk.'

Gefjun kvaþ :

19. (18) 'Hvi it æsir tveir   skuluþ inni hér
sáryrþum sakask ?
Loka þat veit,   at hann leikinn es
ok hann fjörg öll fiar.'

Loki kvaþ :

20. (19) 'Þegi þú, Gefjun !   þess munk nú geta,
hverr þik glapþi at geþi :
sveinn enn hvíti   þér sigli gaf
ok þú lagþir lær yfir.'

Óþinn kvaþ :

21. (20) 'Œrr est, Loki !   ok örviti,
es þú fær þér Gefjun at gremi :
þvít aldar örlög   hykk at öll of viti
jafngörla sem ek.'

Loki kvaþ :

22. (21) 'Þegi þú, Óþinn !   þú kunnir aldri
deila víg meþ verum :
opt þú gaft   þeims gefa né skyldir
enum slævurum sigr.'

19.—Loka, *Gv. S. G.;* Lopzki, **R.**   Fiar, *Kölbing, S. G.;* fría, **R**; fia, *Sv. J.*
20.—Hverr þik, *Gv. S. G.;* er þik, **R.**

Loki.

17. Silence, Idun!   I swear, of all women
    thou the most wanton art;
who couldst fling those fair-washed   arms of thine
    about thy brother's slayer.

Idun.

18. I blame thee not, Loki,   with bitter speeches
    here in Ægir's halls.
I seek but to sooth   the ale-stirred Bragi,
    lest in your fierceness ye fight.

Gefjon.

19. Wherefore, ye gods twain   with wounding words
    strive ye here in the hall?
Who knows not Loki,   that he loathes all beings
    and mocks in his madness of soul?

Loki.

20. Silence, Gefjon!   I will tell that tale
    of him who once stole thy heart,—
that fair swain who gave thee   a shining necklace,
    him thou didst hold in thine arms.

Odin.

21. Wild art thou, Loki,   and witless now,
    thus rousing Gefjon to wrath!
I ween she knows   all the fate of the world
    even as surely as I.

Loki.

22. Silence, Odin!   When couldst thou ever
    rule battles of men aright?
Oft hast thou given   to them who had earned not,
    to the slothful victory in strife.

20.—*Gefjon is only mentioned here in the Poetical Edda. The myth is usually told of Freyja; see Þrк st. 12 and Introd.*

Óþinn kvaþ:

23. (22) 'Veizt, ef ek gaf　　þeims gefa né skyldak,
　　　　　enum slǽvurum sigr:
　　　　　átta vetr　　vastu fyr jörþ neþan
　　　　　kýr molkandi ok kona
　　　　　ok hefr þar börn of borit,
　　　　　ok hugþak þat args aþal.'

Loki kvaþ:

24. (23) 'En þik síþa　　kváþu Sámseyju í,
　　　　　ok drapt á vétt sem völur:
　　　　　vitka líki　　fórtu verþjóþ yfir,
　　　　　ok hugþak þat args aþal.'

Frigg kvaþ:

25. (24) 'Örlögum ykkrum　　skyliþ aldrigi
　　　　　segja seggjum frá:
　　　　　hvat it ǽsir tveir　　drýgþuþ í árdaga,
　　　　　firrisk ǽ forn rök firar.'

Loki kvaþ:

26. (25) 'Þegi þú, Frigg!　　þú'st Fjörgyns mǽr
　　　　　ok hefr ǽ vergjörn verit,
　　　　　es þá Vé ok Vilja　　léztu þér, Viþris kvǽn!
　　　　　báþa í baþm of tekit.'

Frigg kvaþ:

27. (26) 'Veizt, ef inni ǽttak　　Ægis höllum í
　　　　　Baldri glíkan bur,
　　　　　út né kvǽmir　　frá ása sunum,
　　　　　ok væri at þér vreiþum vegit.'

Odin.

23. Know, if ever I gave   to them who had earned not,
    to the slothful victory in strife,
eight winters wert thou   below in the earth
    like a maiden, milking kine,
and there thou gavest   birth to bairns,—
    which I weened was a woman's lot.

Loki.

24. But thou in Samsey   wast weaving magic
    and making spells like a witch:
thou didst pass as wizard   through the world of men,—
    which I weened was a woman's way.

Frigg.

25. Tell ye to no man   the shameful tale
    of the deeds ye did of old,—
how ye two gods wrought   in ancient time;—
    what is gone is best forgot.

Loki.

26. Silence, Frigg! who hast   Earth's spouse for a husband,
    and hast ever yearned after men!
Vé the holy,   and Vili the lustful
    both lay in thine arms, wife of Odin.

Frigg.

27. Know, if I had but   in Ægir halls,
    a son like my Baldr, the slain,   [gods
thou wouldst ne'er come whole   through the host of the
    but fiercely thou shouldst be assailed.

23.—*This strophe perhaps alludes to another version of the myth of Vsp. en skamma,
st. 9.*   24.—*Samsey, modern Samsö, north of Funen.*   26, *line* 1.—*This line has
often been misunderstood, by Snorri and later critics. The literal* thou art Fjörgynn's
maid *has been rendered* thou art Fjörgynn's daughter. *But Fjörgynn is only another
name for Odin in his character as the husband of Fjörgyn or Jörd, the Earth, and mother
of Thor. Vé and Vili, the brothers of Odin, may also be taken as different aspects of the
same god. The name used in the text for Odin is Vidrir, the Stormer; see Grm., st. 51.*

Loki kvaþ:

28. (27) 'Enn vill þú, Frigg!   at ek fleiri telja
          mína meinstafi:
          ek því réþ,   es þú ríþa sérat
          síþan Baldr at sölum.'

Freyja kvaþ:

29. (28) 'Œrr est, Loki!   es þú yþra telr
          ljóta leiþstafi:
          örlög Frigg   hykk at öll viti,
          þót hón sjölfgi segi.'

Loki kvaþ:

30. (29) 'Þegi þú, Freyja!   þik kannk fullgörva,
          esa þér vamma vant:
          ása ok alfa   es hér inni 'rú
          hverr hefr hórr þinn verit.'

Freyja kvaþ:

31. (30) 'Flá's þér tunga,   hykk at þér fremr
          myni ógott of gala;
          vreiþir'u þér æsir   ok ásynjur,
          hryggr munt heim fara.'

Loki kvaþ:

32. (31) 'Þegi þú, Freyja!   þú'st fordæþa
          ok meini blandin mjök:
          síz þík at brœþr þínum   stóþu blíþ regin,
          ok mundir þá, Freyja! frata.'

Njörþr kvaþ:

33. (32) 'Þat's vá litil,   þót sér vers faï
          varþir, hóss eþa hvárs;
          undr's at áss ragr   es hér inn of kominn
          ok hefr sá börn of borit.'

32.—Stóþu, *B. Gv. H. Sv. G. S. J.;* siþu, **R.**

Loki.

28. Wouldst have me, Frigg,   tell a few more yet
    of these shameful stories of mine?
  'Twas I wrought the Woe,   that henceforth thou wilt not
    see Baldr ride back to the halls.

Freyja.

29. Mad art thou, Loki,   to tell thus the shame
    and grim deeds wrought by you gods!
  Frigg knows, I ween,   all the fate of the world;
    though she whispers thereof to none.

Loki.

30. Silence, Freyja!   Full well I know thee
    and faultless art thou not found;
  of the gods and elves   who here are gathered
    each one hast thou made thy mate.

Freyja.

31. False thy tongue is!   Too soon 'twill sing
    its own song of woe, as I ween.
  Wroth are the gods,   and the goddesses wroth,
    rueful thou soon shalt run home.

Loki.

32. Silence, Freyja!   Thou art a sorceress
    all with evil blent:
  once at thy brother's   the blithe gods caught thee,
    and then wast thou frightened, Freyja!

Njörd.

33. Small harm it seems   if haply a woman
    both lover and husband have;
  but behold the horror   now in the halls,
    the vile god who bairns hath borne!

28.—*The only allusion in the Poetical Edda to Loki's share in the death of Baldr;
see Bdr. Introd. Possibly it only refers to Loki's refusal to weep (Nd. Dalt., 41).*
29.—*By you gods: so Gering and Dt. Hl. take yþra.*   32.—*No such myth of Frey or
Freyja is mentioned elsewhere.*   2 L

Loki kvaþ :

34. (33) Þegi þú, Njörþr!   þú vast austr heþan
     gísl of sendr at goþum ;
     Hymis meyjar   höfþu þik at hlandtrogi
     ok þér í munn migu.'

Njörþr kvaþ :

35. (34) 'Sú erumk líkn,   es vask langt heþan
     gísl of sendr at goþum :
     þa ek mög gat   þanns manngi fiar,
     ok þykkir sá ása jaþarr.'

Loki kvaþ :

36. (35) 'Hætt nú, Njörþr!   haf á hófi þik !
     munkak því leyna lengr :
     viþ systur þinni   gaztu slíkan mög
     ok esa þó ónu verr.'

Týrr kvaþ :

37. (36) ' Freyr es baztr   allra baldriþa
     ása görþum í ;
     mey né grætir   né manns konu,
     ok leysir ór höptum hvern.'

Loki kvaþ :

38. (37) 'Þegi þú, Týr!   þú kunnir aldri
     bera tilt meþ tveim :
     handar hœgri   munk hinnar geta
     es þér sleit Fenrir frá.'

Týrr kvaþ :

39. (38) 'Handar emk vanr,   en þú Hróþvitnis,
     böl es beggja þrá :
     ulfgi hefr ok vel   es í böndum skal
     bíþa ragna rökkrs.'

34.—At goþum : *B. suggests af goþum, but at is occasionally used, as here, to denote source (Dt.). G. and others take it in the ordinary meaning* to, *and understand an allusion to Vm. 39.*

Loki.

34. Silence, Njörd! Thou wast eastward sent
  as hostage from hence by the gods;
there into thy mouth flowed the maids of Hymir
  and used thee as trough for their floods.

Njörd.

35. Yet was I gladdened when sent afar,
  as hostage from hence by the gods;
there a son I got me, the foe of none,
  and highest held among gods.

Loki.

36. Silence now, Njörd! Set bounds to thy lying;
  I will no longer let this be hid—
with thine own sister that son thou gottest,
  though he is not worse than one weened.

Tyr.

37. Nay! Frey is the best of all bold riders
  who enter the garths of the gods;
nor wife nor maiden he makes to weep,
  but he breaks the prisoner's bonds.

Loki.

38. Silence, Tyr! Who in truth couldst never
  bring good will betwixt twain;
the tale will I tell of that right hand
  which Fenrir reft from thee once.

Tyr.

39. If I want for a hand for thy Wolf-son, thou;
  we both bear burden of want:
and 'tis ill with the Wolf who must bide in bonds
  till the twilight come of the Powers.

34.—Njörd *figures here in his character of sea god; see Fragments from Sn. E.* 36.—A son, *presumably got with the giantess Skadi, but in Ynglinga S. it is stated that* Njörd *was married to his sister, and had a son and daughter, Frey and Freyja, before even he was sent as hostage by the Wanes to the Æsir.* 38.—*See Introd.* 39.— Twilight of the Powers *or* Ragna rökr: *This is the only use of* rökr *in the poems, which has given rise to the phrase "twilight of the gods." The more usual form was* rök *or* fate.

Loki kvaþ:

40. (39) 'Þegi þú, Týr!   þat varþ þinni konu,
           at hón átti mög viþ mér;
        öln né penning   hafþir þú þess aldrigi
           vanréttis, vesall!'

Freyr kvaþ:

41. (40) 'Ulf sék liggja   árósi fyrir,
           unz of rjúfask regin;
        því munt næst,   nema nú þegir,
           bundinn, bölvasmiþr!'

Loki kvaþ:

42. (41) 'Golli keypta   léztu Gymis dóttur
           ok seldir þitt svá sverþ;
        en es Múspells synir   ríþa Myrkviþ yfir,
           veizta þá, vesall! hvé vegr.'

Byggvir kvaþ:

43. (42) 'Veizt, ef öþli ættak   sem Ingunar-Freyr,
           ok svá sællikt setr,
        mergi smæra mölþak   þá meinkráku
           ok lempa alla í liþu.'

Loki kvaþ:

44. (43) 'Hvat's þat et litla,   es ek þat löggra sék,
           ok snapvíst snapir?
        at eyrum Freys   mundu æ vesa
           auk und kvernum klaka.'

Loki.

40. Be silent, **Tyr**, while I tell of the son
    whom thy wife got once by me :
    not even a penny or ell of cloth
    didst thou get for thy wrong, poor wretch !

Frey.

41. I see Fenrir lying at the mouth of the flood ;
    he shall bide till the Powers perish ;
    and thou, mischief-maker, shalt meet with like fate
    if thou hold not herewith thy peace.

Loki.

42. Wealth gav'st thou, Frey, for Gymir's maid,
    thou didst sell thy sword for Gerd ;
    but how shalt thou fight when the sons of fire
    through the Murk-wood ride, poor wretch ?

Barley.

43. Were I of Ing's race even as Frey—
    owned I a land blest as Elfhome—
    I would crush like marrow yon croaker of ill,
    and break all his bones into bits.

Loki.

44. What is that wee thing whining and fawning,
    snuffling and snapping, I see ?
    Ever at Frey's ear, flattering and chattering,
    or murmuring under the mill !

40.—*A lost myth.* 41.—The flood, *called* Vamm *or* Van *by Snorri, is a river of Hel proceeding from the moisture which flowed out of Fenrir's jaws while the great Wolf lay bound in torture.* 42.—*Frey is slain by Surt, the Fire-giant, at the Doom of the gods ; see Vsp. 54. Gymir, Gerd, see Skm.* 43.—*Ing was the half divine ancestor of the Germanic race who gave his name to the Ynglings or Swedes (Hdl., st. 11) and to the Ingvines mentioned by Tacitus. In Sweden he became associated with Frey, who was there the chief god. Elf-home, see Grm., st. 5.*

Byggvir kvaþ :

45. (44) 'Byggvir heitik,   en mik bráþan kveþa
goþ öll ok gumar ;
því emk hér hróþugr,   at drekka Hrópts megir
allir öl saman.'

Loki kvaþ :

46. (45) 'Þegi þú, Byggvir !   þú kunnir aldri
deila meþ mönnum mat ;
þik í flets straï   finna né máttu,
þá es vágu verar.'

Heimdallr kvaþ :

47. (46) 'Ölr est, Loki !   svát þú'st örviti,
hví né lezkat, Loki ?
þvít ofdrykkja   veldr alda hveim,
es sína mælgi né manat.'

Loki kvaþ :

48. (47) 'Þegi þú, Heimdallr !   þér vas í árdaga
et ljóta líf of lagit :
örþgu baki   þú munt æ vesa
ok vaka vörþr goþa.'

Skaþi kvaþ :

49. (48) 'Létt's þér, Loki !   munattu lengi svá
leika lausum hala ;
þvít þik á hjörvi skulu   ens hrímkalda magar
görnum binda goþ.'

Loki kvaþ :

50. (49) 'Veizt, ef mik á hjörvi skulu   ens hrímkalda magar
görnum binda goþ :
fyrstr ok öfstr   vask at fjörlagi,
þars ver á Þjaza þrifum.'

Barley.

45. Barley, I am named,   too bold and brisk
    I am called by gods and men!
Here am I glorying   that Odin's sons
    all are drinking ale together!

Loki.

46. Silence, Barley-corn!   Never couldst thou
    even serve meat among men:
and when they fought   thou couldst scarce be found,
    safe 'neath the bed-straw hiding.

Heimdal.

47. So drunk art thou, Loki,   thou hast lost thy wits;
    why wilt thou not cease from thy scoffing?
Ale beyond measure   so masters man
    that he keeps no watch on his words.

Loki.

48. Silence, Heimdal!   That hard life of thine
    was settled for thee long since:
with weary back   must thou ever bide,
    and keep watch, thou warder of gods!

Skadi.

49. Blithe are thou, Loki,   but brief while shalt thou
    with free tail frolic thus:
ere long the gods   shall bind thee with guts
    of thy rime-cold son to a sword.

Loki.

50. If in truth the gods   shall bind me with guts
    of my rime-cold son to a rock,
know that first and last   was I found at the death
    when we set upon Thiazi, thy sire.

49.—A sword: *we are told by Snorri that Loki is bound to three sharp stones.*
50.—Thiazi *was slain by Thor; see Hrbl., st. 19; Vsp. en skamma, st. 3.*

Skaþi kvaþ :

51. (50) 'Veizt, ef fyrstr ok öfstr   vast at fjörlagi,
    þás er á Þjaza þrifuþ :
    frá vëum mínum   ok vöngum skulu
    þér æ köld ráþ koma.'

Loki kvaþ :

52. (51) 'Léttari í málum   vastu viþ Laufeyjar sun,
    þás þú lézt mer á beþ þinn boþit :
    getit verþr oss slíks,   ef vér görva skulum
    telja vömm enn vár.'

Þá gekk Sif fram ok byrlaþi Loka í hrímkalki mjöþ ok mælti :

53. (52) 'Heill ves nú, Loki!   ok tak viþ hrímkalki
    fullum forns mjaþar,
    heldr hana eina   látir meþ ása sunum
    vammalausa vesa.'

Hann tók viþ horni ok drakk af :

54. (53) 'Ein þú værir,   ef þú svá værir
    vör ok gröm at veri :
    einn ek veit,   svát ek vita þykkjumk
    hór ok af Hlórriþa
    ok vas þat sa enn lævísi Loki.

Beyla kvaþ :

55. (54) 'Fjöll öll skjalfa,   hykk á för vesa
    heiman Hlórriþa ;
    hann ræþr ró   þeims rœgir hér
    goþ öll ok guma.'

Loki kvaþ :

56. (55) 'Þegi þú, Beyla!   þú'st Byggvis kvæn
    ok meini blandin mjök ;
    ókynjan meira   kvama meþ ása sunum,
    öll est, deigja! dritin.'

Skadi.

51. If first and last   thou wert found at the death
     when ye set upon Thiazi, my sire,
     know that in house   or home of mine
     shall be shown thee little love!

Loki.

52. Milder were thy words   to Loki once
     when thou badst him come to thy bed;
     for such tales, I ween,   will be told of us twain,
     if we own all our acts of shame.

Then Sif came forth, and poured out mead for Loki in the foaming cup.

Sif.

53. Hail now, Loki!   quaff this rimy cup
     filled with the old mead full.
     At least grant that I,   of the kindred of gods
     alone am free from all fault.

Loki took the horn and quaffed:—

54. Thou alone wert blameless   hadst thou in bearing
     been sly and shrewish with men;
     but Thor's wife had one lover   at least, as I know,
     even Loki the wily-wise.

Beyla.

55. All the fells are quaking,   fast is the Thunderer
     faring, I trow, from home!
     He will soon bring to silence   him who thus slanders
     all beings here in the hall.

Loki.

56. Silence, Beyla,   wife of Barley-corn
     all with foulness filled!
     Ne'er 'mid the gods   came one so uncouth,
     thou bond-maid stained and soiled.

52.—*Another lost myth.*   53.—*Sif, Thor's wife; see Introd. to Gm. Hrbl., st. 48.*

þá kom þórr at ok kvaþ :

57. (56) 'Þegi þú, rög vǽttr !   þér skal minn þrúþhamarr
            Mjöllnir mál fyrnema ;
     (57) herþaklett   drepk þér halsi af,
            ok verþr þá þínu fjörvi of farit.'

Loki kvaþ :

58.   'Jarþar *burr*   es hér nú inn kominn :
           hví þrasir þú svá, þórr ?
        en þá þorir þú etki   es skalt viþ ulf vega,
           ok svelgr hann allan Sigföþur.'

þórr kvaþ :

59.   'Þegi þú, rög vǽttr !   þér skal minn þrúþhamarr
           Mjöllnir mál fyrnema ;
           upp þér verpk   ok á austrvega,
           síþan þik manngi sér.'

Loki kvaþ :

60.   'Austrförum þínum   skaltu aldrigi
           segja seggjum frá :
         síz í hanzka þumlungi   hnúkþir þú, einheri !
           ok þóttiska þórr vesa.'

þórr kvaþ :

61.   'Þegi þú, rög vǽttr !   þér skal minn þrúþhamarr
           Mjöllnir mál fyrnema ;
         hendi hǿgri   drepk þik Hrungnis bana,
           svát þer brotnar beina hvat.'

Loki kvaþ :

62.   'Lifa ǽtlak mér   langan aldr,
           þóttu hǿtir hamri mér ;
         skarpar álar   þóttu þer Skrýmis vesa
           ok máttira nesti naa
           ok svalztu hungri heill.'

58.—Burr : *A word is missing in* **R.**

Then came the Thunderer in, and spake :—

57. Silence, vile being!   My hammer of might,
     Mjöllnir, shall spoil thee of speech.
  I will strike that rock-head   from off thy shoulders,
     and soon will thy life-days be spent.

Loki.

58. 'Tis the Son of Earth   who enters the hall!
     Why dost thou threaten so, Thor?
  Ne'er wilt thou venture   to fight with the Wolf;
     he shall swallow the War-father whole.

Thor.

59. Silence, vile being!   My hammer of might,
     Mjöllnir, shall spoil thee of speech.
  I will drive thee forth   to the eastern land
     and no man shall see thee more.

Loki.

60. Of thy eastern journeys   never shouldst thou
     tell unto men the tale;
  how once in a glove-thumb   thou, warrior, didst crouch,
     and scarce couldst think thyself Thor.

Thor.

61. Silence, vile being!   My hammer of might,
     Mjöllnir, shall spoil thee of speech;
  this right hand shall smite thee   with Hrungnir's slayer,
     till each bone of thee shall be broke.

Loki.

62. Though haply thou threat'nest   with thy hammer of might,
     long will my life be, I ween;
  sharp were Skrymir's thongs,   mindst thou, when starving
     thou couldst not get at the food?

Þórr kvaþ:

63. 'Þegi þú, rög vǽttr!   þér skal minn þrúþhamarr
     Mjöllnir mál fyrnema;
     Hrungnis bani   mun þer í hel koma
     fyr nágrindr neþan.'

Loki kvaþ:

64. 'Kvaþk fyr ásum,   kvaþk fyr ása sunum
     þats mik hvatti hugr;
     en fyr þér einum   munk út ganga,
     þvít ek veit at vegr.

65. Öl görþir, Ægir!   en þú aldri munt
     síþan sumbl of göra:
     eiga þín öll,   es hér inni es,
     leiki yfir logi
     ok brinni þér á baki!'

En eptir þetta falz Loki í Fránangrs forsi í lax líki, þar tóku æsir hann. Hann var bundinn meþ þörmum sonar *síns* Narfa, en Váli sonr hans varþ at vargi. Skaþi tók eitrorm ok festi upp yfir annlit Loka; draup þar ór eitr. Sigyn kona Loka sat þar ok helt munnlaug undir eitrit, en er munnlaugin var full, bar hon út eitrit; en meþan draup eitrit á Loka. Þá kiptiz hann svá hart viþ, at þaþan af skalf jörþ öll: þat eru nú kallaþir landskjálftar.

Prose.—Narfa, en Váli, **W**, **r**, *S.*; Nara, en Narfi, **R**.

Thor.

63. Silence, vile being!   My hammer of might,
    Mjöllnir, shall spoil thee of speech.
With Hrungnir's slayer   I will smite thee to Hel,
    down 'neath the gates of the dead.

Loki.

64. Before sons and daughters   of gods have I spoken,
    even as I was moved by my mind:
now at length I go,   and for thee alone,
    for well, I ween, thou wilt fight.

65. Thou hast brewed thine ale,   but such banquet, Ægir,
    never more shalt thou make.
May flames play high   o'er thy wealth in the hall
    and scorch the skin of thy back!

Then Loki went forth and hid himself in Franang's stream in the form of a salmon, where the gods caught him and bound him with the guts of his son Narfi. But his other son Vali was turned into a wolf. Skadi took a poisonous snake and fastened it up over Loki, so that poison dripped from it upon his face. Sigyn, his wife, sat by, and held a basin under the drops. And when the basin was full she cast the poison away, but meanwhile the drops fell upon Loki, and he struggled so fiercely against it that the whole earth shook with his strivings, which are now called earthquakes.

FRAGMENTS FROM THE SNORRA EDDA.

I.

En Skaþi, dóttir jötuns, tók hjálm ok brynja ok öll hervápn ok ferr til Asgarþs at hefna föþur síns; en æsir buþu henni sætt ok yfirbœtr, ok et fyrsta, at hón skal kjósa sér mann af ásum ok kjósa at fótum, ok sjá ekki af fleira. Þá sá hón eins manns fœtr forkunnarfagra ok mælti: þenna kýs ek, fátt mun Gótt á Baldri! en þat var Njörþr ór Nóatúnum. *(Bragarœþur LVI.)* Njörþr á þá konu er Skaþi heitir, dóttir Þjaza jötuns. Skaþi vill hafa bústaþ þann er hafþi faþir hennar, þat er á fjöllum nökkurum þar sem heitir Þrymheimr: en Njörþr vill vera nær sjó. Þau sétuz á þat, at þau skyldu vera níu nætr í Þrymheimi en þá þrjár at Nóatúnum. En er Njörþr kom aptr til Nóatúna af fjallinu, þá kvaþ hann þetta:

(I) 'Leiþ erumk fjöll, vaska þar lengi á,
         nætr einar niu;
     ulfa þytr   þóttumk illr vesa
     hjá söngvi svana.'

FRAGMENTS FROM SNORRI'S EDDA.

I.—How Njörd was made Skadi's Spouse.

Then Skadi, daughter of the giant Thiazi [when she heard how the gods had slain her father], donned helm and byrnie and all her weapons of war, and went to revenge him in Asgarth. For the sake of peace they offered her as weregild the choice of a spouse among the gods, but in her choosing she should behold no more than their feet. And when she saw that the feet of one were exceeding fair and shapely, she cried :—"Him will I choose, for scant is the blemish in Baldr;" but lo! it was Njörd out of Noatun. Thus he took to wife Skadi, daughter of the Jötun Thiazi. She would fain keep the dwellings of her father among the mountains in the land called Sound-home, but Njörd desired to be near the sea, so they made agreement thus :—nine nights they should dwell in Sound-home, and afterwards three in Noatun. But when Njörd came back to Noatun from the mountains, he said :—

'Hateful the hills! though not long I lingered,
　　　nights only nine I dwelt there;
　　the howling of wolves was ill, meseemed,
　　　beside the song of the swans.'

Þá kvaþ Skaþi þetta:

(2) 'Sofa né mákat   sævar beþjum á
     fogls jarmi fyrir:
     sá mik vekr,   es af víþi kömr,
     morgin hverjan már.'—*Gylfaginning xxiii.*

II.

Hana *(Gná)* sendir Frigg í ymsa heima at eyrindum sínum.   Hon
á þann hest er rennr lopt ok lög, ok heitir Hófvarpnir.   Þat var eitt
sinn er hon reiþ, at vanir nökkurir sá reiþ hennar í loptinu, þa mælti
einn:

(1) 'Hvat þar flýgr,   hvat þar ferr
     eþa at lopti líþr?'

Hon svaraþi:

(2) 'Né ek flýg,   þó ek fer
     auk at lopti líþ:
     á Hófvarpni   þeims Hamskerpir,
     gat viþ Garþrofu.'—*Gylfaginning xxxv.*

III.

Því næst sendu æsir um allan heim eyrindreka at biþja, at Baldr
væri grátinn ór helju, en allir görþu þat: menninir ok kykvendin ok
jörþin ok steinarnir ok tré ok allr malmr: svá sem þú munt sét hafa, at
þessir hlutir gráta þá er þeir koma ór frosti ok í hita.   Þá er sendi-
menn fóru heim ok höfþu vel rekit sín eyrindi, finna þeir í helli nökkurum hvar gýgr sat, hon nefndiz Þökk; þeir biþja hana gráta Baldr
ór helju.   Hon svarar:

     'Þökk mun gráta   þurrum tárum
        Baldrs bálfarar;
     kviks né dauþs   nautka karls sonar,
        haldi hel þvís hefir.'

En þess geta menn, at þar hafi verit Loki Laufeyjar sonr er flest
hefir illt gört meþ ásum.

And Skadi spake thus :—

> 'Sleep I could not   on ocean's couch
>   for the wailing cry of the gull :
>   from the wide sea faring,   that bird awoke me
>   when he came each day at dawn.'

II.—Concerning the Goddess Gna.

Frigg sends Gna, the Floater, on errands into many worlds. She rides a horse called Hoof-flinger which fares through the sky and over the sea. Once as she was passing, certain of the Wanes saw her riding in the air, and one said :—

> 'What flies there,   what fares there,
>   what flits there aloft ? '

And she made answer :—

> 'I fly not,   yet am faring,
>   and I flit here aloft,
>   high on the Hoof-flinger,   who was of Hedge-breaker
>   born, and the Fine-flanked steed.'

III.—How the World wept for Baldr.

The gods sent messengers throughout all the world to plead that Baldr might be wept out of Hel. And all beings wept ; men and living creatures, the earth and rocks and trees and metals—even as such things weep when after being fast bound with frost they become warm. When the messengers had well done their errand they returned and found a certain giantess called Thokk sitting in a cave. They bade her weep Baldr out of Hel, but she answered :—

> 'Thokk shall weep   with dry tears alone
>   that Baldr is laid on the bale-fire :
>   Never joy have I had   from man living or dead :
>   let Hel hold fast what she hath.'

Thus they knew that Loki, son of Laufey, had been there, who was ever wont to work most evil among the gods.

IV.

Þá fór Þórr til ár þeirar er Vimur heitir, allra á mest. Þá spenti hann sik megingjörþum ok studdi forstreymis Gríþarvöl, en Loki helt undir megingjarþar; ok þá er Þórr kom á miþja ána, þá óx svá mjök áin, at uppi braut á öxl honum. Þá kvaþ Þórr þetta:

'Vaxat nú, Vimur!   alls mik þik vaþa tíþir
    jötna garþa í:
veiztu ef vex,   at þá vex mér ásmegin
    jafnhátt upp sem himinn.'

En er Þórr kom til Geirröþar, þá var þeim félögum vísat fyrst í gestahús til herbergis, ok var þar einn stóll til sætis, ok sat þar Þórr. Þá varþ hann þess varr, at stóllinn fór undir hánum upp at ræfri; hann stakk Gríþarveli upp í raptana ok lét sígaz fast á stólinn; varþ þá brestr mikill ok fylgþi skrækr; þar höfþu verit undir stólinum dœtr Geirröþar Gjölp ok Greip, ok hafþi hann brotit hrygginn í báþum. Þá kvaþ Þórr:

'Einu sinni   neyttak alls megins
    jötna görþum í:
þás Gjölp ok Greip   Geirröþar dœtr,
    vildu hefja mik til himins.'

V.

Í Ásgarþi fyrir durum Valhallar stendr lundr sá er Glasir er kallaþr, en lauf hans allt er gull rautt, svá sem hér er kveþit, at

'Glasir stendr   meþ gullnu laufi
    firir Sigtýs sölum.'

IV.—How Thor slew the Daughters of Geirröd.

When Thor was faring once into Jötunheim he came to the river Vimur, of all rivers the greatest. There he girt him with his belt of strength, and leant on Gridar's staff as he went down-stream. Loki held on under the belt. When Thor had come into the midst of the flood it had risen so high that it flowed over his shoulders. Then he spake :—

> 'Wax not, Vimur,   I needs must wade thee
>   to reach the Jötun-realms;
> know! if thou wax   forthwith shall wax
>   my god's might high as heaven.'

And when Thor had reached Geirröd's court, he and Loki were taken to lodge in the guest-house. There was but one stool there, and Thor sat down upon it. But presently he became aware that it was rising up to the roof under him. He thrust Gridar's staff against the rafters and pushed the stool down, and then came a great crash, and a shriek was heard ; for the daughters of Geirröd—Yelper and Gripper— had been under the stool, and both their backs were broken. Then spake Thor :—

> 'Once only I used   my god's might all
>   in the realms of the Jötun race ;
> When Yelper and Gripper,   Geirröd's maids,
>   would have raised me high to heaven.

V.—The Glistener.

In Asgarth, before the gates of Valhöll, there stands a wood called Glistener, whose leaves are all of red gold, as here is written :—

> 'Glistener stands   with golden leaves
>   in front of the War-father's halls.'

VÖLUSPÁ.

1. Hljóþs biþk allar   helgar kindir,
   meiri ok minni   mögu Heimdallar:
   viltu at ek, Valföþr,   vel fyr telja
   forn spjöll fira   þaus fremst of mank.

2. Ek man jötna   ár of borna
   þás forþum mik   fœdda höfþu,
   niú mank heima,   niú í viþi,
   mjötviþ mæran   fyr mold neþan.

3. Ár vas alda   þars Ymir bygþi,
   vasa sandr né sær   né svalar unnir;
   jörþ fannsk æva   né upphiminn,
   gap vas ginnunga,   en gras hvergi.

Völuspá.—In **R H**, *No. 1 ; cited in* **Sn. E.**   1.—*B. S. Gv. H.*, vildu Valföþrs vél, *Dt. Hl.;* vildu at ek Valföþr vel, **R**; viltu . . . valföþrs, **H**.   2.—*Í* viþi: *Dt.* *makes this suggestion with hesitation for* ívíþi, **R**.   3.—Ginnunga, *S. G. Dt. Hl.* Ginnunga, *Mk., a proper name.*

COME·FROM·ON·HIGH·TO·THE·GREAT·ASSEMBLY·THE·MIGHTY·RULER·WHO·ORDER·ALL

THE SOOTHSAYING OF THE VALA.

1. Hearing I ask   all holy kindreds,
   high and low-born,   sons of Heimdal!
   Thou too, Odin,   who bidst me utter
   the oldest tidings   of men that I mind!

(The World's beginning.)

2. I remember of yore   were born the Jötuns,
   they who aforetime   fostered me:
   nine worlds I remember,   nine in the Tree,
   the glorious Fate Tree   that springs 'neath the Earth.

3. 'Twas the earliest of times   when Ymir lived;
   then was sand nor sea   nor cooling wave,
   nor was Earth found ever,   nor Heaven on high,
   there was Yawning of Deeps   and nowhere grass:

1.—Sons of Heimdal *or Rig, hence men are called holy; see* Rþ.   2.—Nine
worlds; *see Vm., st. 43.* Fate Tree, Yggdrasil; *see st. 19; Grm., st. 31; Háv., st.*
137; Fj., st. 14.   3.—Ymir; *see Vm., st. 21, 29.*

4. Áþr Burs synir   bjöþum of ypþu
    þeir es miþgarþ   mæran skópu ;
    sól skein sunnan   á salar steina,
    þa vas grund groïn   grœnum lauki.

5. Sól varp sunnan,   sinni mána,
    hendi hœgri   umb himinjöþur ;
    sól né vissi,   hvar sali átti,
    stjörnur né vissu,   hvar staþi áttu,
    máni né vissi,   hvat megins átti.

6. Þá gengu regin öll   á rökstóla,
    ginnheilug goþ,   ok of þat gættusk :
    nátt ok niþjum   nöfn of gáfu,
    morgin hétu   ok miþjan dag,
    undorn ok aptan,   árum at telja.

7. Hittusk æsir   á Iþavelli
    þeirs hörg ok hof   hátimbruþu ;
    afla lögþu,   auþ smíþuþu,
    tangir skópu   ok tól görþu.

8. Tefldu í túni,   teitir váru—
    vas þeim væettergis   vant ór golli—
    unz þriar kvámu   þursa meyjar,
    ámátkar mjök,   or jötunheimum.

9. Þá gengu regin öll   á rökstóla,
    ginnheilug goþ,   ok of þat gættusk :
    hvern skyldi dverga   drótt of skepja
    ór Brimis blóþi   ok ór blám leggjum.

9.—Hvern, *Dt. ;* hverr, **R** : *The sense evidently requires the accusative case.*

4. ere the sons of the god   had uplifted the world-plain,
and fashioned Midgarth,   the glorious Earth.
Sun shone from the south,   on the world's bare stones—
then was Earth o'ergrown   with herb of green.

5. Sun, Moon's companion,   out of the south
her right hand flung   round the rim of heaven.
Sun knew not yet   where she had her hall;
nor knew the stars   where they had their place;
nor ever the Moon   what might he owned.

(Ordering of Times and Seasons.)

6. Then went all the Powers   to their thrones of doom—
the most holy gods—   and o'er this took coun·el:
to Night and the New-Moons   names they gave:
they named the Morning,   and named the Mid-day,
Afternoon, Evening,   —to count the years.

(The Golden Age till the coming of Fate.)

7. Gathered the gods   on the Fields of Labour;
they set on high   their courts and temples;
they founded forges,   wrought rich treasures,
tongs they hammered   and fashioned tools.

8. They played at tables   in court, were joyous,—
little they wanted   for wealth of gold.—
Till there came forth three   of the giant race,
all fearful maidens,   from Jötunheim.

(Creation of the Dwarfs.)

9. Then went all the Powers   to their thrones of doom,—
the most holy gods,—   and o'er this took counsel:
whom should they make   the lord of dwarfs
out of Ymir's blood,   and his swarthy limbs.

4.—The sons of the god, *or sons of Bur; see Vsp. en skamma, st. 2.*   6.—
Thrones of doom, *beneath Yggdrasil; see Grm., st. 30.*   8.—All-fearful maidens:
Cf., this stanza with 60, 61; the Norns, st. 20.   9.—Ymir is here called Brimir.

10. Þar vas Mótsognir   mæztr of orþinn
     dverga allra,   en Durinn annarr;
     þeir mannlíkun   mörg of görþu
     dvergar í jörþu,   sem Durinn sagþi.

11. Nyi ok Niþi,   Norþri ok Suþri,
     Austri ok Vestri,   Alþjófr, Dvalinn,
     Nár ok Naïnn,   Nípingr, Daïnn,
     Bífurr, Báfurr,   Bömburr, Nóri,
     Ánn ok Ónarr,   Aï, Mjöþvitnir.

12. Viggr ok Gandalfr,   Vindalfr, Þraïnn,
     Þekkr ok Þórinn,   Þror, Vitr ok Litr,
     Nýr ok Nýráþr,   nú hefk dverga—
     Reginn ok Ráþsviþr—   rétt of talþa.

13. Fíli, Kíli,   Fundinn, Náli,
     Heptifíli,   Hannarr, Sviurr,
     Frár, Hornbori,   Frægr ok Lóni,
     Aurvangr, Jari,   Eikinskjaldi.

14. Mál es dverga   í Dvalins líþi
     ljóna kindum   til Lofars telja ;
     þeir es sóttu   frá salar steini
     Aurvanga sjöt   til Jöruvalla.

15. Þar vas Draupnir   ok Dolgþrasir,
     Hár, Haugspori,   Hlévangr, Gloïnn,
     Dóri, Óri,   Dúfr, Andvari,
     Skirfir, Virfir,   Skáfiþr, Aï.

16. Alfr ok Yngvi,   Eikinskjaldi,
     Fjalarr ok Frosti,   Fiþr ok Ginnarr ;
     þat mun æ uppi,   meþan öld lifir,
     langniþja tal   *til* Lofars hafat.

11-16.—*Regarded by most authorities as an interpolation.*   14.—Líþi, *Dt. and*
Hl. ; liþi, **R.**

10.   Mead-drinker then   was made the highest,
      but Durin second   of all the dwarfs;
      and out of the earth   these twain-shaped beings
      in form like man,   as Durin bade.

11.   New Moon, Waning-moon,   All-thief, Dallier,
      North and South   and East and West.
      Corpse-like, Death-like,   Niping, Daïnn,
      Bifur, Bafur,   Bömbur, Nori,
      Ann and Onar,   Aï, Mead-wolf.

12.   Vigg and Wand-elf,   Wind-elf, Thraïnn,
      Thekk and Thorin,   Thror, Vit, and Lit,
      Nyr and Regin,   New-counsel, Wise-counsel,—
      now have I numbered   the dwarfs aright.

13.   Fili, Kili,   Fundin, Nali,
      Heptifili,   Hannar, Sviur,
      Frar, Hornbori,   Fræg and Loni,
      Aurvang, Jari,   Oaken-shield.

14.   'Tis time to number   in Dallier's song-mead
      all the dwarf-kind   of Lofar's race,—
      who from earth's threshold,   the Plains of Moisture,
      sought below   the Sandy-realms.

15.   There were Draupnir   and Dolgthrasir,
      Har and Haugspori,   Hlevang, Gloin,
      Dori, Ori,   Duf, Andvari,
      Skirfir, Virfir,   Skafid, Aï.

16.   Elf and Yngvi,   Oaken-shield,
      Fjalar and Frost,   Fin and Ginar.
      Thus shall be told   throughout all time
      the line who were born   of Lofar's race.

11-16.—*A translation of these obscure names has only been given where it seems to suggest the character of the dwarfs.*   14.—*Dallier's song-mead is thus taken by Dt. and Hl. as a synonym for poetry; cf. Snorri's " Dallier's drink." Dallier is a dwarf well known in the Edda, and is chosen to represent his race who brewed the mead (Sn.E.). This dwarf migration from the earth's surface is also suggested by Dt. and Hl.*

17. Unz þrír kvámu   ór því liði
    öflgir ok ástkir   æsir at húsi;
    fundu á landi   lítt megandi
    Ask ok Emblu   örlöglausa.

18. Önd né áttu,   óþ né höfþu,
    lá né læti   né litu góþa;
    önd gaf Óþinn,   óþ gaf Hœnir,
    lá gaf Lóþurr   ok litu góþa.

19. Ask veitk standa,   heitir Yggdrasil,
    hár baþmr ausinn   hvíta auri;
    þaþan koma döggvar   es í dali falla,
    stendr æ of grœnn   Urþar brunni.

20. Þaþan koma meyjar   margs vitandi
    þriar ór þeim sal   es und þolli stendr;
    Urþ hétu eina,   aþra Verþandi,
    skáru á skíþi,   Skuld ena þriþju;
    þær lög lögþu,   þær líf kuru
    alda börnum,   örlög seggja.

21. Þat man folkvig   fyrst í heimi,
    es Gollveigu   geirum studdu
    ok í höllo Hárs   hána brendu,
    þrysvar brendu   þrysvar borna,
    opt ósjaldan—:   þó enn lifir.

19.—Heitir Yggdrasil, **R H W U**; Yggdrasils, **r**, *H. G. Sv. Magn.*   21.—Man,
Mh. S. J.; man hón, **R. H.** *has the third person, as in st.* 27, 28, 29,31, 32, 35, 38
39.

(Creation of Men.)

17. Then came three gods   of the Æsir kindred,
    mighty and blessed,   towards their home.
    They found on the seashore,   wanting power,
    with fate unwoven,   an Ash and Elm.

18. Spirit they had not,   and mind they owned not,—
    blood, nor voice   nor fair appearance.
    Spirit gave Odin,   and mind gave Hönir,
    blood gave Lodur,   and aspect fair.

(The Tree of Life and Fate.)

19. An ash I know standing,   'tis called Yggdrasil,
    a high tree sprinkled   with shining drops;
    come dews therefrom   which fall in the dales;
    it stands ever green   o'er the well of Weird.

20. There are the Maidens,   all things knowing,
    three in the hall   which stands 'neath the Tree.
    One is named 'Weird,'   the second 'Being'—
    who grave on tablets—   but 'Shall' the third.
    They lay down laws,   they choose out life,
    they speak the doom   of the sons of men.

(The War of the Gods.)

21. I remember the first   great war in the world,
    when Golden-draught   they pierced with spears,
    and burned in the hall   of Odin the High One;
    thrice they burned her,   the three times born,—
    oft, not seldom—   yet still she lives.

17.—Elm: *the meaning of Icelandic* embla *is doubtful.*   18.—Hönir: *a god of wisdom.* Lodur *probably stands for Loki, for these three were always companions.* 20.—Weird, *see Gg., st. 7.*   21.—*The story of this war between the Æsir and* Wanes *is never fully told, but is the subject of constant allusions; see Vm., 39.* Golden draught, *see Vsp. en skamma, st. 9.*

22. Heiþi hétu   hvars húsa kvam
völu velspaa,   vitti ganda;
seiþ hvars kunni,   seiþ hugleikin,
æ vas angan   illrar brúþar.

23. Þá gengu regin öll   á rökstóla,
ginnheilug goþ,   ok of þat gættusk:
hvárt skyldu æsir   afráþ gjalda
eþa skyldu goþ öll   gildi eiga.

24. Fleygþi Óþinn   ok í folk of skaut:
þat vas enn folkvíg   fyrst í heimi;
brotinn vas borþveggr   borgar ása,
knáttu vanir vígská   völlu sporna.

25. Þá gengu regin öll   á rökstóla,
ginnheilug goþ,   ok of þat gættusk:
hverr lopt hefþi   lævi blandit
eþa ætt jötuns   Óþs mey gefna.

26. Þórr einn þar vá   þrunginn móþi—
hann sjaldan sitr   es slíkt of fregn—:
á gengusk eiþar,   orþ ok sœri,
mál öll meginlig   es á meþal fóru.

27. Veit Heimdallar   hljóþ of folgit
und heiþvönum   helgum baþmi;
á sé ausask   aurgum forsi
af veþi Valföþrs: vituþ enn eþa hvat?

22.—Hugleikin, *H. B. Gv.*; hón leikinn, **R**, *M. L.*

22.   Men called her 'Witch,'   when she came to their dwellings,
      flattering seeress;   wands she enchanted,
      spells many wove she,   light-hearted wove them,
      and of evil women   was ever the joy.

23.   Then went all the Powers   to their thrones of doom,
      the most holy gods,   and o'er this took counsel:
      whether the Æsir   should pay a were-gild
      and all Powers together   make peaceful offering.

24.   But Odin hurled   and shot 'mid the host;
      and still raged the first   great war in the world.
      Broken then were   the bulwarks of Asgard,
      the Wanes, war wary,   trampled the field.

(War with the Jötuns.)

25.   Then went all the Powers   to their thrones of doom,
      the most holy gods,   and o'er this took counsel:
      who all the air   had mingled with poison
      and Freyja had yielded   to the race of Jötuns.

26.   Alone fought the Thunderer   with raging heart—
      seldom he rests   when he hears such tidings.
      Oaths were broken,   words and swearing,
      all solemn treaties   made betwixt them.

(The Secret Pledges of the Gods.)

27.   I know where Heimdal's   hearing is hidden
      under the heaven-wont   holy tree,
      which I see ever showered   with falling streams   [what?
      from All-father's pledge.   —Would ye know further, and

---

22.—*Witch, or Vala.*   23.—*Lines 2 and 3 are thus understood by Hl.*   25.—
*For Snorri's account, see Introd.   Freyja is here called the bride of Od or Ottar; see
Hdl.*

28. Ein sat úti,　　es enn aldni kvam
Yggjungr ása　　ok í augu leit.

. . . .

Hvers fregniþ mik,　　hví freistiþ mín?

29. Allt veit, Óþinn!　　hvar auga falt,
í enom mæra　　Mímis brunni;
drekkr mjöþ Mímir　　morgin hverjan
af veþi Valföþrs:　　vituþ enn eþa hvat?

30. Valþi Herföþr　　hringa ok men
fýr spjöll spaklig　　ok spá ganda.

. . . .

sá vitt ok vítt　　of veröld hverja.

31. Sá valkyrjur　　vítt of komnar,
görvar at ríþa　　til Gotþjóþar:
Skuld helt skildi,　　en Skögul önnur,
Guþr, Hildr, Göndul　　ok Geirskögul.
Nú 'ru talþar　　nönnur Herjans,
görvar at ríþa　　grund valkyrjur.

32. Ek sá Baldri　　blóþgum tívur,
Óþins barni　　örlög folgin:
stóþ of vaxinn　　völlum hæri
mær ok mjök fagr　　† mistilteinn.

33. Varþ af meiþi　　es mær sýndisk
harmflaug hættlig:　　Höþr nam skjóta;
Baldrs bróþir vas　　of borinn snimma,
sa nam Óþins sunr　　einnættr vega.

34. Þó hendr æva　　né höfoþ kembþi,
áþr á bál of bar　　Baldrs andskota;
en Frigg of grét　　í Fensölum
vá Valhallar:　　vituþ enn eþa hvat?

30.—Fyr spjöll, *Gv.*; fekk spjöll, *E. Mh. G. S. J.*; féspjöll, *B. C. Sv. R.*; fe
spïöll, **R.**

28. I sat lone enchanting   when came the Dread One,
     the ancient god,   and gazed in my eyes :
     'What dost thou ask of me ?   why dost thou prove me ?

29. All know I, Odin,—   yea, where thou hast hidden
     thine eye in the wondrous   well of Mimir,
     who each morn   from the pledge of All-father
     drinks the mead "   —Would ye know further, and what ?

30. Then Odin bestowed on me   rings and trinkets
     for magic spells   and the wisdom of wands.
     I saw far and wide   into every world.

31. From far I saw   the Valkyries coming
     ready to ride   to the hero host.
     Fate held a shield,   and Lofty followed
     War and Battle,   Bond and Spearpoint.
     Numbered now   are the Warfather's maidens,
     Valkyries, ready   to ride o'er Earth.

32. I saw for Baldr,   the bleeding god,
     the child of Odin,   his doom concealed.
     High o'er the fields,   there stood upgrown,
     most slender and fair,   the mistletoe.

33. And there came from that plant,   though slender it seemed,
     the fell woe-shaft   which Höd did shoot.
     But Baldr's brother   was born ere long ;
     that son of Odin   fought one night old ;

34. for never hand   he bathed, nor head,
     ere he laid on the bale-fire   Baldr's foe.
     But Frigg long wept   o'er the woe of Valhöll
     in Fen's moist halls   —Would ye know further, and what ?

28.—Heimdal's hearing *was celebrated. Dt. and Hl. thus correct the hitherto accepted translation* horn *of Icl.* hljóþ.   29.—Mimir, *a water giant. He is the wise teacher and counsellor of the gods, although a Jötun; see Háv., st. 139.*   32-34.— *See Bdr., st. 8-12.*   34.—Fen's moist halls : *the home of Frigg.*

35. Hapt sá liggja   und hvera lundi
    lægjarns líki   Loka áþekkjan;
    þar sitr Sigyn   þeygi of sínum
    ver vel glýjuþ: vituþ enn eþa hvat?

36. Á fellr austan   of eitrdali
    söxum ok sverþum: Slíþr heitir sú.
    . . . .
    . . . .

37. Stóþ fyr norþan   á Niþavöllum
    salr ór golli   Sindra ættar,
    en annarr stóþ   á Ókólni
    bjórsalr jötuns,   sá Brimir heitir.

38. Sal sá standa   sólu fjarri
    Náströndu á,   norþr horfa dyrr;
    fellu eitrdropar   inn of ljóra,
    sá 's undinn salr   orma hryggjum.

39. Sá þar vaþa   þunga strauma
    menn meinsvara   ok morþvarga
    ok þanns annars glepr   eyrarúnu;
    þar só Níþhöggr   naï framgengna,
    sleit vargr vera: vituþ enn eþa hvat?

40. Austr sat en aldna   í Jarnviþi
    ok fœddi þar   Fenris kindir;
    verþr af öllum   einna nekkverr
    tungls tjúgari   í trolls hami.

41. Fyllisk fjörvi   feigra manna,
    rýþr ragna sjöt   rauþum dreyra;
    svört verþa sólskin   of sumur eptir,
    veþr öll válynd: vituþ enn eþa hvat?

(Vision into Hel and Jötunheim.)

35. I saw lying bound in Cauldron-grove
 one like the form of guile-loving Loki.
 And there sat Sigyn, yet o'er her husband
 rejoicing little. —Would ye know further, and what?

36. From the eastward a flood, the Stream of Fear,
 bore swords and daggers through Poison-dales.

37. To the northward stood on the Moonless Plains,
 the golden hall of the Sparkler's race;
 and a second stood in the Uncooled realm,
 a feast-hall of Jötuns, 'Fire,' 'tis called:

38. and far from the sun I saw a third
 on the Strand of Corpses, with doors set northward:
 down through the roof dripped poison-drops,
 for that hall was woven with serpents' backs.

39. I saw there wading the whelming streams
 wolf-like murderers, men forsworn,
 and those who another's love-whisperer had wiled.
 The dragon, Fierce-stinger, fed on corpses,
 a wolf tore men. —Would ye know further, and what?

40. Far east in Iron-wood sat an old giantess,
 Fenrir's offspring she fostered there.
 From among them all doth one come forth,
 in guise of a troll, to snatch the sun.

41. He is gorged, as on lives of dying men;
 he reddens the place of the Powers like blood.
 Swart grows the sunshine of summer after,
 all baleful the storms. —Would ye know further, and what?

35.—*See Ls. prose ending.* 37.—The Sparkler: *a dwarf and forger of the gods'
treasures; see Grm., st. 43.* 39.—Fierce-stinger, *see Grm., st. 35.* 40.—Ironwood:
a famous mythical forest in Jötunheim. Fenrir's offspring: *Skoll, who pursued the sun,
and Hati, who followed the moon; see Grm., st. 39.*

42. Sat þar á haugi   ok sló hörpu
    gýgjar hirþir,   † glaþr Eggþér ;
    gól of hánum   í gaglviþi
    fagrrauþr hani   sás Fjalarr heitir.

43. Gól of ásum   Gollinkambi,
    sá vekr hölþa   at Herjaföþrs ;
    en annarr gelr   fyr jörþ neþan
    sótrauþr hani   at sölum Heljar.

44. Geyr nú Garmr mjök   fyr Gnipahelli,
    festr mun slitna,   en freki rinna !
    fjölþ veitk frœþa,   fram sék lengra
    umb ragna rök,   römm sigtíva.

45. Brœþr munu berjask   ok at bönum verþask,
    munu systrungar   sifjum spilla ;
    hart's í heimi,   hórdómr mikill ;
    skeggjöld, skalmöld,   skildir 'u klofnir,
    vindöld, vargöld,   áþr veröld steypisk ;
    mun engi maþr   öþrum þyrma.

46. Leika Míms synir,   en mjötviþr kyndisk
    at enu gamla   Gjallarhorni ;
    hátt blæss Heimdallr,   horn's á lopti,
    mælir Óþinn   viþ Míms höfuþ.

44.—Veitk, *J. Sv. G.* ; veit hón, **R.**; *so also st. 49, 58.*   46.—Mjötviþr, *Dt. and Hl. (notes)* ; mjötuþr, **R,** *etc.*   47.—Losnar *in H is followed by*

     hræþask allir á helvegum
     áþr Surtar þan sevi of gleypir.

(Signs of Doom.)

42. Sits on a mound   and strikes his harp
the gleeful Swordsman,   warder of giant-wives;
o'er him crows   in the roosting tree
the fair red cock   who Fjalar is called.

43. Crows o'er the gods   the Golden-combed;
he wakes the heroes   in War-father's dwellings;
and crows yet another   beneath the earth,
a dark red cock   in the halls of Hel.

44. Loud bays Garm   before Gaping-Hel;
the bond shall be broken   the Wolf run free.
Hidden things I know;   still onward I see
the great Doom of the Powers,   the gods of war.

45. Brothers shall fight   and be as murderers;
sisters' children   shall stain their kinship.
'Tis ill with the world;   comes fearful whoredom,
a Sword age, Axe age,   —shields are cloven,
a Wind age, Wolf age,   ere the world sinks.
Never shall man then   spare another.

46. Mim's sons arise;   the Fate Tree kindles
at the roaring sound   of Gjalla-horn.
Loud blows Heimdal,   the horn is aloft,
and Odin speaks   with Mimir's head.

42.—The gleeful Swordsman is *the warder of Jötunheim, and corresponds with Heimdal, the watchman of the gods.* 43.—The Golden-combed, see *Fj., st. 17.* 44.—Garm, *the Hel hound; see Bdr., st. 2. He and Tyr fight and slay one another (Sn. E.). Gaping-hel, Icelandic Gnipa-hel, is descriptive of the craggy rock entrance which forms the mouth of Hel.* The Wolf, see *Ls. 39.* 46.—Mim *or Mimir: his sons must be the waters of the well, or the streams that flow from it. Compare Ægir and Hymir's daughters; Hym. st. 2, Ls. st. 34. The story of Mimir's head is told in Ynglinga S. (see Introd.), but here an earlier form of the myth is implied, in which the head is a well-spring of wisdom.* The Fate Tree: *the unemended* mjötuþr *of the MSS. has suggested various renderings—the judge appears; fate approaches.*

47. Ymr aldit tré,   en jötunn losnar,
     skelfr Yggdrasils   askr standandi,

48. Hvat's meþ ásum?   hvat's meþ ölfum?
     gnýr allr jötunheimr,   æsir'u á þingi;
     stynja dvergar   fyr steindurum,
     veggbergs vísir: vituþ enn eþa hvat?

49. Geyr nú Garmr mjök   fyr Gnipahelli,
     festr mun slitna,   en freki rinna!
     fjölþ veitk frœþa,   fram sék lengra
     umb ragna rök,   römm sigtíva.

50. Hrymr ekr austan,   hefsk lind fyrir;
     snýsk jörmungandr   í jötunmóþi;
     ormr knýr unnir,   en ari hlakkar,
     slítr naï niþfölr;   Naglfar losnar.

51. Kjóll ferr *norþan;*   koma munu *Heljar*
     of lög lýþir,   en Loki stýrir;
     fara fíflmegir   meþ freka allir,
     þeim es bróþir   Býleists í för.

52. Surtr ferr sunnan   meþ sviga lævi,
     skínn af sverþi   sól valtíva;
     grjótbjörg gnata,   en gífr hrata,
     troþa halir helveg,   en himinn klofnar.

53. Þá kömr Hlínar   harmr annarr fram,
     es Óþinn ferr   viþ ulf vega,
     en bani Belja   bjartr at Surti:
     þá mun Friggjar   falla angan.

48.—*Placed here by B. G. S.; follows 51 in* **R.**   51.—Norþan, *B. N. G. Sv. Mh. J.;* austan, **R** *and other MSS.* Heljar, *B. N. G. Sv. Mh. J.;* Muspellz, **R** *and other MSS.*

47. Groans the Ancient Tree,   Fenrir is freed,—
    shivers, yet standing,   Yggdrasil's ash.

48. How do the gods fare,   how do the elves fare?
    All Jötunheim rumbles,   the gods are in council;
    before the stone doors   the dwarfs are groaning,
    a rock-wall finding   —Would ye know further, and what?

49. Loud bays Garm   before Gaping-hel:
    the bond shall be broken,   the Wolf run free.
    Hidden things I know;   still onward I see
    the great Doom of the Powers,   the gods of war.

(Gathering of the Destroyers.)

50. Drives Hrym from the East   holding shield on high;
    the World-serpent writhes   in Jötun-rage;
    he lashes the waves;   screams a pale-beaked eagle,
    rending corpses,   the Death boat is launched.

51. Sails the bark from the North;   the hosts of Hel
    o'er the sea are coming,   and Loki steering,
    brother of Byleist,   he fares on the way
    with Fenrir and all   the monster kinsmen.

52. Rides Surt from the South   fire, bane of branches,
    sun of the war gods,   gleams from his sword.
    The rock-hills crash,   the troll-wives totter,
    men flock Helward,   and heaven is cleft.

(The last battles of the Gods.)

53. Soon comes to pass   Frigg's second woe,
    when Odin fares   to fight with the wolf;
    then must he fall,   her lord beloved,
    and Beli's bright slayer   must bow before Surt.

47.—Fenrir, *not Loki. must be intended by* Jötun *of the text, for Loki was always reckoned among the gods.* 50.—Hrym, *the leader of the Frost-giants.* A pale-beaked eagle, *Corpse-swallower; see* Vm. 37. Death-boat *or* Naglfar, *the Nail-ferry, said by Snorri to be made of the nails of dead men.* 51.—Byleist *is unknown except as Loki's brother.* 52.—Surt, *see* Vm., *st. 53.* 53.—Beli's bright slayer, *or Frey. Beli, Snorri tells us, was a giant whom Frey slew with a stag's horn for lack of the sword which he had given for Gerd; see Skm. st. 16, Ls. st. 42.*

54. Kömr enn mikli   mögr Sigföþur,
     Víþarr, vega   at valdýri ;
     lætr megi hveþrungs   mund of standa
     hjör til hjarta :   þá's hefnt föþur.

55. Kömr enn mæri   mögr Hlóþynjar ;
     . . . .
     . . . .
     gengr Óþins sunr   ormi mæta.

56. Drepr af móþi   miþgarþs vëur ;
     munu halir allir   heimstöþ ryþja ;
     gengr fet niu   Fjörgynjar burr
     neppr frá naþri   níþs ókvíþnum.

57. Sól tér sortna,   sígr fold í mar,
     hverfa af himni   heiþar stjörnur ;
     geisar eimi   ok aldrnari,
     leikr hár hiti   viþ himin sjalfan.

58. Geyr nú Garmr mjök   fyr Gnipahelli,
     festr mun slitna,   en freki rinna !
     fjölþ veitk frœþa,   fram sék lengra
     umb ragna rök,   römm sigtíva.

59. Sék upp koma   öþru sinni
     jörþ ór ægi   iþjagrœna ;
     falla forsar,   flýgr örn yfir,
     sás á fjalli   fiska veiþir.

60. Finnask æsir   á Iþavelli
     ok of moldþinur   mátkan dœma,
     ok minnask þar   á megindóma
     ok á Fimbultýs   fornar rúnar.

55, lines 3 and 4.—*A trace of these missing lines is found in* **H**, *but the reading is*
doubtful :—   gínn lopt yfir   liþr *fránn* neþan
     . . . .—**G.**
59.—Sék, *G.* ; sér hón, *R. H.* ; *so also st.* 64.

54. Comes forth the stalwart   son of the War-father,
Vidar, to strive   with the deadly beast ;
lets he the sword   from his right hand leap
into Fenrir's heart,   and avenged is the father.

55. Comes forth the glorious   offspring of Earth,
Thor, to strive   with the glistening Serpent.

56. Strikes in his wrath   the Warder of Midgard,
while mortals all   their homes forsake ;
nine feet recoils he,   the son of Odin,
bowed, from the dragon   who fears not shame.

(The End of the World.)

57. The sun is darkened,   Earth sinks in the sea,
from heaven turn   the bright stars away.
Rages smoke   with fire, the life-feeder,
high flame plays   against heaven itself.

58. Loud bays Garm   before Gaping-hel,
the bond shall be broken,   the Wolf run free ;
hidden things I know ;   still onward I see
the great Doom of the Powers,   the gods of war.

(The new World.)

59. I see uprising   a second time
earth from the ocean,   green anew ;
the waters fall,   on high the eagle
flies o'er the fell   and catches fish.

60. The gods are gathered   on the Fields of Labour ;
they speak concerning   the great World Serpent,
and remember there   things of former fame
and the Mightiest God's   old mysteries.

55.—The Serpent, *see Hym.*, *st. 23.*

61.　Þar munu eptir　　undrsamligar
　　　gollnar töflur　　í grasi finnask
　　　þærs·í árdaga　　áttar höfþu.
　　　·　·　·　·　·　　·　·　·　·　·

62.　Munu ósánir　　akrar vaxa,
　　　böls mun batna,　　mun Baldr koma,
　　　bua Höþr ok Baldr　　Hropts sigtoptir,
　　　vel valtívar :　　vituþ enn eþa hvat ?

63.　Þá kná Hœnir　　hlautviþ kjósa
　　　·　·　·　·　·
　　　ok burir byggva　　brœþra Tveggja
　　　vindheim víþan :　　vituþ enn eþa hvat ?

64.　Sal sék standa　　sólu fegra,
　　　golli þakþan　　á Gimlé :
　　　þar skulu dyggvar　　dróttir byggva
　　　ok of aldrdaga　　ynþis njóta.

65.　Kömr enn ríki　　at regindómi
　　　öflugr ofan　　sás öllu ræþr.
　　　·　·　·　·　·　　·　·　·　·
　　　·　·　·　·　·　　·　·　·　·

65.　Kömr enn dimmi　　dreki fljúgandi,
　　　naþr fránn neþan　　frá Niþafjöllum ;
　　　bersk í fjöþrum　　—flýgr völl yfir—
　　　Níþhöggr naï ;　　nú mun sökkvask.

62.—Vel valtívar, **R**, *Dt.*, *Hl.;* vé valtíva, *R. G. H. S.*　　65, lines 1 and 2.—
Found only in **H.**

---

61. Then shall be found the wondrous-seeming
 golden tables · hid in the grass,
 those they had used in days of yore.

62. And there unsown shall the fields bring forth;
 all harm shall be healed; Baldr will come—
 Höd and Baldr shall dwell in Valhöll,
 at peace the war gods. —Would ye know further, and what?

63. Then Hönir shall cast the twigs of divining,
 and the sons shall dwell of Odin's brothers
 in Wind-home wide. —Would ye know further, and what?

64. I see yet a hall more fair than the sun,
 roofed with gold in the Fire-sheltered realm;
 ever shall dwell there · all holy beings,
 blest with joy through the days of time.

 (Coming of the new Power, passing of the old.)

65. Comes from on high to the great Assembly
 the Mighty Ruler who orders all.

66. Fares from beneath a dim dragon flying,
 a glistening snake from the Moonless Fells.
 Fierce-stinger bears the dead on his pinions
 away o'er the plains.— I sink now and cease.

62.—Valhöll, *called here the victory halls of Hropt (Odin).* 63.—The twigs, *see* *Hym., st. 1.* 64.—Fire-sheltered realm, *Icelandic* (Gimlé *from* gim, fire, *and* hlé, shelter; *Dt. and Hl.), which has often been translated* jewelled; *but the above meaning shows this hall in contrast to the others of st. 37 and 38.*

2 Q

BIBLIOGRAPHY

WITH LIST OF ABBREVIATIONS.

I.
MSS. OF THE EDDA.

R CODEX REGIUS OF THE ELDER EDDA, a parchment
MS. of the 13th-14th centuries, in the Copenhagen Library.
Facsimile by Finnur Jónsson, 1896.

A CODEX ARNAMAGNÆANUS, parchment of the 14th century,
containing fragments of Vm., Grm., Hým., Skm., Hrbl., Bdr.
Copenhagen.

H HAUKSBÓK, parchment of the 14th century, containing Völuspá.
Copenhagen.

r CODEX REGIUS OF SNORRA EDDA, a parchment of the
14th century, containing a few strophes quoted from the
Sæmundar Edda and unknown sources.

U CODEX UPSALIENSIS OF SNORRA EDDA, a parchment
MS. of the 14th century. Upsala.

W CODEX WORMIANUS OF SNORRA EDDA, a parchment
of the late 14th century, containing Rþ. Copenhagen.

F FLATEYJARBÓK, a parchment of the 14th century, containing
Hdl. Copenhagen.

B, C, E, L, N O, S, St. Paper MSS. of the 17th century, containing
Gg. and Fj.

II.
EDDIC POEMS.

Alv.	Alvíssmál.	Hým.	Hýmiskviþa.
Bdr.	Baldrs Draumar.	Ls.	Lokasenna.
Fj.	Fjölsvinnsmál.	Rþ.	Rígsþula.
Gg.	Gróugaldr.	Skm.	Skirnismál.
Grm.	Grimnismál.	Vm.	Vafþrúþnismál.
Háv.	Hávamál.	Vsp.	Völuspá.
Hdl.	Hyndluljóþ.	þrk.	þrymskviþa.
Hrbl.	Hárbarþsljóþ.		

III.

TEXTS AND TRANSLATIONS.

B.　　S. Bugge, "Sæmundar Edda hins fróþa" (Christiánia, 1867). Text.

Bm.　F. W. Bergmann, Hrbl. (Strassburg, 1872), Gg. and Fj. (1874), Bdr. (1875), Rþ. and Hdl. (1876), Háv. (1877), Alv., þrk., Hým., Ls. (1878). Text (greatly emended) and translation.

C.　　Vigfusson and York Powell, "Corpus Poeticum Boreale" (Oxford, 1883). Text and translation.

D.　　F. E. C. Dietrich, "Altnordisches Lesebuch" (Leipzig, 1864). Text, selections.

Dt. & Hl.　F. Detter and R. Heinzel, "Sæmundar Edda," vol. 1 (Leipzig, 1903). Text.

E.　　L. Etmüller, "Altnord. Lesebuch" (Zurich, 1861). Text, selections.

F.　　H. S. Falk, "Oldnorsk Læsebog" (Christiania, 1889). Text, selections.

F. Magn.　F. Magnusen, "Den ældere Edda, etc." (1821-23). Text.

G.　　H. Gering, "Die Lieder der älteren Edda" (Padeborn, 1904). Text.

　　　H. Gering, "Die Edda" (Leipzig, 1892). Translation.

H.　　K. Hildebrand, "Lieder der älteren Edda" (Padeborn, 1876). Text.

Hold.　A. Holder and A. Holtzmann (Leipzig, 1875). Text and translation.

H.　　A. Heusler, "Völuspá" (Berlin, 1887). Text and translation.

J.　　Finnur Jónsson, "Sæmundar Edda" (Reykjavik, 1905). Text.

K.　　Copenhagen Edition (1787-1828).

L.　　H. Lüning, "Die Edda" (Zurich, 1859). Text.

M.　　P. A. Munch, "Den ældere Edda" (Christiania, 1847). Text.

Mb.　Th. Möbius, "Edda Sæmundar" (Leipzig, 1860). Text.

R.   R. Rask, " Edda Sæmundar " (Stockholm, 1818).

S.   B. Sijmons, " Die Lieder der Edda " (Halle, 1888), vol. 2. Text.

Simr.   K. Simrock, " Die Edda, die ältere u. die jüngere " (Stuttgart. 1882). Translation.

Th.   B. Thorpe, " The Edda of Sæmund the Learned " (London, 1866). Translation.

W.   L. Wimmer, " Oldnordisk Læsebog " (Copenhagen, 1889). Text, selections.

IV.

GLOSSARIES.

D.   Dietrich: glossary to " Lesebuch." See *D.* III.

E.   Etmüller. See *E.* III.

G.   Gering, " Vollständiges Wörterbuch zu den Liedern der Edda " (Halle, 1903).

F.Magn. F. Magnusen, Lexicon, 1821.

L.   Lüning: glossary to text. See *L.* III.

N.   M. Nygaard: glossary to text (Bergen, 1882).

V.   G. Vigfusson, " Icelandic-English Dictionary " (Oxford, 1874).

Wk.   E. Wilken, Glossar. (Padeborn, 1883). An abridged edition has been made of this work.

V.

COMMENTARIES.

---

(1)—GENERAL WORKS.

Anderson. " Norse Mythology " (1875).

Bugge, S. " Home of the Eddic Poems " (1899). " Studien über die Entstehung der nordischen Götter- u. Heldensagen " (German trans. by O. Brenner, München, 1889).

Craigie, W. A. "Religion of the Ancient Scandinavians" (London, 1906).

Cox, G. W. "Mythology of the Aryan Nations" (London, 1870).

Detter, F. and R. Heinzel. "Anmerkungen" to text, vol. 2. See *Dt. Hl.* in III.

Frazer, J. G. "The Golden Bough" (1900).

Faraday, Winifred. "The Divine Mythology of the North" (London, 1902).

Gering, H. Introduction to translation. See *G.* in III.

Golther, W. "Handbuch der Germanischen Mythologie" (Leipzig, 1895).

Grimm, J. "Deutsche Mythologie," trans. by J. S. Stallybrass, 1883.

Holzmann, A. Commentary to text. See *Hold.* in III.

Jónsson, F. "Den oldnorske ok oldislandske Literaturs Historie." Copenhagen.

Kauffmann, F. "Northern Mythology" (1900).

Ker, W. P. "Epic and Romance" (London, 1897).

Lang, A. "Myth, Ritual and Religion" (London, 1887).

Meyer, E. H. "Germanische Mythologie" (2nd edition, 1903).

Mogk, E. "Germanische Mythologie" (2nd edition, Strassburg, 1907).

Müller, Max. "Chips from a German Workshop," vol. 4 (1868).

Petersen, H. "Uber den Gottesdienst u. den Götterglauben des Nordens während der Heidenzeit" (Copenhagen, 1876).

Rydberg, A. V. "Teutonic Mythology," English version by R. B. Anderson (London, 1889).

Saxo Grammaticus. "Danish History." Books i—ix trans. by Elton (London, 1894).

Sijmons, B. Introduction to text, vol. 1. See *S.* in III.

Ten Brink. "Quellen u. Forschungen," vol. 10.

York Powell, F. Introduction and Excursus to text. See *C.* in III.

Weinhold. "Altnordische Leben."

(2)—SPECIAL SUBJECTS.

Bergmann. Commentary on *Hárbarþsljóþ, Gróugaldr, Fjölsvinnsmál, Baldrsdraumar, Rígsþula, Hyndluljóþ, Hávamál, Alvissmál, Þrymskviþa, Hýmiskviþa, Lokasenna.* See Bm. III.

Cassel, P. "Eddische Studien" (1856) on *Fjölsvinnsmál.*

Chadwick, H. M. "The Cult of *Othin*," 1899.

Detter, F. "*Die Völuspá.*"

Frauer. "*Die Walkyrien* der skandinavisch-germanischen Götter- u. Heldensagen."

Heusler, A. "Weissagen der Seherin." *Völuspá*, translation and commentary.

Hoffory. J. "Eddastudien" 1889 on *Völuspá.*

Kauffmann. "*Balder*" 1902.

Meyer, E. H. "*Völuspá*" 1889.

Magnússon, E. "Odin's Horse *Yggdrasill*" 1895. "On disputed passages in *Hávamál*" (Proceedings of the Cambridge Phil. Society, 1885). "*Edda :* its Derivation and Meaning" (Saga-Book of the Viking Club, Nov. 1895 ; separate issue : London, 1896).

Rupp, Th. "Eddische Studien," 1869, on *Fjölsvinnsmál, Baldr,* and *Freyja.*

Siecke, E. "Mythologische Briefe," 1901. Criticism of Uhland's study of *Thor.*

Uhland. "Mythus von *Thor*," 1836.

Weinhold. "*Die Riesin* der germanischen Mythus" (in the Acad. der Wissensch. Wien. xxvi., p. 233-306).

Wilkinson. *Völuspá.*

SEE ALSO THE FOLLOWING PERIODICALS :—

Z.f.d.A. ZEITSCHRIFT FÜR DEUTSCHES ALTERTHUM
(*P.P. 4650, 1856, &c.).

Vol. iii., p. 385. Explanatory notes on *Hávamál*, by Dietrich.

---

* *To facilitate reference to these works, we have given their number, shelf-mark and date in the British Museum Library.*

Vol. v.   Interpretations of *Völuspá*, *Hávamál*, *Grimnismál*, *Vafþrúþ-nismál*, by K. Müllenhoff.

Vol. xxx., p. 217. On *Freyja* as a sun-goddess ; myth of *Brisingar-men*, by Müllenhoff.

p. 132. *Skirnismál*, commentary and rearrangement of strophes, by F. Niedner.

Vol. xxxvi., p. 278-295.   Notes on *Þrymskviþa*, *Völuspá*, *Hárbarþsljóþ*, *Skirnismál*, by Niedner.

Vol. xxxviii, p. 1.   *Ymir* as a personification of earth, by R. M. Meyer.

Vol. xli., p. 32.   On doubtful passages in *Völuspá*, by Niedner.

p. 305. On *Baldr* and *Höd*, criticism on Bugge's hypothesis, by Niedner.

Vol. xlii., p. 277. *Fylgienglauben*, by Rieger.

Vol. xlvi., p. 309.   On the historical origin of *Grimnismál*, by Much.

Anz. f.d. Alt.   ANZEIGER FÜR DEUTSCHES ALTERTHUM
(P.P. 4650).

Vol. xviii. *Criticism of Rydberg's Teutonic Mythology*, by Meyer.

Ark. f.n. Fil.   ARKIV. FÜR NORDISK FILOLOGI
(P.P. 5044, e. 1883, &c.).

Vol. vi., p. 108. *Rydberg* criticised by Detter.

Vol. ix., p. 221.   Notes on *Hávamál*, by Olsen.

Vol. x., p. 26. *Svipdagsmál*, by Falk.

Z.f.d.Ph.   ZEITSCHRIFT FÜR DEUTSCHE PHILOLOGIE
(P.P. 5043, af. 1869, &c.).

Vol. iii., p. 1-84.   On the *Home, Date*, and *Characteristics* of *Edda*, by Jessen.

Vol. xviii., p. 156-297.   The myth of *Fenrir* and *Garm* shown as originating in a star-myth, by Wilken.

Vol. xxiii., p. 1.   The original *Völuspá*, by Wilken.

Vol. xxxi.   On the Wonders in the Edda, a study of *Magic* and *Runes*, R. M. Meyer.

Beit.   BEITRÄGE ZUR GESCHICHTE DER DEUTSCHEN SPRACHE (12,962, o, 1874, &c.).

Vol. xii., p. 383.   On the late historical origin of the god *Bragi*, by Mogk.

Vol. xviii., p. 542.   On the correspondence between the *War between gods and Wanes*, and Saxo's history of Fridlevus, by Detter and Heinzel.

Vo. xix.   Odin not Loki the author of *Baldr's death*, by Detter.

Germ.   GERMANIA (P.P. 4652, 1850, etc).

Vol. xxiii., p. 155.   *Sif* as a sun-goddess, by Blaas ; p. 406-440, Hýmiskviþa.

Vol. xxiv., p. 46-64.   On *Völuspá* and the missing strophes in Vafþrúþnismál, by Edzardi.

Vol. xxvii., p. 330-9.   *Frigg* as the goddess of springs and wells, by Edzardi.

Vol. xxviii., p. 17.   On *Hyndluljóþ*.

Act. Germ.   ACTA GERMANICA (12963 dd. 40, 1890).

Vol. 1 on *Loki*.

INDEX.

1.—ICELANDIC TEXT.

2 R

Þegn, 208.
Þekkr, Odin, 20.
——— dwarf, 280.
Þír, 204.
Þjálfi, 194.
Þjazi, 8, 188, 218, 262, 264, 270.
Þjóþnuma, 12.
Þjóþreyrir, 108.
Þjoþvara, 176.
Þjóþvitnir, 10.
Þóra, 230.
Þorinn, 280.
Þórir, 232.
Þórr, 6, 12, 120, 122, 130, 132, 182-200, 226, 244, 266, 274, 284.
Þráinn, 280.
Þriþr, 20.
Þrór, Odin, 22.
——— dwarf, 280.
Þrúþgelmir, 48.

Þrúþheimr, 6.
Þrymgjöll, 166.
Þrymheimr, 8, 264.
Þrymr, 128-134.
Þræl, 204.
Þund, 10.
Þundr, 22, 104.
Þuþr, 20.
Þyn, 12.
Þökk, 272.
Þöll, 12.

Ægir, 20, 112, 124, 244 et seq.
Ækin, 12.

Ölmóþr, 230.
Ökkvinkálfr, 206.
Örmt, 12.
Öþlingar, 228, 230, 232.

———

2.—TRANSLATION.

Ægir, a sea giant, 21, 113, 195, 245-269.
Æsir, the race of gods, distinguished from Wanes, 53, 283, 285.
Agnar, brother of Geirröd, 3, 5.
——— son of Geirröd, 5, 23.
Ai, name of two dwarfs, 281.
Alf, kinsman of Ottar, 231.
Alf the Old, son of Dag and Thora, 231.
——— grandfather of Ottar, 229.
Ali, kinsman of Ottar, 231.
All-father, Odin, 21, 285, 287.
All-fleet, a horse, 17.
All-green, an island, 189.

All-thief, a dwarf, 281.
All-wielder, a giant, father of Thiazi, 189.
All-wise (Alvíss) a dwarf, 25-37.
——— (Alsviþr) a jötun, 103.
Almveig, wife of Halfdan, 231.
Am, son of Dag and Thora, 231.
Andvari, a dwarf, 281.
Angantyr, Ottar's rival, 229, 235.
——— a berserk, 233.
Ann, a dwarf, 281.
Arngrim, father of twelve berserks, 233.
Asgarth, dwelling of the Æsir or gods, 115, 129, 131, 133, 271, 275, 285.

2 T

of Rock-giants, Son of Earth, Steerer of barks, Storm-god, Strength - wielder, Thunderer, Warder, Winged Thunder.

Thora, wife of Dag, mother of many heroes, 231.

Thorin, a dwarf, 281.

Thorir Iron-shield, a berserk, 233.

Thrain, a dwarf, 281.

Thrall, father of the race of thralls, 205.

Thror, Odin, 23.

———— a dwarf, 281.

Thrudgelm, a Jötun, son of Ymir, 49.

Thrym, a Jötun, who stole Thor's hammer, 129-135.

Thund, Odin, 23.

Thunderer, Thor, 7, 11, 13, 27, 115-127, 127-137, 151, 189-195, 199, 265, 267, 285.

Thunder-flood, a river, 11.

Tind, a berserk, 233.

Tree (the), Yggdrasil, 103, 277-283, 293.

Tree-rocker, Odin, 23.

Troth-goddess of oaths and plightings, 135.

True, Odin, 21.

Tyr, god of war, 115-123, 245, 259, 261.

Tyrfing, a berserk, 233.

Ull, a god, 7, 17.

Uncooled-realm, a region in Jötunheim, 289.

Uni, one of the builders of Menglöd's hall, 175.

Uri, one of the builders of Menglöd's hall, 175.

Utterer of gods, Odin, 103.

Valas, wise women, 221, 241-243, 277-297.

Vala-shelf, home of one of the gods,—Odin? 7.

Valgrind, the gates of Valhöll, 11.

Valhöll, Odin's dwelling, 7, 11, 13, 225, 275, 287, 297.

Vali, a god, son of Odin and Rind, 57, 219, 243.

———— son of Loki, 269.

Valkyries, Odin's war-maidens, 17, 287.

Var, one of the builders of Menglöd's hall, 175.

Ve, brother of Odin, 255.

Vegdrasil, one of the builders of Menglöd's hall, 175.

Veiled One, Odin, 21.

Vidar, a god, son of Odin, 9, 57, 59, 245, 249, 251, 295.

Vigg, a dwarf, 281.

Vili, brother of Odin. 255.

Vimur, a river, 275.

Virfir, a dwarf, 281.

Vit, a dwarf, 233.

Völsungs, the race born of Völsung, 233.

Wafter, Odin, 23.

Wand-elf, a dwarf, 281.

Wanderer, Odin, 21.

Wanes, a race of gods, 29-37, 53, 131, 145, 273, 285.

Wane-home, land of the Wanes, 53.

Yggdrasil, the World-tree. *See also* Fate-tree, 13-19, 55, 283, 293.

Ymir, the first-born of Jötuns. *See also* Clay-giant, 19, 29, 47, 49, 221, 277, 279.

Ynglings, a race descended from Yng, 229, 231.

Yngvi, a dwarf, 281.

Youth, son of Churl, 209.

—— son of Earl, 215.

www.ingramcontent.com/pod-product-compliance
Lightning Source LLC
Chambersburg PA
CBHW080538090426
42733CB00016B/2613

* 9 7 8 0 6 9 2 2 0 0 6 5 0 *